AESCHYLUS

THE COMPLETE PLAYS
VOLUME I

ORESTEIA

AESCHYLUS

THE COMPLETE PLAYS
VOLUME I

ORESTEIA

AGAMEMNON
LIBATION BEARERS
EUMENIDES

Translated by Carl R. Mueller
Introduction by Hugh Denard

GREAT TRANSLATIONS SERIES

A Smith and Kraus Book

A Smith and Kraus Book
Published by Smith and Kraus, Inc.
177 Lyme Road, Hanover, NH 03755
www.smithkraus.com

First Edition: November 2002
10 9 8 7 6 5 4 3 2 1
Manufactured in the United States of America

Cover and Text Design by Julia Hill Gignoux, Freedom Hill Design
Cover Illustration: Nike, goddess of victory, loosening her sandal
in order to bring victory offering barefoot.

The Library of Congress Cataloging-In-Publication Data
Aeschylus
[Works. English. 2002]
Aeschylus : the complete plays / translated by Carl R. Mueller ; introduction by Hugh Denard. —1st ed.
p. cm. — (Great translations series)
Includes bibliographical references.
ISBN 1-57525-312-7 (v.1) — ISBN 1-57525-313-5 (v.2)
1. Aeschylus—Translations into English. 2. Mythology, Greek —Drama. I. Mueller, Carl Richard. II. Title. III. Great translations for actors series.
PA3827.A2 M84 2002
882'.01—dc21
2002070807

For
THE EUROPEAN CULTURAL CENTRE OF DELPHI
and its devotion to the
Spirit of Attic Theater

CONTENTS

Aeschylus and the Athenian Theater of His Time

I

Aeschylus was born most likely in 525 B.C.E. and died in the year 456. Although we are not certain, his birthplace was probably Eleusis, up the coast of Greece, not far from Athens, the same Eleusis that was the seat of the Eleusinian Mysteries, making it one of Attica's most sacred spots and Athens' most famous deme. We also know that Aeschylus was born of an aristocratic family and that at the age of forty-five he fought in one of the decisive battles of the Persian Wars, the Battle of Marathon, in 490—that conflict between the Athenians and the Persians. In 480 he either fought in or was an eyewitness to the final defeat of Persia at Salamis, an island off the western coast of Attica. His description of that battle in *Persians* is the only firsthand account that survives of the historical event that freed the Athenian state to pursue its own agenda and become one of the cultural pinnacles in the history of Western civilization.

Aeschylus' first tragic production was in 499, and his first victory with a tragedy came in 484. Thereafter it is not unlikely that he was almost always victorious in the tragic competition at the City (or Great) Dionysia, the annual Athenian religious festival that centered around the presentation of tragedy and eventually comedy, as well as other musical and choreographic events. In any case, he won a total of thirteen first prizes. His first extant play, *Persians,* was written in 472 and enjoyed so great a success that he was invited to restage it in Syracuse at the invitation of the Sicilian dynast Hieron, and also to write for him his *Women of Aitna* in celebration of the founding of that city. *Seven Against Thebes,* Aeschylus' second extant play, was first produced in Athens in 467 and was followed in 463 by the Danaïd-tetralogy of which the extant *Suppliants* is a part and which won first prize over Sophokles. Aeschylus' final production during his lifetime, *Oresteia,* was first produced at Athens in 458, a tetralogy with which he honored his beloved Athens and its bold experiment in democracy. This behind him, he again visited Sicily, where he died at Gela in 456. It will likely never be known, but it's possible that it was in Sicily that he wrote *Promêtheus Bound,* the play that was produced posthumously by his son Euphorion.

The extent of Aeschylus' work is not certain, but it is likely to have been somewhere between seventy and ninety plays. The seven that have survived the twenty-five-hundred years since their creation come to us not as originals but in the form of medieval copies. We do know, however, that a good number of his productions were tetralogies, three tragedies united by a single theme and followed by a satyr play that dealt comically with the same material. Just how many such tetralogies he composed is unknown, though there is certainty regarding at least four: the *Oresteia,* the Theban-tetralogy, the Danaïd-tetralogy, and *Lycurgia.* Only *Oresteia* survives, though only as a trilogy (the satyr play having been lost), and one play each from the Theban and Danaïd tetralogies, with none from *Lycurgia.* But it is also possible to reconstruct from the names of the plays that have been lost at least seven additional tetralogies.

The *Vita,* the ancient source that records the life of Aeschylus, notes that his epitaph makes no mention of his art, but—as Sommerstein notes in *The Oxford Classical Dictionary*—refers "only to his prowess displayed at Marathon; this estimate of what was most important in Aeschylus' life—to have been a loyal and courageous citizen of a free Athens—can hardly be that of the Geloans and will reflect his own death-bed wishes . . . or those of his family."

II

One of the fascinating questions in regard to Aeschylus and his work is what was his theater like? The fact is we know virtually nothing about it, as little as we know about the origin of Athenian tragedy. What we do know is that the first performances of Athenian tragedy in the mid-sixth century took place in the Agora, the Athenian marketplace—a place of general assembly—and that spectators sat on wooden bleachers. Then, around 500, the theatrical performance site was moved to the Sacred Precinct of Dionysos on the south side of the Akropolis. At first spectators may have sat on the natural slope of the hill to watch the performance, an arrangement most likely superceded by wooden bleachers introduced for greater audience comfort—but even this is guesswork, logical as it sounds. From here (or perhaps even before we arrive here) the general public image of the Athenian Theater of Dionysos makes a great and very wrongheaded leap some one hundred and fifty years into the future to the middle of the fourth century and the most esthetically harmonious of all Greek theaters, that at Epidauros. There we have a stone skênê building to serve as backing for the action, a building with from one to three doors and fronted by a line of pillars, the proskênion; possibly there is a second story to the skênê building and a logeion—the skênê's roof for the appearance of gods and even mortals. We then perhaps see a raised terrace or low stage area in front of the skênê where some if not most of the action takes place. Then, in front of all that, the most crucial element of all, a perfectly round and very large orchestra made of pounded earth and circled in stone. And, not least, the vast reaches of a stone auditorium, in Greek the theatron. Certain as that structure may still be at Epidauros, it has no precedent in Athens until the 330s when stoa, skênê, and auditorium were finally finished in stone. There is evidence, however, that the oldest stone skênê in Athens dates from some-time between 421 and 415. We know that for some years prior to that the skênê was made of wood, torn down at the end of each festival and rebuilt (perhaps newly designed) the next year. Just when, however, that wooden skênê was first introduced is a mystery that may never find an answer, if for no other reason than the fragility of such a structure and/or the fact that it was regu-larly demolished at the close of each festival.

About the only thing that is certain in all this speculation is that the ear-liest extant plays of the Athenian Theater of Dionysos are those of Aeschylus and that they require no skênê building, suggesting that none existed. The earliest play, *Persians,* in 472, requires only a raised mound to serve as the grave or tomb of Dareios, whereas *Seven Against Thebes* needs only a representation of statues and altars of gods, and *Suppliants* requires much the same, except in place of statues of gods are symbolic representations of them. It is frequently believed that a raised area was required for *Suppliants,* an area that would serve as a place of sanctuary on which the symbols were placed and to which the Chorus retired for safety. This, however, is dubious inasmuch as the Chorus could not with any great facility perform its choreographed dance on such a platform, and therefore we are left again with a large playing area on a single level as the most logical possibility. It is not until *Oresteia* in 458 that an extant play of Aeschylus calls for a skênê with at least one and perhaps more doors, and in front of that skênê it is possible that there was a raised acting area, per-haps the first. But it is only in the late fifth and early fourth centuries that there is evidence in the form of vase paintings of a low, raised platform for the performance of tragedy, a platform raised about a meter (roughly forty inches) and mounted via a flight of steps in the center, steps suggesting that action was not confined to the platform but spilled out into the orchestra. This, of course, still tells us nothing about the positioning of theatrical action in the earlier period from the late sixth to well into the fifth century, nor is it conclusive evidence that such a raised level actually existed in Athens in the fifth century. Nothing short of archeological evidence could do that, and of that there is none. From a purely practical standpoint it must be asked what if anything would have been served by such a raised level, especially considering that the action of the play was looked down upon by a steeply raked auditorium of spectators, and that even the first row of seats, the thrones for priests and dignitaries, was itself raised above the ground-level playing area.

But there is another issue involved here that goes well beyond a question of sight lines, and that is the nature of Aeschylus' plays. They don't lend themselves to a separation between character and chorus, for the simple reason that it is precisely the relationship between them that is at the heart of the plays—they are inextricably bound up. Eteoklês in *Seven Against Thebes* is who and what he is by virtue of his relationship with the people of his polis, his city; it is how they treat each other that determines the sort of hero that Eteoklês is, and that relationship has inevitably to be at close quarters. To see Eteoklês on a raised platform speaking like any orator to the city, or castigating the chorus from there, is unheard of if one has any real understanding of the nature of Aeschylus' play. The same is true of Klytaimnêstra and Agamemnon in *Oresteia*. For Agamemnon to enter at ground level and confront Klytaimnêstra situated an entire meter above him on a platform is to say in semiotic terms that Klytaimnêstra needs elevation to register (maintain, generate) power: It weakens rather than strengthens her. Let them meet at ground level and our sight tells us without recourse to words that they are equals and that Klytaimnêstra knows it even if Agamemnon doesn't. Tigers don't stalk their prey from a distance.

It is also not known what the original shape of the early Athenian orchestra might have been, that area where the Chorus sang and danced elaborate choreographies. There are examples of smaller, outlying Attic theaters of the later fifth century, whose orchestras were other than circular. Both Thorikos and Trachones had tiny provincial deme-theaters in which the audience was seated on wooden benches in a rectangular arrangement in close proximity to the acting area, which, as well, may have been loosely rectangular, or, even more likely, trapezoidal, with only two sides being parallel. It is possible that the early shape of the theater at Athens was the same, with the exception that it would have been on a much grander scale. Where does all this lead? Not much of anywhere except more speculation. Some scholars maintain, for example, that there is no evidence for a circular orchestra in Athens before the 330s, whereas others argue that the choreography performed by the Chorus required a circular area and thus there must have been one from the start. Who knows?

III

There are several conventions of classical Athenian tragedy that must be considered, namely masks, the chorus, music, and dance.

Whatever the layout of the early Athenian Theater of Dionysos, it is a fair guess that in order to accommodate the numbers of male citizens of that thriving metropolis and many from its outlying demes, not to mention important foreign visitors, the structure could not have been less than sizable. Size brought with it distance from the theatrical event as the eventual auditorium at Athens in the 330s still demonstrates, rising as it does to touch the fortified walls of the Akropolis some hundreds of feet away. The capacity of the theater has been judged to be somewhere between fifteen and twenty thousand.

Whether distance served as an incentive to the use of masks (some have speculated that they served as a megaphone to project the voice to the farthest rows) is not known, nor is it the most salient reason for the use of the mask, for there are others. There is ample evidence, for example, that in Greece the use of the mask in cult ceremonies was widespread. Adolescent rites of passage, puberty rites, known from Sparta, made use of masks of considerable grotesqueness; and the cult of Dêmêtêr and Dêspoina at Lycosura is known for its use of animal masks. Then, of course, there is the mask used closer to home, in the cult of Dionysos, from which the mask in Greek tragedy most likely derives. Whether amplification had any part in the use of masks on the Athenian stage, they at least gave a greater presence to the actor wearing one, for they were large enough to cover the entire head. Made generally of linen, the fifth-century mask represented types rather than individuals. Perhaps the most compelling reason for them is the need for two and later three actors to act out all of the speaking roles.

The rationale might also have been one of economy. Considering that tragedy was a masked entertainment, it was only practical to confine the number of speaking parts in any one scene to three actors, the reason most likely being, as Easterling suggests, to enable the audience to tell "where the voice is coming from," inasmuch as facial movements were obscured by masks. This practical limitation, however, permitted an actor to be double- and perhaps even triple-cast, a practice much used and most often, one must assume, to very good effect. In any case, even though the primary reason for only three actors was very likely a financial consideration, to have a single actor play, for example, the roles of Klytaimnêstra, Êlektra, and Athêna in *Oresteia;* or, in the same play, the roles of Agamemnon and Orestês; or in Euripides' *Bakkhai*

Pentheus and his mother Agavê, and in Sophokles' *Women of Trachis* the roles of Dêianeira and Heraklês—each of which possibilities offers resonances that are far-reaching and highly intriguing. One must also not forget that masks were helpful in disguising the male actor who traditionally assumed female roles, women being excluded from theatrical performance. As for the numbers of non-speaking actors on stage there was no limit and exciting stage effects with scores of "extras" would not have been unusual.

IV

Of all the elements of theatrical practice the importance of the Chorus cannot be overestimated. In Athens especially there was a long tradition (even before tragedy) of and emphasis on the competition of dithyramb choruses that consisted of both song and dance. Even in the days of tragedy, there were separate competitions devoted to the dithyramb in which each of the ten demes of Athens participated. In Aeschylus' day the tragic Chorus numbered twelve, then Sophokles added three more for a total of fifteen. In his *Tragedy in Athens* David Wiles gives a brilliant and convincing exposition of the degree to which the tragic Chorus participated in the theatrical event. He posits (with help from other scholars) that not only was the choreographed movement of the Chorus not in straight lines or highly formalized, as previously thought, but that it was often particularly active. When, for example, the Chorus of Young Theban Women in *Seven Against Thebes* makes its first entrance, it is anything but sedate, it is disordered in the extreme (choreographed disorder, to be sure), but their terror of the encroaching war outside their city gates is such that it prompts the agitated reentry of Eteoklês who deals harshly with them for their civic disturbance. In Sophokles' *Oedipus at Kolonos* there is a similar entry by the Chorus of Old Men who dart wildly about the orchestra in search of the intruder into the Sacred Grove.

Wiles makes a most insightful deduction when he posits that the subject of each choral ode is acted out by the Chorus in choreographed dance. Even more startling, that during long narrative speeches, such as the Persian Herald's speech in *Persians,* in which he describes the defeat of the Persian forces in the naval battle at Salamis, the Chorus was actively acting out a choreography that visually complemented the verbal narration. The brilliance of this deduction is staggering in indicating the participation of the Chorus in Athenian tragedy: They were seldom inactive, and not only did they wear the persona of their first function as Old Men of Kolonos or Young Theban Women, but they served also as an abstract or distanced body that acted out the subject of others' narration of which in no event could they have had any foreknowledge. It helps to understand why when Athenians attended the theater at festival times they spoke of going to the "choreography" rather than to the play.

V

Of music in Archaic and Classical Greece we know very little. Some music scores survive, but they are largely fragmentary and date from the Hellenistic period or later. Although the Greeks were knowledgeable about a great many musical instruments, especially from their eastern neighbors, they adopted only two main sorts: stringed instrument (lyre) and wind instrument or pipe (*aulos*), not a flute but sounded with a reed (single and double). In tragedy of the fifth century the double-pipe *aulos* was the instrument of choice to accompany the musical sections of the dramatic action.

The musical element in the performance of fifth century tragedy was of primary importance, and its similarity to modern opera is not unnoticed. Every one of the extant tragedies has built into it a number of choral sections (usually five) that cover generally short passages of time and in which the singing and dancing Chorus holds the center of attention in the orchestra. In addition, there are sections in which song is exchanged between characters, as well as an alternation between spoken dialogue and recitative or song, the latter often between a character or characters and the Chorus. As Easterling rightly points out, these sections exist in the same time frame as the scenes of exclusively spoken dialogue. The rationale behind this practice being "to intensify emotion or to give a scene a ritual dimension, as in a shared lament or song of celebration." To what extent music was employed in performance is not known, but it is intriguing to speculate that its role was enormous and went far beyond those sections of the plays that call unequivocally for music.

VI

What we know about the production of tragedy in Greece is almost totally confined to Attica, though other areas were also active producers. In any event, from the close of the sixth and throughout the fifth century, tragedy was primarily performed as part of the Great or City Dionysia in Athens, though tragedy was also a part of the Rural Dionysia during the winter months when access to Athens was inhibited because of weather. But tragedy was not the sole reason for these festivals. They also scheduled processions, sacrifices in the theater, libations, the parade of war orphans, and the performance of dithyramb and comedy. As summary, the final day was devoted to a review of the conduct of the festival and to the awarding of prizes.

Three tragedians competed with three plays each plus a satyr play, all chosen by the archon, a state official who also appointed the three *chorêgoi* who undertook the expense of equipping and training the choruses, the actors and playwrights being paid for by the state. One judge from each of the ten tribes or demes of Athens was chosen to determine the winners of the competition, and the winning playwright was crowned with a wreath of ivy in the theater. Till about the middle of the fifth century, the three tragedies of each day's performance comprised a trilogy; eventually each of the three plays had a different subject and were independent of one another, but always there was a satyr play.

And then there was Dionysos.

VII

Dionysos. What had the theater to do with Dionysos, and Dionysos with the theater? How did the two become one and mutually express one another as an indigenous Athenian institution? What is it that is quintessentially associated with Dionysos that makes him the appropriate representative of the art of drama, and in particular of tragedy?

Some scholars believe that, since the subject of the dithyramb chorus was Dionysos, tragedy, developing out of the dithyramb (as Aristotle conjectured), simply took with it its subject. Now, of course, we are less than certain of that succession, especially when one considers, as Herington puts it, the "catholicity of the art form" of tragedy in the subjects it treats; for, though Dionysos plays a significant part as a subject, he has considerable competition. Or is it his Otherness that makes him tragedy's apt representative, his transformative aspect (both animate and inanimate), or simply his inability to be pinned down as being either this or that? Some would say that his cult ritual, which existed long before tragedy, possessed aspects that made it prototypical of drama: the use of masks for disguise, ecstatic possession and the capacity to assume alternate personalities, mystic initiation. Then there is wine, discovered by Dionysos, and the wildness of nature, the power of his ambivalent sexuality, his association with dance in partnership with satyrs and maenads. These are only a few of the possibilities that may have led to this inexhaustible god's association with drama. Which it was, of course, we will never know; but a fair guess might be that each of these attributes, and perhaps others, had its share.

One thing, however, is certain, that in the early period of tragedy, from the late sixth and well into the fifth century, tragedy was associated with the satyr play, that light send-up of a classical mythological subject. What's more, once tragedy emerged, the same playwrights who wrote the tragedies also wrote the satyr play that culminated the day's dramatic event.

Easterling finds that all three of these forms (dithyramb, satyr play, and tragedy) share one thing: song and dance, and, as she says,

> among them it was satyr play that was the most obviously Dionysiac element, since the chorus of satyrs, far more than any other choral group, was explicitly and by definition part of the god's entourage, and satyrs of various types, as we have known from vase-paintings, had been associated with Dionysus well before the dramatic festivals were established.

The question remains: What made Dionysos the god uniquely suited to drama? Authentic, testable proof from the time of its formation doesn't exist and we have only the extant plays (a small remnant of the total production of those years) to look to for possibilities.

Perhaps one of the most salient reasons for Dionysos as god of theater is the mask, for at its core it is the very essence of the Dionysiac, which, ultimately, is escape. But who would think of Greek tragedy as escapist fare, the means of leaving reality behind? And yet, is it so impossible that tragedy's removal from real life gave the same satisfaction, then as now, albeit of a different kind? Greek tragedy, after all, is filled with Alienation devises. Just as the Elizabethan playgoer didn't in the street speak the language of Shakespeare's stage, the diction, the vocabulary, the very syntax of Attic tragedy (not to mention the emotional manipulation possible through various skillfully applied metric systems) was even more removed from the daily patter of the Athenian Agora.

And as far as the mask and its Dionysiac potentialities, it permits an actor to take on not just one but as many roles as needed in the course of the tragic trilogy and its culminating satyr play. In the early days of tragedy there was one actor, then Aeschylus added a second, and Sophokles a third. No matter how many actors (one or three), he/they were required to play as many speaking roles as the play called for, each time changing his mask to assume another character. Since only males were permitted to act, a male would as easily perform a female as a male role. Pentheus, for example, in Euripides, also plays his mother Agavê who at the end enters carrying her son's severed head. In other cases an actor could play four or even five roles. Furthermore, each of the four choruses in a tetralogy would assume another, separate, identity, finally and inevitably ending up as a band of cavorting and lascivious satyrs. Then, of course, there is the distancing of the music as well as the elaborate choreography of the chorus.

So fictive is this convention of masks in the Attic theater that it is as iconoclastic in regard to everyday reality as is the Epic, anti-illusionist, theater of Brecht. No Athenian in that Theater of Dionysos could have failed finally to be aware of the game openly and unashamedly being played on him and he must have relished it, knowing by subtle means, by the timbre of a voice, by delivery, or some other telltale sign that Pentheus was now (in the terrible/wonderful deception that was theater) his mother carrying his own head. Which doesn't mean that theater couldn't also be the bearer of weighty messages, such as: As you sow, so also shall you reap—a lesson Pentheus learns too late. In any event, an illusion of reality was deliberately broken that said to that vast audience that this is not life as you know it, and, besides, there's always the down-and-dirty ribaldry of the satyr play to send you home laughing at its unmediated escapist function, just in case you fell into the trap of taking things a bit too seriously.

One other thing regarding the mask needs saying. As we know from Greek pottery (in particular large kraters for the storage of wine), in the cult rituals of Dionysos the god was frequently "present" in the form of a large suspended or supported mask, suggesting two intriguing possibilities: 1) that he served as an observer, and 2) that he observed the playing out in the ritual of many of his characteristics. It is fascinating to associate that spectatorship of the "ritual" Dionysos with the fact that at the beginning of every City Dionysia at Athens a large statue of Dionysos was placed dead center in the auditorium to oversee the day's theatrical representation of himself in the form of mask, transformation, disguise, ecstatic possession, dance (to name only a few), and, in the satyr play, debauchery, drunkenness, and general ribaldry.

And then there was sex.

VIII

The sexual import of Dionysos and his cult is quite beyond refutation. His most formidable aspect in absentia is the giant phallos, a sign of generation and fertility, a ritual instrument that was prominently displayed and carried through the streets in procession on various holidays, as well as ritually sequestered in a small, cradle-like enclosure and treated at women's festivals as the product of its fertility, a baby. In small, it was a piece of polished wood looking like nothing so much as a dildo.

As a subject for Attic tragedy sex cannot be denied; it appears so often as not only a motif, but as a catalytic motivational force in one play after another, so significant an element that Attic tragedy could scarcely do without it.

One has only to think of Phaidra and Hippolytos, of the Suppliants and their Egyptian suitors, Mêdeia and Jason, Laïos and Iokastê, Oedipus and Iokastê, Heraklês and Dêianeira, Pentheus and Dionysos. In each of these relationships sex is dark, disruptive, tragic, leading inevitably to the solution of all problems: Count no man happy till he is dead.

Dionysos and death? The Dionysos who gives wine, who causes milk to flow from the earth and honey to spout from his ritual thyrsos, who carouses with his satyrs and maenads in the mountains? The answer can only be yes, as much death as freedom, as much death as liberation, as escape, as dissolution, as sex itself—no infrequent carrier of the death motif as rapture in destruction. Death is, after all, the only total escape, the only true liberation from pain and distress and dishonor and fear, the only unalloyed pleasure that ultimately is nothing less than the paradoxical absence of that pleasure in Nothingness.

When we consider how often the death expedient is invoked in Athenian tragedy and how often it is the only answer to the dark plague of sex that enfolds these plays, we come to the realization that the Dionysos situated commandingly dead center in that Athenian theater that bears his name, watching himself onstage in every event that transpires on it, from the playful to the tragic. Dionysos is not only watching, not merely observing from his place of honor, but, like the gods in various of his plays, directing, manipulating the action and the fate of his characters—like Aphroditê and Artemis in *Hippolytos,* like Athêna in *Aias,* like Dionysos himself in *Bakkhai.* In the end, Dionysos is the god of the theater because Dionysos is Everything, All: light-dark, hot-cold, wet-dry, sound-silence, pleasure-pain, life-death. If he lures his Athenian audience unsuspectingly into his theater in order to escape "reality" by raising life to a level that exceeds, indeed transcends, reality, whether by means of language, or dimension, or poetry, or the deceptively *fictive* games he plays with masks and actors playing not only their own characters but others as well, he does so with a smile (he is, after all, known as the "smiling god," though at times demonically, eyes like spiraling pinwheels, tongue hanging lax from tightened lips), knowing what they don't know, that that really is life up there on his stage, a mirror of him, and as a mirror of him it is a mirror of all things, of his all-encompassing fertility (that also includes death), and as such there can be no question why he is the god of theater, but most specifically of tragedy, because in the end death is the only answer, and sex, life's greatest pleasure, becomes the catalyst that ultimately leads to death, which is the greatest pleasure of all, and has everything to do with Dionysos.

Carl R. Mueller
Department of Theater
School of Theater, Film, and Television
University of California, Los Angeles

INTRODUCTION
Oresteia
by Hugh Denard

*Poetry is the product either of a man of great natural ability or of
one not wholly sane; the one is highly responsive, the other possessed.*
Aristotle, Poetics

I. SEEING THINGS

It is Easter 2001. Together with several of my students, I am making my way
up to the Akropolis, the stronghold and sacred center of ancient Athens. Behind
us, the Agora, Pnyx, and Areopagos: mercantile, executive, and legal centers
of Athens. The path up the hill is paved with stones so well worn that they
gleam in the sun; it would be easy to slip. Passing between the colossal columns
of the entrance vestibules, the little temple of Nike perched high to the right,
we come out into the sun again, and there across an expanse of rock, we finally set eyes on what is perhaps the most famous building in the world: the Temple of Athêna Parthenos or, simply, the Parthenon.

Athêna's massive Doric temple must be unimaginably heavy, yet somehow it seems to rest lightly on the hilltop as if it could drift off into the Athenian sky at any minute—the effect of the culmination of centuries of architectural
refinement. We press past those engaged in reassuring themselves that the view
will, after all, fit in a camera lens, and join the individuals or small groups of
people who sit or stand gazing toward the temple in reverie.

The cult rites and rituals of Athêna are now long forgotten. The Panathenaic procession in her honor began every August in the northwestern section of the city known as the Keramikos, the district in which the potters lived
and worked. It proceeded through the Agora, the marketplace—the city's nerve-
center, and then finally wound its way up the formidable hill to the Akropolis. It was here, from around 461 B.C.E., that the colossal bronze statue of
Athêna Promachos stood, so tall that the tip of her helmet and the point of
her spear could be seen as far away as Sunion, the southernmost point of Attica that ends at the sea. Every four years the Panathenaia expanded to become
the Greater Panathenaia, and it was on this occasion, most likely, that the city

presented its protective goddess with a newly made robe woven with scenes of the Battle of Gods and Giants. The Panathenaic procession is still with us, however, in the form of the frieze that once wound its way around the upper reaches of the Parthenon, and today rests captive in the British Museum.

The sheer scale, antiquity, and architectural eloquence of the Parthenon still seem to demand of visitors that they measure themselves against some timeless, ineffable truth or sensed perfection—all the greater because the temple is now a fragment of its former self. The mastery and mystery of this temple is that this transcendental perspective is an illusion. Inscribed in every inch of the Parthenon is the paradox that "timelessness" is the creature of the ephemeral: Each line, contour, and detail is dictated by the vagaries of the fleeting human eye. Columns that seem straight are in fact slightly curved outward to counteract the eye's natural tendency to see straight lines as concave. The very steps upon which the temple rests are subtly arched so that they *seem* perfectly straight. Again and again, the apparent unbending assertiveness of this building is compromised, compensating for our optical system's determination to distort and foreshorten all that we behold. A perfect rectangle, for instance, should be twice as long as it is wide, but the Parthenon is eight columns wide and *seventeen* long. A closer look at the spacing of the decorative motifs above the columns reveals that they, too, are ingeniously distorted so as to *seem* regular. The apparently natural harmony of the building is achieved through myriad imperfections; the cold stone of the Parthenon is a living testament to this great paradox of perfection.

Several hours later, we have completed our tour of the Akropolis. We rest on the long wall that runs the length of the south face of the hill parallel to the Parthenon, marveling at the size of the pieces of column shaft and capital lying on the ground that archaeologists have not yet restored to their original positions. Each upturned capital is taller than a person. The afternoon light has given way to a softer, golden glow that transforms the stones into mezzotints.

If the Parthenon occupies the summit of Athenian architectural achievement, then grafted to its slopes is the *Oresteia*. As we sit on the south wall, we are only a stone's throw from the very site upon which Aeschylus' spectacular dramatic trilogy was first performed in 458 B.C.E. So, when the last stragglers have caught up, before starting on the downward journey, I turn their attention to tomorrow's destination. Several hundred feet below us, on the far side of the wall, lies a curious stone structure: a paved, elongated semi-circle truncated by a low platform. Radiating outward on three sides, like ripples from a disturbance, are the wide-curving lines of cut stone approaching toward us up the steep hillside. The higher up the slope, the more decrepit the remains, until they peter out well short of the Akropolis walls. This is where Western drama began. Theatre, television, cinema, musicals, opera: These and others among the dramatic forms that dominate cultural and leisure activities across much of the globe trace their origins to this single space. It is the Theatre of Dionysos.

II. A THEATRE FOR DIONYSOS

Walking off the previous night's *retsina,* we finally arrive at the gates of the Theatre of Dionysos and are soon admitted to the precinct. I use the word "precinct" because this was a sacred area, demarcated by a boundary (*temenos*), and dedicated to the great god Dionysos. Walking though a dusty area, shaded by occasional pine trees and punctuated by fragments of ancient stone, we see to our left the outline of the Temple of Dionysos. A single course of blocks laid out on the ground is all that survives. Glancing up we see the sheer rise of the Akropolis itself, with the pediment of the Parthenon just visible over the south wall upon which we sat yesterday. Lowering our eyes, we find ourselves gazing at the theatre itself, just some fifty meters or so away. We simultaneously realize how close we are to the theatre, and how intimately connected are theatre and temple; the theatre, too, is within the god's *temenos*. At the time of the *Oresteia,* tragedy was performed in Athens at the festival of Dionysos early each spring: the City (or Great) Dionysia.

Some of the group have pressed ahead, eager to experience the theatre for themselves. Gradually the rest of us follow, threading our way through the ruins until we stand, hushed, center-stage, gazing out into an imagined crowd of perhaps 15,000 to 20,000 Athenian men awaiting our performance. There is not one of us that does not feel the *frisson* of being in this extraordinary place where Aeschylus performed. He and his contemporaries, of course, never saw the theatre in this broken state. Nevertheless, for us the space is still charged with a kind of electricity. The auditorium itself, the *theatron,* provides an immensely intense focus upon the central, curved "dancing area," the *orchestra.* The cult statue of Dionysos occupied the central position among the front row seats of honor (*prohedria*) flanked by priests, the two chief executive officers of the city (the *archons*), the ten generals (*strategoi*), and other prominent individuals—some dedicatory inscriptions can still be seen. Five hundred seats were reserved for the members of the *Boule:* the executive council. Each of Attica's ten *demes* (political-administrative groupings) contributed fifty men to this council, selected annually by lot. The rows of seats, receding up the hillside toward the Akropolis, wrap around the *orchestra* like slightly extended, concentric semicircles. Even today they create an atmosphere of expectation that visitors itch to fulfill by walking into the *orchestra* and addressing the vacant *theatron*. Lines of steps extend outward from the center, dividing the three tiers of seats into thirteen wedge-shaped sections, with subdivisions higher up for ease of access. Each of the ten *demes* sat in its allotted section. In the remaining blocks, areas were set aside for visiting dignitaries, resident aliens (*metics*) in special robes, and young trainee-warriors (*ephebes*) whose fathers had died fighting for Athens—"war orphans" who were educated and armed at public expense. It remains unclear whether slaves, women, or children were entitled to attend the theatrical performances at the City Dionysia in this period.

This seating arrangement acted as a vast and potent visible sign of the sovereign people of Athens, arrayed to the world and to themselves in their democratic splendor. At the same time, the *theatron* was a powerful visual amplifier that channeled and intensified focus upon the *orchestra*. It is difficult to imagine just how compelling this space is unless you place yourself at its center. Standing here, we intuit why the Greeks were compelled to call the seating area the *theatron,* the "seeing place," rather than our term, the auditorium, "the hearing place." While we are "those who hear" (the *audience*), the Greeks who sat in this place were *theatai*: "those who see." Only in the word "*theatre*" itself do we remember to look to the Greeks.

At this moment you are reading a book that purports to contain the *Oresteia*. But a text is only a trace of performance: Tragedy was the word made flesh. All that is left to us are traces: stones in a field, pigment on vase shards, scratches on papyrus. But tragedy is not in the traces. Tragedy was that annual time and space where thousands gathered on the hillside. Tragedy was the sum of forms flashed onto the mental retinas of its spectators, and the forms deposited by these impressions within the sub-structures of culture: impression turned instinct. Tragedy was these "instinct-forms" becoming implicated in other events and forms.

As we stand here, our imaginations begin to populate the vacant theatre with ghostly figures: Aeschylus himself teaching the chorus their choreography; the chorus of twelve or fifteen men stepping into the *orchestra* to perform for Dionysos before their fellow citizens; the *theatai* rapt in horror as they see a drama unfold in which a woman kills her husband and his royal sex slave; in which a city attempts to rise up against tyranny only to be cowed into servitude; in which a son kills his mother and her lover; in which the dark, avenging spirits of the Underworld track him down to the foot of the statue of Athêna on the Athenian Akropolis; in which a cosmic conflict erupts between old and new gods that threatens to destroy the city of Athens; and in which the outcry finally resolves into the birth-cry of democracy. This is the *Oresteia*.

And yet all is not as it seems. Although the theatre in which we are standing occupies virtually the same site as the fifth-century theatre, it was not until the 330s—about a century and a quarter after the *Oresteia*'s debut—that the statesman Lykurgus had these stone seats built. Aeschylus' audience sat on wooden benches or on the hillside. As for the stage and stage building, we do not even know for certain whether there was a raised stage behind the dancing place. A stage façade (*skênê*) of some sort, yes: This is attested by the various ancient sources, not least those surviving plays that require an architectural backdrop. But even here one must be careful, for in the seven extant plays of Aeschylus only the *Oresteia* requires a *skênê*. When exactly it was introduced is not known. It might be that the *Oresteia* was the first to call for one. In any case, the *skênê* that Aeschylus used for the *Oresteia* in 458 was a painted wooden structure, torn down at the end of the festival. Each year, a new *skênê* was built for the new plays to be staged. Not until some time between 421 and 415 did Athens have its first stone *skênê*.

The ornately carved stage base depicting events in the life of Dionysos that we see today is the product of the much later Roman reconstruction of the playing area. The Romans also utilized the Theatre of Dionysos for events other than dramatic presentations, spectacles such as wild beast hunts and gladiatorial contests, even flooding the orchestra to play out miniature sea-battles: sacrilegious conflations of theatrical performance and blood entertainments that dismayed the Athenians. What we see today is at a yet further remove. The archaeologists who "restored" this Greco-Roman theatre to its present state could not help but bring their own cultural and historical assumptions to bear on their reconstruction of the space. In *Tragedy in Athens*, David Wiles describes how excavators of the theatre had in their minds a preconception of how they wanted the space to look and rearranged it accordingly. Rather than a totally symmetrical construction that bespeaks architectural perfection, the area may have been irregular: The past was made to conform to what later cultures needed it to have been.

Time and time again as we begin to peel back the layers of the past, we will undergo these disorientating double takes: the immediate apprehension of trans-historical connection and of the "authentic," followed by the shocking realization of the distance and "otherness" that lies between *them* and *us*, between *then* and *now*, together with an ever increasing sense that (as the creators of the Parthenon knew) what we see is as much the product of our own ways of seeing as of "the past itself."

III. INVENTING AESCHYLUS

Some time later, resting on ancient seats about a quarter of the way up the hillside, we read from the final play of the *Oresteia* of Athêna's arrival in Athens to resolve the dispute between Orestês and the Furies. It is eerie to hear Aeschylus' words in this space, temporarily liberated from the deathly clutches of world literature, reading lists, newspaper reviews, and book clubs (the flesh made word). Overlooked by the sacred citadel in which the scene is set, we seem to sense the ghosts crowding around, willing us to re-experience for them the wonderment of the trilogy's first performance.

But instead, we immediately find ourselves caught up in yet more double takes: The words we read are no more those of Aeschylus than this theatre is the one for which he wrote. Like the ruins of the Theatre of Dionysos, the script has been "restored." Each edition of the original Greek text is an amalgam of variant texts involving painstaking scholarship over hundreds of years, with no guarantee that we have got it right: The variants add up to a million possible versions.

The plays have been captured and colonized, too, by our dictionaries—by words, ideas and images amenable to our own, very different and (counterintuitively) much *more* ancient culture. Translation is a kind of reconstructive archaeology, with all the inevitable interpretative distortion and tacit vested interests that this involves. The analogy is worth pursuing. Should we strip away the remains of the Roman theatre to reveal the Hellenistic stage? Why stop there? Why not go back to the Lykurgan theatre of the 330s? But surely we should remove even this: clear the site of all stone, to recover the pure earth of the golden age of Athenian theatre in the fifth century? In translation as in archaeology, each decision obscures as much as it reveals: The quest for "authenticity" can be as destructive as it is creative.

So alien to us are ancient Greek language and theatre that we cannot simultaneously give equal weight in our own translations to their poetic imagery, linguistic economy, dramatic pace, linguistic register, and cultural connotations, much less offer "equivalents" for the ideological, social, and religious functions that the ancient plays may have fulfilled. One thing *is* clear: Whatever we are reading, it is not the play as written or imagined by Aeschylus or his contemporaries. Insofar as each translation attempts to be loyal to some particular aspects of our understanding of Aeschylean tragedy, it will necessarily betray others. If a modern translator's ethic requires us to renounce the "dream of the master text," it also requires us to acknowledge and take responsibility for the partiality of our decisions. What is less frequently recognized is that it also calls for an equally rigorous reader's or theatre practitioner's ethic that apprehends, even embraces, the partiality of *all* interpretation.

Does this disorientation, this loss of the "authentic" disappoint us? Only if we think that "the authentic" is what we are really hoping to find. But perhaps what we are pursuing (however we may choose to imagine it) is an experience authentic *to ourselves in response to* the fragments we assemble as "the past." The ghosts that we encountered in the Theatre of Dionysos may be the projections of our own impressionable imaginations; they are no less moving or provocative for that. Is this an invitation to "ignominious relativism," as one scholar has recently phrased it? Not quite. There is nothing ignominious about recognizing that dialogue with "the past" is a two-way communication— or that *we* are the ones asking all the questions.

IV. THE CITY DIONYSIA

The City Dionysia did not simply evolve out of folk tradition; it was invented in cold blood. Dionysos, the young death-and-resurrection god, was honored in towns and villages throughout Attica by annual festivals of song and dance: the Rural Dionysia, Anthesteria, and Lenaia. A deity of supernatural creative and destructive force who presided over the pleasures and perils of phallus and wine, civilization and the wilds, he was deemed safer friend than foe, better domesticated than ostracized. At the heart of this powerful enactment of agricultural and communal renewal was the *dithyramb* (sung and danced religious choruses). In each of the ten tribes, or *demes*, two groups of fifty—one of men, one of boys—performed their sacred hymns dancing in a vast circle. These dithyrambs perhaps expressed a vision of the human community as part of a natural order eternally alternating between regeneration and death, each the condition of the other. It is also, Aristotle tells us, the origin of tragedy.

In the couple of centuries leading up to 458 B.C.E., the year in which the *Oresteia* won the first prize at the City Dionysia, Athenian self-fashioning advanced by welding a loosely associated gathering of urban and rural centers into a unified Athenian City-State. At some point in the sixth century, the city annexed the Dionysia, instituting an urban version of the rural festival that all of Attica was to attend. The City Dionysia was a spectacular expenditure of economic, artistic, and ideological capital, and rapidly became one of the greatest annual festivals of the Greek-speaking world.

The days preceding the theatrical performances were marked by lavish processions. From the early fifth century, each year's festival began with the triumphant arrival of the cult statue of Dionysos from outlying Eleutherai into a sanctuary within the city. The altars were made to burn with precious sacrifices, and hymns in honor of the god were sung. This procession simultaneously symbolized and effected the transformation of Dionysos into a major patron of the city. Another resplendent procession, the *pompe*, culminated with the highest possible sacrifice to Dionysos: bulls. In addition to the male citizens of Athens, others who, like Dionysos, were honored outsiders yet central to the life of the city—females and resident aliens—were also represented, their symbolic presence marked by the carrying of cult objects and the wearing of special robes. Dionysos reciprocated with the gift of the *komos:* the riotous, alcohol-enhanced revel the god of wine and the wilds inspired in his followers.

Tragedy and Control

The City Dionysia appropriated the dithyramb. A total of twenty dithyrambs were performed in the course of the festival: two from each *deme,* involving a thousand dancers in all. It was also for the City Dionysia that the benevolent tyrant Peisistratos commissioned the first standardized text of Homer. The festival was thus defined, at least in part, by the civically controlled performance of Greek mythical heritage, and by a concern to transform the fluidity and variability of that heritage into an officially sanctioned, communally shared version. Like the Rural Dionysia itself, a fluid folk tradition was thus made worthy of a *civic* festival by being subjected to the city's regulatory control.

At least from 444, but probably from the earliest days of the festival, playwrights and performers were required to present themselves and the subject of their plays in public for formal approval before the performances could take place. The ceremony was called the *proagon.* Given the many months of preparation and tremendous costs that went into staging a tetralogy (three tragedies and a satyr play), it is likely that the *proagon* was usually a routine procedure, but we cannot discount the possibility that the power of veto implicit in such an event might have been used in certain instances. Nor did the city's control end there: The city chose ten judges by lot—one from each deme—to award prizes for the best playwright, the best *choregos* and, after 449, the best tragic actor. Despite the great significance past scholars have placed on the outcome of these awards, only a random five of the ten verdicts were actually counted. Except in the case of an overwhelmingly outstanding winner, this is hardly to be considered a secure gauge of the views of the many thousands gathered on the hillside, and there is some evidence to suggest that prominent individuals may have influenced the judges for their own ends. The random element in the vote tactfully allowed the god a hand in choosing the winners (perhaps echoed in Athêna's decisive, casting vote in the *Eumenides*). Finally, on the last day of the festival, the people assembled in the Theatre of Dionysus to discuss and pass resolutions on the conduct of the festival. Theatre was thus seen and experienced as one of the organs of democracy. What is important is that each specific performance had to be formally *authorized, judged,* and finally *deliberated upon* by the city. The playwrights, patrons, performers, and the city therefore were obliged to recognize their responsibilities to each other. Above all, the makers of theatre had carefully to observe the civic limitations within which they could function.

Probably some time around the middle of the fifth century (although possibly as late as the fourth century), a festival fund called the *theorikon* was established, which distributed money so that even the poorest citizens could afford to attend the theatre. The implication seems to be that festival going, and theatre going in particular, were seen as part of what it meant to be an Athenian citizen—perhaps even part of a person's duties as a citizen. Meanwhile, at the other end of the socioeconomic scale, each tetralogy was lavishly funded by a wealthy backer, a *choregos,* as a form of ostentatious service to the city.

In return for laying on a rich and wondrous display, the *choregoi* could expect to win personal glory and influence in the city. Less glamorously, this *liturgy* could be viewed as the democracy's super-tax designed to keep would-be oligarchs in their place. Once appointed, a *choregos* could require citizens to perform in the chorus, even to the point of insisting that they be exempted from military service, although their participation would add more greatly to the honor of the *choregos* if contributed willingly. The *choregos* was expected not only to hire actors, musicians, extras, stage props, and costumes, but also to house, feed, and train the chorus at his own expense during the rehearsal period. Much prestige could be gained by visibly providing for the performers and for the production itself far beyond the call of duty. In the event that the tetralogy won the competition, the *choregos* paid for the masks used in performance to be dedicated to Dionysos—they were hung about his temple—and for the setting up of a monument dedicating the victory to the god. On occasions it seems that *choregoi* came close to bankruptcy in their desire to excel each other and win the approval of the city.

The evidence available to us also suggests that to sponsor a tragic tetralogy cost the financial equivalent of funding a fully equipped, fully manned warship (*trireme*) for about eight months (also a form of *liturgy*).[1] Indeed, the connections between military and theatrical domains are striking, and are made repeatedly by ancient commentators—not always favorably. In about 115 C.E., Plutarch recorded a certain Spartan criticizing the Athenians for "lavishing so much on their love for play, in effect pouring the expense of large fleets and the provisions of armies into the theatre." It is no coincidence that the term *liturgy* used to describe the honor/duty of funding the dramatic choruses could also be used to describe the funding of a warship or of an athletic team. The colossal scale of investment of state resources in theatre asserted that theatre's importance to the life and survival of Athens was deemed comparable, perhaps even coterminous, with the city's capacity to defend and extend itself.

In a century in which Athens spent at least as much time at war as at peace, military prowess was the supreme signifier of a man's worth as a citizen. Greek religion stipulated few sexual taboos and thus allowed a relatively free interlinking of social and sexual desire. In a comprehensively militarized citizenship, male beauty was held at a premium, and in this socially informed aesthetic, beauty was largely associated with athletic fitness. Unsurprisingly, the gymnasium in which men trained and competed naked is often referred to by contemporaneous sources as a prime place in which to observe and be observed by potential social and sexual partners: The vignette at the opening of Plato's dialogue, *Lysis,* is not untypical of such accounts. Within this male-orientated aesthetic, close friendships between like-aged youths played an important part in the social and sexual development of future citizens. A more formally codified form of social-sexual relationship was that between an older man, typically in his twenties, and a younger, beardless boy, enacted through gift-giving rituals, and patrolled by clear understandings (and in some cases laws) regarding the way in which each partner (*erastes* and *pais,* respectively) was expected to behave. It is quite probable that these relationships would have been subject to some form of family approval, and in time the older of the couple might well have been instrumental in helping his younger protégé find a suitable wife.

The City Dionysia was directly associated with the coming-of-age of warrior-youths. From at least the middle of the fifth century, part of the triumphal pageant preceding the theatrical performances was the presentation to the assembled *theatai* of those young trainee soldiers, *ephebes,* whose fathers had died fighting for the city. They had been brought up and educated at state expense, and they were now formally presented by the city with their weapons. In return, they solemnly swore an oath to fight and die in the service of Athens as their fathers had done before them.

The festival was thus a time of change: People came of age, changed their bodies, their status, and their roles. Boys' bodies were transformed in the eyes of the city into those of men. Acquiring weapons, they became living signs of civic service and patriotic death.

The festival was about civic regeneration, which is to say, about the annual succession of life and death. We recall that Dionysos, characteristically resident upon such borders, was also a fertility god. In the urbanization of the Rural Dionysia, an ancient, rural fertility ritual was being cast in a civic context, and regeneration thus acquired new dimensions: economic, political, poetic. Ideas, beliefs, understandings had to be regenerated too. The city had to be reborn. This involved a fascinating and complex bifurcation: The festival both looked back to the past—bidding farewell, remembering the dead—and to the future—forging anew its faith, values, forms, and practices.

Much excellent scholarship has concentrated upon the way in which tragedy increasingly came to incorporate the language of political and legal vocabulary of the democratic law-courts or citizen's assembly (*ekklesia*). It has been argued that tragedy assumed the role of providing exemplary and persuasive displays of rhetoric, "training" its citizen-audience to adjudicate the merits of argument and counterargument. But tragedy also offered exemplary displays of *physical* discipline and skill akin to those required in the "theatres" of war and athletics. Whether the tragic choruses were composed of *ephebes* as J. J. Winkler argued, or of older men, theatrical choreography was a highly demanding display of group discipline and skill—that is to say precisely the same virtues that were valued within a highly militarized culture. The martial connections of dance for the Greeks were clear. Plato, writing around 350 B.C.E., describes a type of dance that "has to do with war and beautiful bodies engaged in violent struggle," and Plato's teacher, Sokrates, is said to have written that "those who honor the gods most beautifully with choruses are best in war." The correspondence was so close that, for Athenaeus, dancing was "virtually like military maneuvers." During the performances, the ten generals in charge of the city's armies were present in honorific seats in the front row of the *theatron*. They, too, participated in the absorption of the dramatic performances into the military ideology of the city by collectively pouring a libation. Theatre, therefore, along with war and athletic competition, was a time and place in which Athens self-consciously "performed" its citizens' excellence, publishing to the Greek world its citizens' supremacy as warrior-citizens.

In return for receiving lavish funding, high cultural status, and full military honors, tragedy was expected to add new artistic treasures to the city's other riches. New hymns, dances, poems, plays, speeches, ritual practices, and monuments entered the life of the city through the dramatic festivals. Aeschylus, for instance, is reputed not only to have directed and acted in his own tragedies, but also to have introduced a new "comeliness and magnificence of dress" that was subsequently absorbed into religious worship at the Eleusinian Mysteries. According to Athenaeus, Aeschylus invented and taught his chorus-members many new dance steps. Tragic dance evidently fulfilled an important narrative function within specific plays. "Telestes, Aeschylus' dancer, was such a consummate artist, that in dancing the *Seven against Thebes* he was able to communicate the events with his dancing," records Athenaeus.[2] But its value also extended beyond that as new dances became absorbed into the broader social and cultural life of the city. The texts of the victorious plays themselves were memorized by Athenian citizens. As "memory-texts," these plays acted as shared cultural referents, contributing to a communal experience of Athenian identity. So potent was tragedy as a sign and agent of cultural regeneration that within his own lifetime Aeschylus' successor, Euripides, saw certain Athenians reprieved from slavery in Syracuse because they could recite from memory choruses that he had composed.

By acquiescing to civic control, along with other (athletic, political, and military) forms of public performance, theatrical performances acquired prestige, wealth, and an enlarged range of official, cultural functions. For its part, tragedy assumed the task of defining, consolidating, and at times challenging the city's dominant values. By producing rituals of affirmation and of contestation, tragedy reproduced the city within a dialectic of critique and congratulation. But by the same token, theatre became an agent of civic control, with all curtailments and changes attendant upon assuming new responsibilities. Unfree, implicated in a strident patriotic pageant of military and economic might, fettered to political patronage, financially and ideologically likened to a warship, and made to compete for favors before a bench of judges, Tragedy, Comedy and Satyr Play bowed to necessity and became indentured servants.

Distance

With that strange, Dionysian combination of belonging and not quite belonging, tragedy generally preferred to confront questions of moment through distanced, "mythistorical" narratives ("plot," "myth" and "history" were all *mythos* to the Greeks). Where recent historical events did appear, as in the *Persians* of Aeschylus, they were edited to yield a different order of "truth"—supernatural interventions estranged and elevated them to the status of myth. Eschewing the politics of directness, tragedy avoided the directness of politics: Tragic estrangement offered the city critique without divisiveness. *The Capture of Miletos* proves the rule: In 493 B.C.E., Phrynichos' play allowed its audience to mourn the previous year's catastrophe and to set it within a collective frame of understanding that would strengthen Athens in wisdom and resolve. But in doing so, it collapsed the crucial distance between tragedy and politics and in turn became a political casualty. Herodotus' *Histories* (6.21.2) records that Phrynichos was fined a thousand drachmas for distressing the city and his play permanently banned. (Even *katharsis*, it seems, has city limits.)

The revisionist mythistoricism of the *Oresteia* itself is audacious. Allusively connecting with currents in contemporaneous sociopolitical discourses—most notably the reform of the Areopagos court, current gender debates, and military and diplomatic relationships with Argos—the *Oresteia* culminates with the invention of a new charter myth for Athenian democracy based upon the personal intervention of the city's patron goddess. There was nothing neutral, safe, or routine about tragedy such as this. Each play was a forceful, persuasive intervention in the material, cultural, and ideological life of the city, serving its citizen masters by simultaneously connecting with and challenging their most basic assumptions and "reforming" the stuff of their beliefs according to the pressure of their most urgent needs.

V. THE TROUBLE WITH CHILDREN . . .

There are an amazing number of children in Greek tragedy, most of them either dead, dying, or . . . disposing of someone. Approaches to the social aspects of Greek tragedy for many years now have concentrated upon representations of women, and to a lesser extent barbarians. A fraction of that effort has gone into thinking and writing about representations of children. But the *Oresteia* begins with the slaughter of children, and the revenge of mothers.

There are two child-stories in the history of the House of Atreus of concern to the *Oresteia*. The first has to do with Agamemnon's father, Atreus. Eager to secure the throne of Mykenê for his heirs, Atreus summoned his rival brother Thyestes to a reconciliation banquet. Their children played outside while the two brothers chatted, or so Thyestes thought. In fact, Atreus had Thyestes' children killed. Not content with that, in macabre mimicry of child-swallowing, sky-god Kronos, he had the young bodies chopped and boiled into a sweet-tasting stew that the boys' unwitting father ate. On finding some identifiable body parts at the bottom of his bowl, Thyestes realized the dreadful truth and let loose a deadly, eternal curse upon the House of Atreus. Of Thyestes' sons, only one, Aigisthos, escaped his father's banquet.

In the *Oresteia*, Aigisthos has returned to Mykenê to avenge his brothers' deaths. Atreus has been succeeded by his son Agamemnon. While Agamemnon is away in the east leading the Greek troops in the war against Troy, Aigisthos becomes the lover of Agamemnon's wife, Klytaimnêstra. It is now ten years since Agamemnon set out for Troy, and Klytaimnêstra has her own good reasons for wanting to see her husband Agamemnon dead. Together, Klytaimnêstra and Aigisthos plan how best to kill the king when he returns from Troy.

Child-story 2: Agamemnon is truly his father's son. Like Atreus, he will stop at nothing in the pursuit of power and glory—especially not at the killing of children. This time it is worse: This time it is his own child.

Agamemnon's brother Menelaos was stupid enough to let his wife, Helen, elope with a pretty Trojan prince named Paris. The Greeks, relinquishing their famed fondness for moderation and proportion, amassed a great army under the command of Agamemnon and set off to reduce the whole city of Troy to rubble, kill every living man and boy, and enslave the women and girls. If the Trojans felt this was a rather tough penalty to pay for a Greek woman's wayward ways, consider the alternative: Greek women might think they could go off with any charming Persian with half a ship of gold who smelled better than their husbands. Above all, the story of the Trojan War is about the importance of keeping women in their place.

There was a problem, however. The Greek fleet was stormbound at Aulis and could not sail to war. Reading the omens, the prophet Kalchas declared that the goddess Artemis required Agamemnon to slaughter his own daughter upon her altar if he wanted to lead the Greeks to glory at Troy. After some weeping and regal stick thumping, Agamemnon bowed to Necessity (*Necessity*—a useful word in Greece for defending the indefensible). Aeschylus tells the rest:

> Madness took hold.
> His mind changed course in the evil blast
> and reeled in its utter ruthlessness.
> From that moment he could stop at nothing.
> His mind, sickened by Necessity,
> grew bold with evil.
> Only then did he have the heart
> to seek his daughter's death,
> first sacrifice to a war to win back a whore,
> the life of a child for a fair wind.

The whole gory sacrifice scene is recounted in some detail by the Old Men of Argos in the opening chorus of the *Agamemnon,* with a combination of death and sexual desire that is typical of tragedy, not least of the *Oresteia*. Agamemnon should have known better than to sacrifice Klytaimnêstra's daughter on the altar of his ambition: From that point on, he is caught in a trap between the twinned hatreds of his cousin, Aigisthos, and his wife, Klytaimnêstra. This is where the plays begin.

Agamemnon

The trilogy opens on the palace roof where a Watchman waits for a signal announcing the fall of Troy. Ten years have elapsed since the Greeks sailed to war. The signal arrives and, jubilant, he calls the good news to the household. A Chorus of Old Men of Argos enters to report that all the altars in the city are ablaze with sacrificial offerings. Having recounted the story of Iphigeneia at Aulis, they call on Queen Klytaimnêstra, regent in her husband's absence, to explain the burning altars. She tells them of the fall of Troy. At first skeptical, they are won over. They sing of Helen and Paris, the grief and civil unrest that this empty war has brought to Greece.

A Herald arrives announcing the imminent return of Agamemnon, victorious from Troy. The Old Men hint darkly that all is not well in Argos, but Klytaimnêstra sends him back with a message of innocent welcome for Agamemnon. Before going, the Herald reveals that most of the Greek fleet has been lost in a terrible storm on the voyage home. The Chorus sing of the evils of Helen.

Agamemnon arrives in a chariot, with Kassandra, a Trojan priestess of Apollo, in tow. The Chorus welcome him, again hinting that those who seem faithful may have something to hide. Agamemnon salutes the city's gods, describes his victory at Troy, and determines to enter the palace. Instantly, Klytaimnêstra stalls him. Having declared her faithfulness to him, and her loving relief to see him safe and sound, she informs him that she has sent their son, Orestês, to an ally for safekeeping against possible revolt in Mykenê. She then orders slaves to lay out a rich purple tapestry carpet between Agamemnon's chariot and the palace doors so that Agamemnon can enter in kingly dignity. Agamemnon appears offended. The tapestries are vastly expensive. To damage them by stepping on them would be wasteful and arrogant; it would incur the disapprobation of the city and the wrath of the gods. Klytaimnêstra persuades him that, as conqueror of Troy he deserves no less, and she enables him to walk upon them by presenting it as a concession to her. As he does so, she expresses her pleasure at his homecoming. The Chorus are full of foreboding, however. They sense that something is terribly wrong.

Klytaimnêstra then instructs Kassandra to enter the palace too. Kassandra is agitated, but she says nothing. Klytaimnêstra enters, leaving the Chorus to attempt to communicate with Kassandra. She, however, suddenly bursts into sounds of lament, directed at the god who does not accept laments: Apollo. The Chorus are distressed by this ill omen. They know that Kassandra is a princess of the royal house of Troy. Gradually, as Kassandra becomes more comprehensible, she reveals that, because she accepted and then rejected the god Apollo's sexual advances, he first gave her the gift of prophecy, and then cursed her so that, while she would accurately foretell the future, no one would believe her. Thus, she was able to foresee the doom of Troy, but not avert it. She demonstrates that she knows the bloody history of the House of Atreus, and prophesies that Klytaimnêstra is even now preparing to kill Agamemnon inside the house, and her with him. She rips from herself the prophetic garments of Apollo and tramples them underfoot. Knowing that she cannot escape death, she approaches the palace, but she recoils at the horrors within. Steeling herself once again for death, she finally enters.

The Chorus barely have time to draw breath before Agamemnon is heard to cry out. The Chorus panic. They realize what is happening, but they cannot agree on whether to storm the palace or wait for further information. Klytaimnêstra appears, spattered with blood, and the bodies of Agamemnon and Kassandra are displayed. He is enmeshed within a net-like material, having been hacked down with an axe like a sacrificial animal. Klytaimnêstra now openly declares her hatred for him, and her joy at having paid him back for the death of Iphigeneia. There is a bitter exchange with the Chorus, in which she seeks to justify herself in their eyes, not least by invoking the curse upon the House of Atreus. They are not convinced.

Finally, Aigisthos arrives with a cohort of guards. To justify his part in planning the killing of Agamemnon, he recounts the gruesome story of the child-banquet in which all his brothers perished. The Chorus accuse him of cowardice for having left the killing to a woman. He threatens them with death unless they show him respect. A massacre is only averted by the intervention of Klytaimnêstra who persuades him to ignore the Old Men, and to enter the palace with her to commence their reign.

Libation Bearers

The second play takes place several years later, when Orestês, son of Klytaimnêstra and Agamemnon, now a young man, returns from exile to avenge his father's murder. He is with his companion-mentor-lover, Pyladês, whose father has raised Orestês from childhood. Orestês places a lock of his hair on his father's grave as a funeral tribute. At the approach of Êlektra and a Chorus of Women Captives from Troy, Orestês and Pyladês move out of sight. Êlektra and the Chorus have been sent by Klytaimnêstra, who has had an ominous dream, in order to propitiate the dead king with tomb offerings. Instead, the Chorus convince Êlektra to pray for the return of Orestês as avenger. Pouring the libations on the grave mound, she notices the lock of hair and footprints that she believes are those of her brother. Orestês reveals himself to her and proves his identity when he shows her a piece of tapestry that she had woven for him when he was a child. He tells her of Apollo's command that he avenge his father, and of the unspeakable punishments to which he will be subject should he fail to do so. Together, brother and sister and Chorus pray at length in order to summon the vengeful spirit of their father, Agamemnon, until they are convinced that the dead king has heard them and will aid them from beyond the grave. Orestês then lays out his murder plan. Left alone, the Chorus sing of the wickedness of women in the past and of the advent of Justice.

Following the ode, Orestês and Pyladês enter in the disguise of travelers from Phokis. After a brief encounter with the Gatekeeper, Klytaimnêstra enters and receives from them the news of Orestês' death in exile. Believing the tale, she welcomes them into the palace. Enter then Kilissa, the nurse who tended Orestês as a baby, in tears at the news. She has been sent to fetch Aigisthos and his bodyguard. The Chorus, however, have no trouble persuading her to alter her message and have Aigisthos come alone. Aigisthos arrives following a choral ode and proceeds into the palace. Not long after, an offstage cry announces his death. Klytaimnêstra enters to face Orestês. With the encouragement of Pyladês (who speaks his only three lines in the entire play at this point), Orestês forces Klytaimnêstra, step by step, back into the palace.

After an ode of joy sung by the Chorus, the doors open and Orestês is seen standing over the bodies of Klytaimnêstra and Aigisthos. Orestês orders slaves to throw down the net-like tapestry robe used in the murder of his father so that all can see it. Unlike Klytaimnêstra in the *Agamemnon*, standing over the bodies of her husband and Kassandra, elated and proud of her conquest, Orestês here betrays no evidence of triumph, only anger, then sadness, and finally frenzy as in his mind's eye he sees his mother's Furies closing in as the result of her curse. Tortured by the vision, he sets out for Delphi to seek Apollo's protection. The Chorus wonder when the end to suffering will come.

Eumenides

The final play of the trilogy opens in front of the temple of Apollo at Delphi. The Prophetess Pythia prays before commencing the day's activities, and enters the temple, only to crawl out a moment later in a state of abject terror.

In the god's sanctuary, she says, is a man dripping blood, and surrounding him a swarm of sleeping female Furies too horrible to be endured. She summons Apollo before leaving. Apollo and Orestês enter. The god sends Orestês on a journey that will last years but will culminate with his arrival at Athens. The vengeful spirit of Klytaimnêstra insinuates itself into the dreams of the Furies, harshly instructing them to resume pursuit of Orestês. The Furies awake only to be confronted by Apollo who threatens them with his bow and arrows and expels them from his sanctuary. They round on him for having created a matricide and for having ignored their ancient rights. After a brief exchange, the Furies leave in pursuit of Orestês.

The scene changes to the Athenian Akropolis and the monumental statue of Athêna where Orestês, after his lengthy wanderings, seeks sanctuary. Almost immediately the Furies enter and surround him. Ignoring his claims that he has been purified of all blood-pollution, they begin to sing a song of power that will bind and destroy him. At this point Athêna enters. Having ascertained the identity of both Furies and Orestês, she determines that only a trial can settle the issue. She leaves to select a jury of the best of Athenian male citizens.

Following a song by the Furies, we understand that the scene has now moved to the Areopagos, the Hill of Arês next to the Akropolis, where the trial commences. The Furies serve as prosecution, Apollo as defense. The issue is matricide: Can a son kill his mother to avenge his father? Before the vote is taken, Athêna establishes the institution of trial by jury, and principles of justice for all time. The jurors vote but, hemmed in on one side by the Furies' threats of terrible curses upon Athens should they lose the vote, and on the other by the authority of Zeus as represented by Apollo, the vote is even. Athêna exercises her casting vote, and Orestês is acquitted.

Orestês in gratitude pledges his and his city's eternal friendship with Athens. The Furies protest the injustice of the decision, enraged that their age-old rights have been usurped by the new gods of Olympos. Appealing to Night, their mother, they threaten to blight the land of Athens. However, over a lengthy scene, Athêna calmly persuades them to relinquish their claims and accept an honored place in the Athenian state where they will forever be worshipped as fertility goddesses and protectors of justice; they will live in the rock beneath the Areopagos, the site of the Court. A triumphant musical dialogue follows between the Furies and Athêna. Now transformed from Erinyës (Furies) to Eumenides (Kindly Ones), they are dressed in purple robes by a Chorus of Athenian women and girls. The trilogy ends as they leave in a blaze of flaming torches and a song blessing their new home. Justice has been served, fertility is the land's blessing, and civic peace is established.

Proteus

There then followed a satyr play: a burlesque, mock-tragic play involving a combination of "serious" mythological characters and satyrs (bibulous, sexually avaricious goat-men). Each tragedian wrote a satyr play to follow his trilogy of tragedies as a light-hearted end to a long day's theatre going. Although we have many tragedies, only one satyr play—the *Cyclops* by Euripides—survives. We know the satyr play that Aeschylus wrote to follow the *Oresteia* was called *Proteus*, and it may have dramatized the story of how Menelaos and three of his companions disguised themselves as seals to trap the shape-changing, prophetic sea-divinity, Proteus.

VI. TRAGEDY AND ELITISM

The Chorus as Citizen Community

Aristotle holds Aeschylus responsible for having "cut down the role of the chorus, and give[n] the first place to the dialogue." If the chorus originally had "the first place," then we realize that this is not drama as we (have come to) know it. We have to do a 180-degree shift in our expectations of these plays until we understand that the chorus is no mere bystander-commentator, or human wallpaper for the "lead" actors. Rather, the chorus is at the theatrical and conceptual epicenter of the *Oresteia*.

In the *Agamemnon*, for instance, it is the chorus that is given the critical role of retelling the story of the sacrifice of Iphigeneia at Aulis. This story is so central to understanding the actions of Klytaimnêstra in the *Oresteia* that French director Ariane Mnouchkine prefixed her production of the *Oresteia* with a production of *Iphigeneia at Aulis* by Euripides, in which the tragic plight of Klytaimnêstra is given great prominence. In the last play the chorus *is* the central character: the Erinyës, later called Eumenides, after whom the play is named.

Each chorus in the trilogy has its own distinct identity and function. Even the conventional constraint to which the chorus is usually subject—that it can observe but not affect the action—does not apply here. The vast expanses of choral odes that seem to stretch out forever on the page, in performance are spectacular virtuoso displays of song and dance; and we recall that the chorus may also have been viewed as an idealized display of quasi-military drilling. The *theatai*, who in the course of the festival would watch a total of twenty dithyrambs, must have looked forward to these theatrical choruses as some of the theatrical highlights of the plays.

It has often been argued that the chorus is simply a vicarious audience on stage, expressing, amplifying, and shaping the responses of the *theatai* to the action. There must be an element of this: If the chorus cannot win the empathy of the *theatai,* much of the emotional power of the plays is lost. But that alone is not enough. Are the sovereign people of Athens really to identify themselves straightforwardly with the Old Men of Argos who equivocate at every opportunity and who ultimately fail in their resolution to withstand tyranny? Or are they to be identified with the barbarian slave women who aggressively encourage the young elites to murder their own mother and the tyrant-king, and then when the plan is set in motion retreat to the sidelines muttering that they cannot be held responsible for whatever happens next? And *surely* they are not to be identified with the hideous Furies—daughters of Night—upon whom the gods can scarcely bear to look, and whom the city of Athens and its patron goddess somehow have to neutralize? On the contrary, insofar as the choruses do act as a vicarious audience, it is to present the Athenian citizens with *negative* models of itself: The choruses of the *Agamemnon* and *Libation Bearers* are examples of slavish behavior that guarantee (and thus in a sense justify) their subjection to tyranny.

The real counter-image to these *unfree* choruses is the silent chorus of Athenian citizens that appear in the *Eumenides.* Here Athêna calls upon the "best" of the citizens of Athens to vote in the homicide court and thus to decide the fate of their city: whether it will incur the wrath of the Furies or defy the Olympian gods; whether it will uphold justice over self-interest. Here the most admirable citizens of the city's male order are displayed hearing out both sides of the case, understanding the implications of rejecting either plaintiff or accused, and accepting responsibility for their city's future through voting. By doing so, they make themselves citizens worthy of mastery over their own affairs. The court system established by their patron goddess thus both recognizes, and enables Athenians to exercise, their "innate" masterful nature. Sovereign citizens of a democratic city-state, they are deemed worthy and able to control their own destiny.

And if these Citizen Jurors, who speak only through their votes, are the perfect response to the verbose but slavish Chorus of Old Men in the *Agamemnon,* then the women of Athens, redressing the placated Furies in robes of honor and leading them with song to their new home within the city, are a potent counter-image to the barbarian slave women of the *Libation Bearers.* In contrast to these slave women, urging natives to take violent retribution upon their fellows while seeking to remain immune from the implications of their actions, the final image of the *Oresteia* is a patriarchal society's idealized vision of "free" women in a democratic state, accepting their role within the symbolic and religious order of the city by finding songs of rejoicing to placate and win over ancient, defeated goddesses. Nine years after he had done so for the first time in the *Seven Against Thebes*, in the *Oresteia* Aeschylus again offered the city negative and positive models of both female and male citizenship.

A Theatre of Elites

No less central to the fashioning of the audience's citizen-subjectivity, however, were the roles played by the actors. If the choruses modeled the city as community, those characters who stand out from the choruses modeled the capacity of the individual citizen to shape the life of that civic community.

The interplay between collective and individual is perhaps the single most important axis around which the life of Athens revolved. Each citizen was at once a member of *and* an agent within the various collectives that made up the social and political life of the city. But this axis was also one of the most fraught. While powerful individuals could lead the city to glory, their very power could equally pose a threat to the democratic values in whose name and interests they purported to act. An attempt to neutralize this apparently irreconcilable conflict between individual and collective took the form of powerful rhetorical and institutional assertions that personal glory *in the eyes of the democratic city* was the ultimate attainment to which an individual citizen could aspire. In practice, relationships between powerful individuals and the collective were less than stable, indicated not least in the extraordinarily high number of the outstanding men in fifth-century Athens who were sooner or later killed off by the city.

The tension is implicit in tragedy, which addressed itself to the concerns and interests of the democratic city primarily through producing narratives of elites: Heroes and leaders drawn from the myths of the Homeric age. Athenian tragic representation was predicated upon the assumption that these troubled, ruling-class figures could iconically stand for the conflicts and contradictions that were part of the Athenian male's citizen life. Invidiously, the ruling-class bias slipped like poison into the bloodstream of the democratic city.

Take, for instance, the tragic treatment of the Battle of Salamis in Aeschylus' *Persians* in 472, *seven* years after a maritime force led by democratic Athens beat off the much larger fleet of the great monarchical enemy, Persia. This would seem to be a natural site upon which to build an encomium of the democratic city-state, and indeed the play is greatly concerned to assert the superiority of the masterless men of Athens and their democratically manned (if elite-funded) navy over the defeated forces of the Persian monarchy. But the play is set in the court of the Persian monarch, and it is largely concerned with whether the young king, Xerxês, has proven a worthy successor to his regal father, Dareios. While on one level a validation of Athenian democracy is present, what is much more remarkable is that, even in this most "democratic" of tragic subjects, the "natural" topic of tragedy is still to be identified with the fate of the ruling elites.

A similar structure can be observed in the *Oresteia*. The *Agamemnon* opens with a lowly house slave on night-watch duty on the rooftop:

> Gods, I pray for an end,
>> an end to my pain,
>> an end to my yearlong watch!
> I crouch here,
>> dog-like,
>>> on the roof of the palace
>>>> of Atreus' sons,
>> and know by heart
>> the gatherings of the stars,
>>> those glittering lords,
>>> dazzling in the firmament,
>> that bring us winter and summer.

From these opening moments to the eventual torch-lit procession of goddesses in which the citizens of Athens are invited to participate, the trilogy is concerned with gods and rulers, wars and death. The "little people"—slaves, citizens and soldiers—appear only to confirm that the "important" events are those that concern the "important" people. Even the gods leave off their pursuits to answer the call of kings.

At some level, the *Oresteia* is concerned with whether Orestês can become a worthy son and heir to his father, soldier-king Agamemnon. If the *Libation Bearers* is largely a study of Orestês' entry into manhood by learning, with the help of Pyladês, to assume the duties of an adult, the *Eumenides* is a study of his entry into the duties of Kingship. By the end of the trilogy, Orestês has enlisted gods on his side, has made treaties on behalf of Argos, and has promised in time to become one of the powerful, vengeful dead: He is truly his father's son. Thus, the ruling-class bias permeates every fiber of the dramatic texture.

The pervasiveness of this ruling-class perspective within tragedy's choice

an inhuman *hero*. Note, the only grounds on which the Chorus surrender to him their right to gripe (though not their gripes) and offer up to him praise is that he is now a conquering hero:

> Ten years ago,
>> when you marshaled the armies
>> to repossess that worthless whore,
>> you threw all Greece into a panic,
>>> we thought you evil,
>>>> a man gone mad with power,
> sending so many young lives to their graves.
>
> And then that sacrifice
>> to save your demoralized men
>>> from desertion and mutiny.
> Horrible, we said,
>> a mad man's desperate decision!
>
> But times change, and so do minds.
> And I welcome you now in friendship,
>> and praise you for this victory you have brought us.

The *Oresteia* is very greatly concerned with "bowing to the yoke of Necessity." Look through the text: Again and again, Necessity is held up as something that the wise will do. The whole slave-economy depends upon it. So does the subjugation of women. I'm not suggesting that heroes were justified on all counts: Gods and mortals both reserve the right to take umbrage at sacrilegious behavior. But in terms of social and political dominance, the simple law of life in ancient Greece was "winner takes all." Here, the Chorus recognize that they are subject to the victor's rule, and they must bow to it and give praise where praise is necessary.

Women, however, *can* have no heroic victories, no glory. A glorious woman is an oxymoron (the only glorious woman is one who has an ox sitting on her tongue, as the Watchman might say). A woman, therefore, has never had *any* justification for being troublesome. Consequently, Aeschylus allows Klytaimnêstra to bear the full brunt of his misogynistic narrative. So pervasive and persuasive is this rampant patriarchalism that the most potently *just* words in the trilogy are discredited simply because they are spoken by a women seeking glory for her deeds. Standing over Agamemnon's dead body,

Aeschylus' blood-spattered fiend of vengeance, Klytaimnêstra, addresses the outraged men of the Chorus:

KLYTAIMNÊSTRA: *(Speaks.)*
                    My, how pious we are,
        so suddenly!
Judge and jury all in place.
Passing judgment.
            Curses,
                hatred,
                    condemnation,
                        exile!
Where were you then,
            where were *they,*
            these citizens,
        when *this* man,
                at Aulis,
        raised the knife to his daughter's throat,
                                        Iphigeneia,
            his daughter and mine,
            caring not an iota that this was his child—
        she was no more to him than a goat
            from a flock of thousands!—
        this sacrificial creature torn from my womb,
                        and for what?
To charm away the cutting winds of Thrace
        and make some sailors happy!

        Why not have exiled *him,*
        driven *him* from the land,
                for his vicious, polluting act that soiled us all?
No, you never gave it even a *first* thought,
            let alone a second.
                        But of me and my *just* actions
            you are a cruel and exacting judge.

So powerful is the alliance of the play's philosophical, rhetorical, thematic, symbolic, and dramatic structures to the ideological substructures of its patriarchal host-culture, Athens, that the indisputable moral velocity of Klytaimnêstra's challenge is neutralized (at best). No matter what she says, all that the Chorus hear is the sick logic of a woman who does not know her place:

LEADER: *(Sings.)*
You're mad, with ambition,
with pride, with arrogance.
This bloody murder has fired your mind.
I see it in your eyes flecked with blood.

So invidious and overwhelming is the pro-male bias in this trilogy that, when asked to consider the significance of Agamemnon's dilemma at Aulis, an amazing number of my students concede that, in Agamemnon's place, they too would finally, reluctantly, have surrendered Iphigeneia. I will never forget the chill that gripped a lecture theatre when one student, a mother of three, said: "I would cut every last soldier's throat with a smile on my face before I let one of them lay his hands on a child of mine." That small dose of reality was delivered calmly, but with a conviction that left nobody in any doubt that she meant exactly what she said. The depth of feeling made it merely a cool statement of fact. Such glimpses allow us to peel back, for a moment, the rhetorical, cultural, and dramatic layers of the tragedy, and to expose its underlying suave, monstrous, patriarchal brutality.

To sustain one's own consciousness against the subtlety and beauty of a masterwork of the intellectual and artistic magnitude of the *Oresteia* is a difficult task. It's not so much that the conclusions are disturbing. In fact it's doubtful that there are any hard-and-fast conclusions: Nobody in the trilogy concedes that Agamemnon was right to kill Iphigeneia. On the contrary, the question is posed as a genuine dilemma, inviting the audience to think about the kind of qualities that a leader must have in order to command respect. What is disturbing, then, are not conclusions, but the way in which the structures of the plays formulate the questions. Tragedy's sole reason for existence is to reproduce itself. Or to put it differently, it is a story designed to make itself come true. Before delivering up its pleasures, tragedy requires its spectators to capitulate to the naturalness of its tragic vision. (Tragic truth demands tragic assuredness: Only an art form so sure of itself could produce the paradox that naturalness must be acquired through estrangement.) How, then, should we view these displays that desire to render themselves invisible—to be discovered to be so "natural" that they enter into Truth? The making of theatre, criticism, approaching the canon, become less a matter of reading between the lines than between the lies.

In this case, the audience is systematically conditioned by the dramatic narrative to privilege certain questions that are of interest and importance to males (preferably socially elite males). The problem of acquiring consciousness is made all the more difficult given that we ourselves are working within a set of cultural and linguistic parameters that are frequently gender biased. (Why, for instance, does the term for "hatred of females" (*misogyny*) have such widespread cultural currency, while the term for "hatred of males" (*misandry*) is a relatively unknown newcomer?)

We saw how, through its concern to ensure that Orestês grows to kingly stature, the *Oresteia* promulgates a vision of the world that is very much centered upon the concerns of social and political elites. Now, too, we can see that Orestês is fully his father's son in his willingness to sacrifice family and female rights to those of the dominant male. Indeed, by the end of the *Eumenides* not only has he overcome his mother, but through his petition to Athêna he has also succeeded in having inscribed a law *for all time* that females of the family are expendable in the pursuit of male glory. At the same time, in Athêna's universalization of Athenian justice, we see the ancient, powerful female divinities subordinated to the male rule of Zeus, all the more sinister and final for having been achieved through the agency of Zeus' warrior-daughter, Athêna. There's a curious circularity to all this when we note that in *Agamemnon,* Klytaimnêstra was already a protector of paternity: Did she not, ultimately, punish Agamemnon for his failure as father?

VII. FIRE AND TAPESTRY

Fire

Let's start with a detour: Promêtheus and Pandora. This story is curiously similar to the Judeo-Christian narrative of the "Fall" as recounted in Genesis. The Greek and Judaic narratives are both stupendously patriarchal: God/The Gods invent woman in the guise of Oscar Wilde ("I can resist everything except temptation"), and woman (Eve/Pandora) promptly ensures that all humankind is exiled from paradise (Eden/the Golden Age). Both narratives, interestingly, are intimately connected with the human thirst for knowledge, and its price.

In the Greek version, as related in Hesiod's *Works and Days* (53–105), it all starts with Promêtheus, a friendly Titan, who steals fire from Olympos to give to humans against the express command of Zeus. Fire is the source of all civilization. With fire, humans suddenly become like little gods (the Greek equivalent of the serpent and apple in Genesis, although the Greek version at least has the grace to allow that most of the world's problems tend to begin with men). Zeus, slightly upset by the frustration of his grand plan to exterminate the human race, punishes Promêtheus by chaining him to a mountainside for a few thousand years and dispatches an eagle to chew on his liver every day (don't mess with Zeus *whatever* the reason, seems to be the message). Meanwhile Zeus sets his mind to wreaking the most deadly havoc upon humankind he can conceive. The gift of fire will soon seem small recompense for what they are about to suffer. What catastrophe, what cataclysmic devastation does Zeus have in store for mankind? Fire? Plague? Earthquake? Flood? War? No, *much* worse: Woman! Fashioned from earth and water by Hêphaistos and Athêna, and armed by each of the gods in turn with some secret weapon: Irresistible beauty, deceit, charm, persuasiveness, and a kleptomaniac disposition, Pandora is loosed upon the unsuspecting world of men, and loses no time in distributing from her box the malign gifts with which she has been endowed:

> For the tribes of men had previously lived on the earth
> free and apart from evils, free from burdensome labor
> and from painful diseases, the bringers of death to men.
> In the power of these evils men rapidly pass into old age.
> But then woman, raising the jar's great lid in her hands and
> scattering its contents, devised anguishing miseries for men.
> Only Hope was left within, securely imprisoned,
> caught there under the lip of the jar, unable to fly
> out and away, for before this could happen she let the lid drop,
> as the Lord of the Aigis, Zeus of the Storm Cloud, decreed.
> But as for those others, those numberless miseries, they wander among men,
> for the earth is abounding in evils and so is the sea.
> And diseases come upon men by day and by night,
> everywhere moving at will, bringing evil to mortals
> silently, for Zeus of the Counsels has deprived them of voices.
> Thus in no way can anyone escape the purpose of Zeus.[3]

Tremendously entertaining as this saga of woe is, how does it help us with the *Oresteia*? The opening scene of the trilogy is set on the last morning of a Watchman's ten-year-long night patrol on the palace roof. He waits for the day he will see a pyre lit on a distant watchpost that will finally signal that the Greeks have sacked Troy, and they will soon be returning home. This scene establishes many of the conceptual, dramatic, and thematic preoccupations of the trilogy. The Watchman emphasizes that he acts on the instructions of

Queen Klytaimnêstra. It is she who presides over the cunning device of this relay beacon-signal from Asia to Greece. Fire and woman; woman and fire. Promêtheus and Pandora . . .

The Promêtheus myth draws attention to the problem of fire. Fire is a double-edged gift. It is the source of all that makes life worth living, but it comes with the terrible price of much that makes life miserable. That's the tricky thing about fire: It always carries this dual creative and destructive potential. Fire is the center of human life. It is the hearth: cooking, warming, protection against wild animals, the central point around which the life of the house revolves. From the fire of the forge comes the craft of metalwork: hunting, defense against enemies, the conquest of new territories, technologies for agriculture, tools and utensils for everyday use, and beautiful things to adorn private and public spheres. It is the hub of the community's shared life. In religious terms, fire comes to signify purification: burning away the impure, and carrying holy gifts up to the gods in the scent of precious oils, or the smoke of animal sacrifice. This is why fire is the ultimate symbol of inspiration, enlightenment.

But fire is also the destroyer. It is the uncontrollable blaze that a chance accident sets tearing through the city. It is the volcanic torrent of molten stone that consumes town, village, and farmland. It is the wargod's breath: the homestead burnt by marauding enemies, the distant haze of a smoldering harvest, the black smoke of a burning city—a none-too-distant memory for the Athenians, watching their play in the shadow of the burnt-out Akropolis.

Fire is therefore always symbolically (and thus mythically) ambivalent. Fire signifies a potential for creation and destruction, defense and attack, culture and its annihilation, spiritual purification and transgression of divine law. This ambivalence is written into the social practices surrounding the use of fire. The hearth-fire is the living flame at the center of the life of the *oikos* (household), to be kept alight at all times. But that fire has to be brought into the house from outside. Fire is thus simultaneously an intimate and an alien element in the *oikos*—the most creative and enabling, and also the most potentially destructive and damaging.

The Pandora episode of the Promêtheus-Pandora myth suggests a direct correlation between fire and the female. Woman is indeed a *fitting* punishment for the human possession of fire: She, too, is the heart of the life of the *oikos*. She, too, has to be brought into the house from outside as a wife. She, too, is simultaneously most intimate and most alien to the house, most creative and enabling through childbirth and the fulfillment of her domestic duties, and *therefore* also the most potentially destructive—best placed to damage and destroy that interior world.

The Promêtheus-Pandora myth encapsulates the insight (if that's what it is) that the creative and destructive elements in human life are each the necessary, inextricable condition of the other. The mythical narrative's seemingly simple duality of fire (creative) and female (destructive) is actually embedded within a more complex symbolic structure: By making the arrival of fire contingent upon the arrival of the female, the myth draws attention to the underlying duality of creative and destructive energies that exists within *both* fire *and* the female.

When the Athenian audience watches the opening scene of the *Oresteia,* with its woman-awaited fire, these theatrical signs are loaded with an ambivalent symbolic value. The Watchman greets the fire with whoops of exultation, but almost in the same breath hints darkly that something is rotten in the state of Argos:

> But I'll say no more.
> > "An ox sits on my tongue,"
> > as the adage has it.
> O if these walls had a voice,
> > what tales they could tell.

The Watchman is a character immersed within the everyday pragmatics of duty, and as such fails to recognize the dual symbolic potential of the fiery beacon. To him the only important duality is between the absence and the presence of the King: The fire promises welcome relief from the Queen's tyranny. The audience, however—aware of the beacon as a theatrical, and therefore symbolic construct (rather than a pragmatic reality)—will be mythically and culturally attuned to recognizing that the fire may well *both* be a triumphant messenger of destruction abroad *and* an ominous harbinger of doom at home.

In the later scene in which Klytaimnêstra jubilantly describes the brilliance of the relay-beacon system, the audience may have recalled another variant of the Trojan War homecoming myth, also concerning beacons. The story goes that the Greek fleet was shipwrecked not, as here, by a storm sent by angry gods, but rather by *false* beacon lamps lit by a grudge-bearing Greek. In one version, they are lit by Nauplius, whose son, Palamedes (associated with the invention of the alphabet—very Promêthean), was stoned by the Greeks at Troy at the instigation of Odysseus on trumped-up charges of treason. In one telling version, it was also Nauplius who was responsible for persuading the wives of the Greek commanders to take lovers while their husbands fought at Troy. This version is particularly suggestive, not least when we discover at the end of *Agamemnon* that Klytaimnêstra has formed an intimate alliance with her husband's mortal enemy and cousin, Aigisthos. But whether or not the *Oresteia's* beacons function as an ingenious allusion to the story of the shipwrecking father-Fury and of his promulgation of adultery among Greek wives, the mythically literate audience would have been alert to the possibility that beacons do not always contribute to a happy ending for Greeks returning from Troy.

The Chorus of Old Men are also aware that there is something fishy about Klytaimnêstra's behavior. They indicate more than once that they know Klytaimnêstra has not been behaving as a wife ought. Their description of Klytaimnêstra's boast of marital fidelity to the Herald as "innocent words to innocent ears" presses the protective courtesy of ambiguity to its limits. Their muted greeting to Agamemnon is an elaborate warning: "There are many who are not honest / who play at seeming, /… / And these transgress against Justice." The warning culminates in a compliment: "But you can see through that, Majesty," that they intend to be self-fulfilling. It is also a barely veiled threat to Klytaimnêstra: "You will learn soon enough / which of us stay-behinds / have been loyal to your cause, / and which have not." After ten years of subjection to this overweening female's harsh rule, they pleasure themselves with the prospect of ensuring that Klytaimnêstra will receive her due reward.

Long before Agamemnon's entrance, however, Klytaimnêstra's fabulous description of the beacon-relay diverts the attention of the Chorus from the important questions. She focuses their interest and their skepticism only on the beacons as a wondrous mastery of technology and men, and upon the news of the fall of Troy. The real question, of course, is not how the beacons work or whether they truly announce Agamemnon's return, but whether Klytaimnêstra herself will be true or false to Agamemnon. Reluctant to credit a woman's fantasy, the Chorus fail to consider even for an instant why this particular woman might want advance notice of this particular man's return, or why this adulterous wife seems to be so pleased at the prospect of her husband's imminent return. By playing on their desires and prejudices, Klytaimnêstra ensures that the Old Men, obsessed with what the beacons signal, are blind to what they might *signify*. She thus acquires sufficient mastery to ensure that she will be able to transform these apparent symbols of victory into sacrificial flames.

Fire opens and ends the trilogy as an ambivalent sign. In *Eumenides*, destructive ambivalence—the deathly symbols of fire and tapestry—is transformed into creative ambivalence—justice underwritten by violence. This symbolic transformation is a microcosm of the tragedy's ambivalence: Tragedy formulates conflicts but refuses to provide complete (discursive) closure. In that respect, the particular ambivalence of *Eumenides* is a microcosm of tragic ambivalence in general. *Eumenides* serves the *patriarchal* city by exemplifying how female voices and duties can be integrated into the civic order without surrendering male control (indeed, in order to underpin male control). It serves the *blessed* city by exemplifying how to worship the gods and accept their blessing *and* to keep control of the city in the hands, not of divinely ordained kings such as Agamemnon or of priests such as Kalchas, but of the people. It serves the *democratic* city by exemplifying how to accommodate several competing voices or points of view within the city without eschewing responsibility to choose between them when necessary.

Tapestry

For the Greeks of the fifth century, woven material had a high cultural value and significance. Textiles were intimate documents of an individual woman's expenditure of time, devotion, duty, expertise, creativity. As a sign of female productivity and duty, textiles displayed the woman's subordination to the corporeal needs of the male, and the good stewardship of the house. Textiles such as those laid out on the command of Klytaimnêstra for Agamemnon's return were "public" documents: They were one of the very few ways in which the female could display herself and enhance her honor without incurring disapprobation for having attracted attention to herself. As head of the household, Klytaimnêstra would have been responsible for supervising the creation of these tapestries.

But crucially women's industry and its product belonged to their *kurios*: their male, legal guardian (typically father, brother, or husband). The fact that her industry belonged to husband or the god (for example Athêna's *peplos*), ensured that a woman's personal pride and honor could only be achieved when refracted through those of her *kurios* and his city; females could only acquire glory through the benefit they brought to the dominant male within their household. Counterintuitively, textiles were both a potent symbol of *both* dutiful female productivity within the male order *and* patriarchal control and ownership of the female, her labor, skill, and stewardship of the domestic sphere. The quantity and quality of the labor that a female gave to her male *kurios* directly correlated to (and indeed effected) the degree to which that female was subordinate to that male. Each domestic product was a symbolic (and actual) surrender of female labor to the male: the greater the labor, skill, and artistry, the greater the surrender.

A kind of social equilibrium was reached: The "dutiful" and "excellent" wife received honor and respect for her "dutiful" and "excellent" productivity. But note, it was a patriarchally conceived equilibrium. Female happiness was always measured in terms primarily amenable to male interests: The productive woman was approved of exclusively insofar as she contributed herself and her labor to the male. For a woman to desire personal recognition or glory, rather than the reflected glory of her husband, is itself systematically represented in Greek literature as the gravest violation of female propriety. The stories of Klytaimnêstra and Mêdeia, as narrated by Aeschylus and Euripides, are perhaps the ultimate Greek horror stories of female insubordination. The ideal woman, then, sought no glory at all: "the greatest glory of a woman is to be least talked about by men, whether they are praising you or criticizing you"[4] as the historian Thucydides has the Athenian statesman, Perikles, say.

What Klytaimnêstra does is to manipulate the signs of this complex set of socioeconomic transactions. Klytaimnêstra's tapestries are the antithesis of faithful Penelopê's tapestry. Penelopê, wife of Odysseus, fends off the unwelcome host of importunate suitors during her husband's long absence following the Trojan War by winning one concession from them: sufficient time to complete weaving a funeral shroud for Odysseus' father, Laertes. By day she weaves; by night, she unpicks what she has woven. Her tapestry is incomplete, deferring publication. Reversing the traditional sign of the wanton, wasteful, unindustrious wife, Penelopê's unfinished tapestry is a document in which she secretly records her fidelity to her absent husband. Klytaimnêstra's tapestries, however, are complete, persuasive. Apparently an ostentatious display of her good stewardship of the city to her returned husband, they purport to speak of her wifely obedience working industriously to create wealth and honor for him even while away. But, in contrast to Penelopê's perpetually unfinished tapestry, Klytaimnêstra's splendid tapestries betray their "lord and master."

Klytaimnêstra thus exploits a deadly chink in the patriarchal armor. If the male gained wealth and honor through controlling female labor, this gave the female rather too much power: If a dutiful, productive wife could add to a man's wealth and glory, a "malfunctioning" wife could equally detract from it. A woman's lack of productivity in transforming the raw materials produced by male labor into valuable produce meant that the fortunes of the house would decline. Worse still, an ill-kept house could incur scandal. But worst of all, an extramarital affair could introduce a genetic impostor into the house, thereby threatening male control of inheritance. Of course, through their exclusive control of the legal systems, males had good ways of protecting their own interests against dysfunctional wives: They could divorce them by sending them back to their fathers, or, if caught in the act of adultery possibly even kill them (the male adulterer could be killed with impunity). But that was never quite enough to eradicate the danger that women pose. For an Athenian audience, women were always somehow "outsiders," dangerously situated at the heart of the family and city-state. Athenian women, unlike their Spartan counterparts, were barred from citizenship and almost all forms of public life, so they did not necessarily share the values of male citizens. They were deemed irrational and susceptible to illicit and excessive desires. Slave-like, they had to be mastered by men in order to remain healthy in themselves, and to contribute to the health and wealth of the city.

Having ruled the city in Agamemnon's absence, Klytaimnêstra has achieved a degree of personal public status that is abnormal for a woman—even an elite woman. Although this prominence has been necessary, it has also violated the fundamental gender codes of this society: Public status is, or should be, an exclusively "male" domain. The ambivalence of this necessary evil is registered in the descriptions of Klytaimnêstra by the Watchman and the Chorus of Old Men of the *Agamemnon* as a woman with masculine traits. (An anxiety about the roles of women in a society deprived of men through military duty figures largely in many of the comedies of Aristophanes, most notably the *Lysistrata* and *The Women at the Assembly*.)

Now, at Agamemnon's return, Klytaimnêstra seems poised to surrender her political power and public status to her *kurios*, Agamemnon, and to return to the private sphere of the domestic interior. The arrival of Agamemnon in front of the palace marks a cataclysmic moment in the life of the city: The powerful female will surrender her labor—her excellent, dutiful stewardship of the city—to her *kurios*, the king. When he enters the palace and once again assumes control of household and city, he will in the same instant transform this sovereign Queen, who has ruled the city with an iron fist for ten long years, into a subordinate, silent wife—a virtual social and political sub-entity.

Purple was precious. It was the most costly dye. In Greece, it was associated with the truly heroic and regal. As such, Klytaimnêstra's purple cloths symbolically link the domestic and the public worlds: They are, in effect, Klytaimnêstra's dramatic display of the value of her labor in stewarding the city as an extension of her royal household. Her request, while she clings onto these last moments of power within the city, that Agamemnon tread these tapestries, is an insistence that he publicly acknowledge the excellence of her labor—that he recognize her as a good and faithful wife. That is why she presses the point: She requires him to accept her token of good faith. That is why he contests it: As male of the house, he and he alone is responsible for mastering her labor and the uses to which the wealth it creates will be put. As a concession to her—a reward for her evident industry—and to his own vanity as general and husband, Agamemnon finally allows his wife her hard-earned moment of reflected glory, accepting what simultaneously is a symbolic surrender of her labor to his own greater glory.

If, as I have suggested, each domestic product is a symbolic and actual surrender of female labor to the male, then Klytaimnêstra's tapestries, spread under Agamemnon's feet such that the very act of treading them will damage or destroy them, is the ultimate, spectacular display of her total subordination to him, which she demands he accept.

Agamemnon would have this transaction take place quickly, invisibly, without ceremony. That the city was left in the hands of his wife was an unfortunate aberration of war. The sooner it is rectified and his mastery over her and the city is reasserted, the better. His first words to his wife after ten years are less than heart-warming:

> Guardian of my house, of my palace,
>   queen,
>   daughter of Lêda—
> your speech was like my absence:
>
>   long.

The formal build-up and sudden, condescending reproof is an attempt publicly to belittle her and her role. She has been his mere puppet; he has been in power all along:

> I have no need of footwipes and tapestries;
>   my fame speaks aloud,
>   speaks for itself,
>   without the aid of such crutches.

Agamemnon's message is clear: Klytaimnêstra has never really had any power of her own; she has but exercised *his* kingly authority. So while this scene is ostensibly about an internal conflict within Agamemnon—between desire for approval in the eyes of men, and desire for the kind of absolute power that renders such approval unnecessary—for an Athenian audience it is framed upon another conflict, intuitively understood rather than expressed directly. A rich and complex range of social and economic significations underlies this exchange making it meaningful to its audience as a multilevel transaction within the field of gendered power.

At least from Perikles' citizenship law of 451–450 , in order to introduce a son or adopted son into the honor of citizenship, a father had to swear a sacred vow that the child had been born of an Athenian woman from a legitimate union. In part, such an oath functioned as a husband's public affirmation of his wife's sexual fidelity, an acknowledgement that she had fulfilled her duty by providing the household with children. Control of female sexuality was thus central to the city's capacity to confer or withhold the considerable honors and obligations of citizenship. The *Oresteia* makes no claim to the historical accuracy of its representation of the heroic age, but for a fifth-century audience, Klytaimnêstra's repeated claims of sexual fidelity to Agamemnon are socially charged. In fifth-century Athenian terms, sexual fidelity of the female was synonymous with good stewardship of the house and, in Klytaimnêstra's case, of the city. These tapestries are the visible sign she offers him of her fidelity, embodied in dutiful industry on his behalf, dyed in the precious purple of blood signifying the perpetuation of life through childbirth into the house.

With the ghost of Iphigeneia hovering between husband and wife, the tapestries appear to signify Klytaimnêstra's willing subjection to Agamemnon of her own most precious labor, and her most intimate product: her flesh and blood, body and offspring. Just as the Chorus relinquish their criticisms of Agamemnon in the face of his god-granted victory, so Agamemnon understands her purple path as a belated acceptance of his complete mastery over life and death within the household. So complete is that acceptance that she invites him symbolically to kill their child all over again: urges him to exercise his absolute rights by treading the purple underfoot. He must accept it if he is to accept her belated, but now eloquent, recognition of his right to shed her daughter's blood. It is a royal woman offering a face-saving acquiescence. In Katie Mitchell's *Oresteia* for the UK's National Theatre in 1999, a silent Iphigeneia watched from the sidelines as Klytaimnêstra's house slaves laid before the feet of Agamemnon a purple pathway of young girl's dresses. It is in this context of Klytaimnêstra's total, and yet proud, surrender to a more worthy master that Agamemnon is required by her to accept all that she has produced for him, and to acknowledge before the people her claims of fidelity. If those claims are false, then to accept their sign will be fatal.

Agamemnon, riding the crest of his own recent mythologization as Sacker of Troy, wrongly presumes that his conquest of Klytaimnêstra is as complete as his conquest abroad. How can any mortal withstand him, before whom the walls of great Troy itself have fallen?

In a version of the myth later to be taken up by Euripides in his *Iphigeneia at Aulis*, Agamemnon lures Iphigeneia to her death at Aulis with a false message, summoning her on the pretext that she is to marry Achilles. Iphigeneia's death through the sign of the false message both enables and symbolically foreshadows Agamemnon's conquest of Troy through the false sign of the Trojan Horse. Master of fatal stratagems, Agamemnon fails to see his wife's Trojan Horse for what it is. Both of his false messages are chillingly recalled and inverted by Klytaimnêstra through her own false sign: the tapestries.

Klytaimnêstra appears to have created this "play," complete with props and speeches, in order to perform to Agamemnon her spectacular, proud surrender, with all the aristocratic vanity he would expect to find in Helen of Troy's sister. But in fact, Klytaimnêstra is setting up another play in which he, not she, is the true performer. Enticing Agamemnon to walk on the costly, delicate tapestries, she makes him perform before the city the bloodthirsty sacrilegiousness that spurred him to pave his own path to immortal glory with innocent blood. Destroyer of the household's and the city's most precious possessions, first he killed his own daughter, and then a generation of young men, "the flower of Argos." The tapestries are the "set" upon which Klytaimnêstra has Agamemnon play out his violent nature. By knowing him better than he knows himself, she acquires control over him, and kills him. (To be mastered by a woman is already a kind of death for a patriarch.) Agamemnon enters the palace, would-be conqueror carried upon a false sign of victory.

When she has perfected her vengeance—massacred him in the bath and slaughtered his war-trophy, elite sex-slave Kassandra—she can display to the audiences, both onstage and offstage, her final tableau. Having had Agamemnon himself perform to them his violations of civic and familial rights, Klytaimnêstra can now justify her own actions. Klytaimnêstra's elaborate performances, both as "actor" and "*choregos*," constitute a symbolic re-enactment of the past in order to shape the present.

In the male Athenian civic order, for a man to kill his daughter is disturbing; but for a woman to kill her husband is unforgivable. However, Klytaimnêstra's mastery of the situation, symbolic and actual, is complete: Enter Aigisthos, with all the military muscle necessary to quell any stirrings of dissent, and a chip on his shoulder large enough to want to do so.

Tapestries recur in all three plays. The story of the *Libation Bearers* is that of the return of Agamemnon, as replayed by his son. But this time, it is Orestês who is in control of the performance, playing the deceiver—the secretly intimate stranger. At the end of *Libation Bearers*, Orestês orders slaves to display the net-like tapestries in which Agamemnon died, and which themselves evoke (if indeed they are not the selfsame material as) the tapestries upon which Agamemnon trod on his fateful, fatal journey into the house. Whereas in the *Agamemnon* they were the portal between past and present, in *Libation Bearers* the tapestries become the retrospective justification for Orestês' murder of Klytaimnêstra in the sight of gods and people, and his passport to kingship.

The first part of the *Eumenides* is set in Delphi before the temple of Apollo. In front of the temple is a statue of Athêna. Of all the places that in classical antiquity laid claim to be the "center of the earth," Delphi is the most sacred. Marking it is the great *omphalos*: the Navel Stone. It is almost invariably depicted in sculptures, vase paintings and later Roman wall-paintings, covered with a net-like weave. When the Pythia enters the temple, it is at the sacred *omphalos* that Orestês sits, seeking sanctuary from the Furies. It is possible that the interior of the temple, with the sleeping Furies surrounding the *omphalos*, is displayed after the Pythia exits. This may have been achieved using the *ekkyklema*, the same low, wheeled platform eased out of the central doors of the *skênê* upon which the dead bodies had been displayed at the end of the *Agamemnon* and the *Libation Bearers*. Indeed, Apollo abuses the Furies in terms reminiscent of the fate of the House of Atreus: "You belong where / men are slaughtered, heads / chopped, sentences passed . . ." But whether physically present or not, the *omphalos* is at the very least rhetorically and imaginatively present, both through the cultural knowledge of the play's audience, and through the words of both the Pythia ("there at the / Navel Stone, I saw him") and the Furies:

> Omphalos,
> Earth Navel,
> stained with pollution,
> evil blood from evil men,
> evil deeds,
> evil, evil!

This blood-stained *omphalos*, covered in its net-like weave, coheres eerily with the audience's immediate visual memory of Agamemnon trapped in Klytaimnêstra's net. It coheres not least because Delphi is the site of a prior war between chthonic (subterranean) female divinities and Olympian (sky-dwelling) male divinities, of which the *Oresteia* is the mortal aftershock. According to the Homeric *Hymn to Apollo*, which dates from the seventh century

B.C.E. or earlier, the origins of Apollo's prophetic priesthood at Delphi go back to the day that Apollo arrived in Delphi and slew Python, the sacred serpent that protected the shrine of the Earth Goddess, and appropriated the role of prophetic intermediary between gods and mortals for himself. Sometimes Python and the Earth Goddess seem to be one and the same. Euripides (in one of his two Iphigeneia plays, *Iphigeneia in Tauris*) calls her Themis. A more ancient divinity than Zeus and his children, she is the goddess of righteousness. She is also associated with Ge or Gaia, the Earth Mother. (In that sense, Orestês is not only spurred on by, but he is fully the mortal counterpart of, Mother-attacking Apollo.) What is important here is that the power and influence of the new, male, sky-gods depends upon the silencing and immolation of the old, female, earth goddesses: Apollo does not communicate the will of the Earth Mother, but that of Zeus: "it is for Zeus he / speaks; for none but Father Zeus."

We have already seen the grim equations of *male speech* = *female silence* and *male power* = *female death* played out in mortal terms in the *Agamemnon* and *Libation Bearers*. So strong are the correspondences between the ancient narrative of cosmic warfare and the new theatrical narrative of mortal combat, that Aeschylus can weave an intertextual counterpoint: In Aeschylus' version, Apollo's priestess eradicates all trace of cosmic conflict, tracing the origins of the Oracle to a gladly-given gift from the elder goddesses to Apollo:

PYTHIA:

To Mother Earth

I give pride of place in my prayer,

Gaia,

prophet,

first of gods;

then to Themis, her daughter,

protector of Law and

Tradition, the second, as legend

tells, to hold her mother's

prophetic seat;

and third in line is Phoibê,

Bright One, Titaness and

daughter of Earth,

a seat given in peace and

calm.

And she in turn gave it, a birthday

gift, to Apollo, along with her

name:
Phoibos Apollo he is,
god of prophecy and light.

This narrative attempts to transform the myth of cosmic conflict and sex-war into one of happy families exchanging presents of mutual affection and respect. In doing so, it sets up the pattern that the rest of the *Eumenides* will enact: The ancient blood-grudge between male and female, and the catastrophic fissure between the will of Olympians and the ancient rights of the powerful Chthonic divinities, will be voted into the past by the smooth mechanism of a new-born Athenian judicial system.

This attempted return to Eden is short-lived, however. The priestess almost immediately pierces her own serene narrative of Golden Age mythology with nauseous, horrified howls as the true face of the ancient goddesses is revealed. Nor does Apollo's savagery toward the Furies in the ensuing rout do much to win the audience's confidence in the Priestess' revisionist mythology of cosmic harmony:

Out of this temple,
out of this precinct,
away from here, all of you,
this ground is a place of prophecy!
Out!
Get out!
Now!
Or my winged arrows will
sting you like snakes and fire your
bowels to disgorge black curds of
blood that you suck from your victims!

In his threats we note how absolutely he has usurped the rights and powers of the primordial goddess and her guardian serpent: "my winged arrows will / sting you like snakes."

The middle section of *Eumenides* is set on the Akropolis in Athens where Orestês clutches at a statue of Athêna for protection. The statue of Athêna referred to by the Pythia in the previous scene, now signifies one of the Akropolis statues. It is possible that, in a moment of creative anachronism, Aeschylus was in part evoking the great statue of Athêna Promachos by Phidias, commissioned either shortly before or shortly after 461. When the *Oresteia* was performed in 458, the Akropolis itself was still a charred ruin, having been sacked by the invading Persian force of Xerxês in 480. The old temple of Athêna had been witness to sacrilege: Citizens who had taken up defensive positions in the Akropolis were massacred by the Persian army, and the temples burnt; a painful memory for the audience that is echoed in the *Oresteia*'s references to the Greek desecration of Trojan temples. This scene, then, is probably set before the old temple of Athêna (later superceded by the Parthenon, upon which work began in 447). The statue of Athêna is perhaps clothed, recalling the *peplos* that the women of Athens wove and presented to the goddess every four years at the Greater Panathenaia. The weaving of the *peplos* for Athêna signifies the women of the city surrendering their labor, expertise—and not least their children—to the "male" cause of glory in battle and the city's well-being. Athêna and her *peplos* act as the intersection of male and female, and they symbolically display the male order's victory by inducting female consciousness into patriarchal ideology. If the weaving and presentation of the *peplos* to Athêna represents the acquiescence of Athenian female industry to the public male order, it is a fitting counterpart to Athêna's own glad and obedient acquiescence to her father Zeus, and her judgment in favor of her brother, Apollo, against more ancient goddesses. When Athêna appears as a character in the *Eumenides*, she, too, will have been clothed in both a *peplos* and the armor in which she sprang, fully clad, from the head of Zeus. By transgressing every social convention regarding the role of mortal women in Athens, Athêna becomes the divine, living sign of the male conquest of the female, proudly subject in body and mind to patriarchal interests.

At the end of *Eumenides*, after the action of the play has moved to the Areopagos, purple tapestries are produced again to transform the Erinyës (Furies) into Eumenides (Kindly Ones). They thus evoke, if indeed they were not the same as, the robes used to lure Agamemnon to his death, and the netted weave in which he was finally trapped—displayed again on the command of Orestês at the end of the *Libation Bearers*. The repeated symbolic use of textiles at the end of each play to mediate between past and present provided a powerful visual mnemonic allowing each instance to be mapped onto the other in the mind of the audience. Whether the transcendent or the transformative was emphasized, by the use of different or the same textiles, respectively, is not known. In either case, the closure of the *Oresteia* remains symbolically ambivalent: that which brings blessing appears hideous, and is robed in tapestries that recall past bloodshed. This equilibrium of harmony and horror is achieved through mastery of the symbolic order—not by stripping that order of its polysemy ("multi-signifyingness"), but by harnessing it: In the new democratic Athens, order is revealed to be strangely conditional upon ambivalence and contradiction.

VIII. METATHEATRE

So we arrive at a law of sorts: within the world of the play, whoever is in control of the symbolic order—whoever can create signs and manipulate the way in which they will be interpreted (or even more deadly: whoever can render invisible their capacity to signify)—thereby acquires control of reality.

What makes this intriguing is the conflation of the symbolic order *within* the play and *of* the play. Let me put that slightly differently: The way in which Klytaimnêstra, and later Orestês, and finally Athêna master the symbolic order within the play can be characterized as "theatrical." Klytaimnêstra lays on a performance for Agamemnon of the dutiful wife, complete with speech, props, and plot (in both senses of the word). And it is his incapacity to recognize it *as* a performance that disempowers him. In the *Libation Bearers*, Orestês and Pyladês act the role of travelers from Phokis, bringing their tale of the supposed death of Orestês. This time it is Klytaimnêstra who fails to identify the difference between fact and fiction and fatally allows them access to the palace interior. Athêna, in the *Eumenides*, does not fictionalize herself. But from the moment she enters, she assumes responsibility for stage-managing events. She devises the homicide court, populates it with its cast of jurors, and inaugurates it with a formal speech in which she sets out the charter according to which it will operate. She also establishes which rhetorical and symbolic languages are appropriate to it: music and silence, voting tablets and urn, the order of speakers, and the types of considerations that may be brought to bear on the jurors' dispensation of justice. What makes this specifically "theatrical" is that her control of the legal event within the fiction of the play *is produced by and is the same as* her control of the theatrical event: that is to say, her control of *Eumenides* in which she herself is a character.

Having finally determined the outcome of the court's deliberations, and having pacified the Furies, she calls forth a new performance: new costumes for the Furies to transform them, symbolically and thereby actually, into benevolent divinities:

> Children, young women, venerable ladies,
> come, hang them with purple robes of honor.
> Lead on with the light,
> let the torches flare high.
> Honor them, the Kindly Ones,
> that in years to come they will
> bless our land
> with men of glorious courage.

This chorus of Athenian non-citizens—children and women—create a hymn to sing the new resident alien divinities to their new places within the civic order. At this moment, Athêna is at once divine patron, festival magistrate (*Eponymous Archon*), *choregos*, playwright, performer, and character. Her production echoes the theatricality of the City Dionysia, but also hints at the giving of a new *peplos* to Athêna herself at the Greater Panathenaia, and the grand processions that attended both festivals. The worlds of Athêna and Dionysos thus fittingly merge in the Theatre of Dionysos under the wing of Athêna's temple on the Akropolis.

As we have seen, the first two plays in the trilogy *thematically* connect the problem of symbols and signification to the reality of their fifth-century audience. But in these final moments, the last play *actually* connects the symbolic with the real: tapestries and torches, creation and destruction, females and males, gods and mortals, earth-gods and sky-gods, past and present—all coalesce into a unified civic procession in which tragedy, the dramatic festival, and the living city fuse into an indivisible entity. This movement through and between levels of fictionality and reality reaches toward the insight that whoever is in control of the symbolic order of theatre to some extent acquires the capacity to influence the reality of the city. This is true not only during the specific moment of the theatrical event: Theatre exerts a more lasting influence through its transubstantiation of "the past" into a symbolic order in which the image of possible futures may be formed.

The visual economy of the ancient theatre was such that highly complex, and even contradictory, ideas could be suggested by carefully deployed symbols. But reality, too, from the idea of language to the most elaborate rituals of collective social life, is constituted by signs. In a world of signs, or more to the point, in *the world-as-sign*, the limited, fictional world of the theatre expands to become nothing less than a metaphor for reality. Furthermore, while theatre, as a consciously created, and self-conscious sign-system, finds that it has itself become a paradigm for the world at large, it also discovers that it is *itself* a part of that world. Theatre is thus *hyper*-real: refracting and reflecting upon reality even while conscious of itself as part of reality.

Finally, theatre inexorably reaches the conclusion that it cannot reflect upon the nature of the real without reflecting upon itself. Nor, conversely, can it reflect upon itself without reflecting upon the world. Out of this self-begetting, self-consuming, loop of self-conscious reality is born metatheatre: theatre *of* theatre. Or, to put it more prosaically: theatre in/or about theatre—self-referential representation.

If the world is constituted, or made meaningful, through signification, the objectification of signification *as such* in theatrical representation offers the world a *discourse of signification*. In the case of the *Oresteia*, this tangled relationship between the theatrical and the real is played out in the form of a thematic concern with ambivalent signification.

Metatheatricality begets intertextuality. Intertextuality is that associative depth achieved when one text draws into itself new dimensions of suggested meanings by hinting or referring in some way to another text. When the bodies of Klytaimnêstra and Aigisthos are revealed at the end of the *Libation Bearers*, for instance, the audience, recalling the bodies of Agamemnon and Kassandra similarly displayed at the end of the previous play, are implicitly invited to ask whether Orestês' murders resemble those perpetrated by his mother more than superficially. This is only the most obvious example. As Oliver Taplin and others have shown, a fundamental dramatic building-block of the *Oresteia* is the parallel scene. Each parallel is, by definition, an intertextual reference; the plays thus gorge on themselves and each other in an intertextual feeding frenzy. Each moment of the *Agamemnon* overlays each other moment in the play, while the last moments of the *Libation Bearers* only exist to "re-member" those of the *Agamemnon*. This pervasive network of intertextual correspondences allows the conceptual and theatrical eruptions of the *Eumenides* to be seen as an emphatic *coup d'état* to the fatalism of its parent plays.

But the trilogy's deep, over-layering of "false signs," and the machinations of its cast of powerful "sign-masters"—Klytaimnêstra, Orestês, Athêna—call into question whether there can ever be such a thing as a "true sign." If not, then not even the trilogy's own status as a "true sign" for the city can be taken for granted. Tragedy thus both is concerned with *and* constitutes a questioning of the paradigmatic value of new mythological narratives, i.e., their value as "true" models of some aspect of reality.

Paradoxically, the tragic problematization of signification itself offers a paradigm for just such an evaluative process. Through the *Oresteia's* insistent self-referential intertextuality, we see laid out before us not only problematic signs, but *the problem of signs*. In this way, the *Oresteia* affirms its own role, and by implication that of tragic representation, as a teacher of signs—theatrical and "real"—even as it seems to subvert the very object, and means (signs) through which it fulfils that role.

Ultimately, however, the Oresteian narrative stipulates that the production and reception of signs both operate within a dialectic of freedom and responsibility. The voting, citizen audience must become "true" creators and interpreters of the symbolic world of the theatre, and of their own ever-shifting world of signs.

IX. THE REINVENTION OF TIME

Through tragedy, Athens imagines its future in the past tense, impressing the disjointed miscellanea of its present onto the templates of historical-mythological narratives. At the same time, as we have seen, Athens regards the past with an eye to the future, molding narratives of the past according to the shape of contemporaneous needs. The Athenians enjoyed the tension between looking to the past for authorization while refashioning the past with considerable freedom. By reinventing their sense of who they had been, they enabled themselves more creatively to invent who they might become. The dramatic retellings of "Homeric" myths are the most manifest examples and agents of that dual process: rewriting both past and present, each in the image of the other.

Not only does each play in the *Oresteia* configure the relationship between past and present differently, but each is also *thematically* concerned with the reciprocal operations of past and present upon each other. The dark *daimon* pursues the House of Atreus through the generations. Klytaimnêstra, Aigisthos, Agamemnon, Êlektra, Orestês . . . these vengeful revenants are the shadows of a seemingly inescapable past, which in turn shadows them. But tragedy, by reshaping those myths to serve the city, and by providing new mythological narratives to authorize the present (most dramatically in the *Eumenides'* Areopagos), tames and makes fecund the past. All the while, the plays themselves compete to win the city's approval—to become immortalized as effective, shared memories.

Timelessness

Like the Parthenon, tragedy strives to create the illusion of "timelessness." It is not enough that those men on the hillside should shudder and weep: Tragedy insists on becoming a paradigm for all time. Choral odes labor to yield their gnomic utterances, while dying words, poised between worlds, instill into civic consciousness "true" insights into the human condition:

> Success, good fortune,
> is only a shadow,
> and man's grief the scribble of chalk on a board,
> cancelled by a wet
> sponge.

The tragic vision is, it seems, as inescapable as Oedipus' fate: Tragedy will track us down. Rather than an "historical" effect, tragedy thus produces a "Universality Effect." Past and present are conflated into "mythical time." As with many historically based religious narratives, tragedy claims to embody *both* mythological/historical truths *and* immediate spiritual truths. Through performance, the narratives of the past are experienced fully in the present. The actor speaking through the mask becomes the living sign of a transcendent spiritual truth speaking through the bodily presence of the merely mortal actor. Finally, as the spiritual truth becomes incarnate, mythical time elides with universal time. The Universality Effect is rooted in the very premise of tragic representation: Narratives of people and places suspended between the parallel words of myth and history can be summoned forth by tragedy to produce valid paradigms of contemporary, fifth-century life and death. In that sense, tragedy is indeed the true heir to Homer.

These paradigms depend upon a belief in the fixity of human nature: only then can ancient narratives be deemed universally valid. Whether this essentialist belief is literally or ("only") poetically held, it must reproduce itself within the worldview of the audience if the dramatic performance is to be successful. Ironically, tremendous energy is required in order to transform these supposedly "transcendental" truths into "particular" narratives applicable to the fifth-century moment, as the radical revisionism of the plays of the *Oresteia* abundantly demonstrates. In Tragedy, seismic cultural paradigm shifts are represented as seamless elucidations of timeless truths about humanity. Nevertheless, tragedy's self-perpetuating myth of universality, compounded by later assertions such as Aristotle's influential dictum that "poetry speaks . . . of universals," has succeeded in ensuring that positivist-essentialist views have dominated the historical reception of Greek tragedy in the West even after most of their enabling philosophical and cultural foundations have been destabilized or dismantled.

By stripping tragedy and the contemporary moment of their historical specificity, latter-day essentialism too frequently leads to modern performances that are overwhelmed by the desire to absorb the emotions of the character into the actor's or audience member's own capacity to "feel." Such productions tend to mark cultural difference only superficially. It is often difficult for us to concede that the intuitively felt "authenticity" of our emotions is a fiction, one that masks an altogether less stable reality: The emotions operate and acquire meaning within a multiplicity of elaborately constructed, and ever-shifting parameters. If we view the canvas broadly enough, we *can* perceive what seem to be transtemporal, transcultural points of connection in human experience (we all experience "pain," "fear," "loss" and so on). But within the holistic, interlocking mesh of consciousness, even seemingly elemental conditions such as these continually change in inflection and meaning: No one element can change without changing the aspect and our experiences of every other contingent element. When we surrender to the illusion that we are connecting with an artwork in "essentially" the same way as the ancients did, we authorize, by design or default, the notion of an "essential," shared, "human nature" existing unchanged across the boundaries of time, culture, and language. This highly political-aesthetic stance privileges the capacity to identify association, but erodes the equally generative desire (perhaps even capacity) to perceive diversity and alterity. Essentialism relies upon producing and reproducing a fixed view of human nature that, in refusing to acknowledge the created, and continually "recreated," nature of consciousness, locks the creative and critical paradigms through which we invent present, past, and future, into a self-circling spiral of eternal regression.

The illusion or "conceit" of timelessness is a fascinating phenomenon in its own right. The cultural currency of positivist essentialism is a powerful part of the ideological and aesthetic "texture" of cultural artifacts within contemporary discourses surrounding the uses of the past. And we do unquestionably debilitate ourselves when we cut ourselves off from the capacity to create suggestive associations between past and present and to wrestle the past into a fertile relationship with the present. But, equally, we violate ourselves when we attempt to annex the past without paying sufficient attention to its alienness, and to all the variables that circumscribe the infinite possibilities of consciousness (the contradiction is only apparent).

Never in or since antiquity has Greek drama been performed as much as in our own day: Tragedy has found its feet and treads the boards. Out of a dream of origins emerge both atavism and originality, equally molded to the shape of present desires. Part of our challenge is to recognize that the tragic rhetoric of universality, human consciousness, even time itself are constructs; that when we read, study, watch or perform the *Oresteia*, the way in which we allow past, present, and future to shape each other must be of our own choosing.

Hugh Denard
School of Theatre Studies
University of Warwick
Coventry, United Kingdom

[1] Csapo, Eric and William J. Slater. *The Context of Ancient Drama*. Ann Arbor: The University of Michigan Press, 1995, p.139 ff.

[2] Athenaeus. *Deipnosophistae* 21d – 22a. Translated (and annotated) in Csapo, Eric and William J. Slater *The Context of Ancient Drama*. Ann Arbor: The University of Michigan Press, 1995, pps.359–360. All quotations on dance are from Csapo & Slater, p.367.

[3] Hesiod. *The Poems of Hesiod*. (Translated by R.M. Frazer.) Norman: University of Oklahoma Press, p. 198, lines 90–105.

[4] Thucydides. *The Peloponnesian War*. (Translated by Rex Warner.) Harmondsworth: Penguin Classics, 1972, p.151.

A Note on the Translation

Every translator feels obligated to explain his or her aim in making a translation, and that is a salutary endeavor, for at least it tells the innocent reader what to expect as well as what not to expect. As a translator for many years, I have always (perhaps even before deciding whether or not to buy a particular volume of translations), insinuated my fingers between the covers to peek briefly at the obligatory *Note on the Translation* that I know cannot help but be there. What am I looking for? Usually only one word—the word that must be the *bête noire* of the true translator: ACCURACY. What's accuracy to him or he to accuracy that he should lust for it? A flippant query perhaps, but perhaps not. For it is a question that boggles the mind of all but the pedant. And it is in the name of ACCURACY that many a translator's hour (lifetime?) has been wasted, not to mention the hours wasted on their product by the unsuspecting reader who sets out to enjoy a Dante or a Homer or a Goethe, only to plow his way through by means of will and in the end wonder what all the fuss has been about.

There is no question that there is a place for literal translation, for translation that is bound to the word. The most convenient example that comes to mind is the long-lasting and successful Loeb Classical Library that publishes the original text and the translation on facing pages. The aim of its volumes is to aid the reader with a little Greek (or Latin), or a lot of Greek (or Latin) but not quite enough, to read the original by casting a glance at the translation when knowledge fails or falters. David Kovacs is completing a new six-volume Euripides in that series that admirably fulfils its function as support in reading the original. He says about his translation: "I have translated into prose, as literally as respect for English idiom allowed." And he's correct. He's also "accurate." But that's what the series' mission is to be, and for good reason. Yet what his translations are not (and I suspect he would agree) are performable versions for the stage, and for one reason: "Accuracy" has destroyed the poetry.

But enough of this.

What is good translation? And the answer to that question is different with each "good" translator who has ever wrestled with the problem. Listen to St, Jerome, the great fourth-century translator of the Bible into the Latin Vulgate, in speaking of Plautus and Terence and of their translations of Greek plays into Latin: "Do they stick at the literal words? Don't they try rather to preserve the beauty and style of the original? What men like you call accuracy in translation, learned men call pedantry . . . I have always aimed at translating sense, not words." Fourteen hundred years later the body of translators of the King James Bible of 1611 expressed their thoughts on literal translation: "Is the kingdom of God become words and syllables? Why should we be in bondage to them?" And in the later seventeenth century, John Dryden, the translator of many a classical text, from Plutarch to Virgil and Ovid, expressed his theory of translation at length, but most succinctly when he said: "The translator that would write with any force or spirit of an original must never dwell on the words of the author."

To bring it now to our own day and to the prolific translator of many classical and modern texts, William Arrowsmith: "There are times—far more frequent than most scholars suppose—when the worst possible treachery is the simple-minded faith in 'accuracy' and literal loyalty to the original." To read an Arrowsmith translation, say, of a classical Greek play, side by side with the original, is to see a fertile and poetic mind undaunted by the mere word of the original. He realized that he was translating a fifth-century B.C.E. Greek play for a middle- to late-twentieth-century English-speaking audience and had one obligation: to make that ancient play work on the contemporary stage for an audience that had few if any ties to the play's original context or audience. His duty was to make it work, and to make it work with style and the best poetic means at his disposal.

And finally the contemporary Roger Shattuck: "The translator must leave behind dictionary meanings and formal syntax . . . Free translation is often not an indulgence but a duty." And to that one must add that dramatic texts require perhaps even greater freedom than non-verbal texts (and poetry in whatever form is a verbal text). On the stage, rhythm is every bit as important as what is being said—at times even more important. A stinging line has to sting not merely with what it says, but with how it says it, with its rhythm. One phrase, indeed one word, too many in a sentence, destroys a moment that in the end can destroy an entire scene. Effect on the stage is everything, whether one is Aeschylus or Tennessee Williams. What to do with that rebellious word or phrase? Cut it if it adds nothing of importance. And if it is important, and can't be cut, then write a new sentence that gets it all in, just be certain that it has grace and style and wit, or horror if that's what's needed, and serves the moment in the best and most theatrical way possible.

AGAMEMNON

(ΑΓΑΜΕΜΝΟΝ)

Cast of Characters

WATCHMAN

KLYTAIMNÊSTRA *queen of Argos*

HERALD *of the Greek forces at Troy*

AGAMEMNON *king of Argos*

KASSANDRA *Trojan prophetess*

AIGISTHOS *lover of Klytaimnêstra*

GUARDS

ATTENDANTS

SLAVES

CHORUS OF OLD MEN OF ARGOS

FIRST OLD MAN *chorus leader*

AGAMEMNON

Night.
Mykenê, in Argos.
Outside the royal palace.
A WATCHMAN sits on the palace roof.
GUARDS stand below.

WATCHMAN:
 Gods, I pray for an end,
  an end to my pain,
  an end to my yearlong watch!
 I crouch here,
  dog-like,
   on the roof of the palace
    of Atreus' sons,
  and know by heart
  the gatherings of the stars,
    those glittering lords,
    dazzling in the firmament,
  that bring us winter and summer.
 I know them all,
  their comings and their goings.

 I search even now
  for a gleam, a beacon flash
   in the dismal vault,
 news from Troy that the city
     has fallen.
 Mykenê's queen, my mistress
  Klytaimnêstra,
  who rules here now
 with the confidence and the hard
  will of a man—
 how she waits for that word!

At night
>when I wander the roof
>to ease my pain,
>my boredom,
>>restlessly, endlessly,
or lie down on my dew-drenched bed,
>no dreams come.
But Fear is there,
>never leaving,
>never relenting,
>>a cruel guard against flagging eyes,
>>>insidious sleep.

And so I whistle, I hum,
>to guard against sleep,
I moan, I sigh with the thought
>of how once this house
>>was blessed by the gods,
>but now is cursed.

Gods, let it come,
>the end,
>let it come,
>the end to my pain,
>>let the good news come!
Break through the dark!
A beacon in the dismal night!

(A distant pinpoint of light cuts through the dark.)

A light!
>A light!
>>>There in the dark!
>A light in the sky!
>A beacon in the night!
Blessèd, blessèd light!
>Holy, blessèd light!
>>Beam of day,
>>beacon of hope,

        bringing dawn to Argos!
Argos will thank you with
     dancing for your blessing!

IOOOO! IOOOO!

(To the GUARDS below.)

The sign has come!
    The beacon!
       Run! Tell her!
          Agamemnon's wife!
The sign she's waited for!
    Wake her from sleep!
        Let her dance through the palace!
         Shout for joy,
         shouts of jubilation,
         for the beacon is here,
   flaming in the night!
Tell her come greet the flame!
              Troy has fallen!

(The GUARDS hurry into the palace.)

If only it's true.
O I pray to the gods it's true,
    this flame,
    and Troy is taken,
       for then
I'll dance and sing,
    for my master's throw
    will have been lucky and I'll
       turn it to my own good,
for this flame has thrown me triple sixes!

If only he were here now,
         my master, Agamemnon,
    and I could hold his dear hand in mine.
But I'll say no more.

"An ox sits on my tongue,"
    as the adage has it.
O if these walls had a voice,
    what tales they could tell.
      As for me,
I speak to those who know,
      you know?
    To those who don't,
      I don't.

(Exit the WATCHMAN through the palace roof. Enter through the central doors of the palace MALE SLAVES with burning torches who light fires on various altars. Then enter through the palace's central doors KLYTAIMNÊSTRA and a formal procession of FEMALE SLAVES with paraphernalia for a ritual. Once the ritual is in progress, enter the CHORUS OF OLD MEN OF ARGOS, slowly, helped along by their sticks, chanting individually and in varying groups. The ritual continues throughout.)
(Music. Song. Dance.)

OLD MEN OF ARGOS: *(Chant.)*
    Ten years now since the sons of Atreus,
      Menelaos and brother Agamemnon,
        kings,
      kings by divine fiat,
        twin-sceptered,
        twin-throned,
    summoned an army of the youth of Hellas
      to challenge Priam
  and sail for Troy with a thousand proud ships,
    men whose fierce hearts uttered a warcry
      like vultures,
        soaring,
  rowing the air with the oars of their wings,
      enraged,
    grieved at the plunder of their nest,
      their nestlings gone.
    And someone hears,
    some god in the heavens,

Apollo or Pan or Zeus hears,
and hearing,
sends Vengeance,
in pity sends Fury,
in answer to cries
tearing his heaven,
of pain,
of loss,
sends Vengeance,
though late,
to hunt down the doer.

So Zeus Protector,
Zeus Guardian of Host and Guest,
sends against Paris the sons of Atreus.
And so it begins,
the struggle for Helen,
the woman of many men,
the wrestling,
the grappling,
arms locked in conflict,
bodies torn,
worn down to destruction,
knees broken,
bloodied in the dust,
spears splintered in writhing bodies,
the sacrifice begun,
for Greeks and Trojans alike.

And what must be *is*,
and what happens *must* happen,
cannot be otherwise,
cannot be changed,
for no tears,
no offering,
no secret sacrifice
can end the gods' anger.
But we are too old,
too old to fight,

too old even then when the warcry sounded
and Arês leapt high in the blood of youth,
too old even then,
withered stalks now we walk on three legs,
no fighting,
no blood-bath in battle,
our flesh decayed,
weak as a child,
we wander like phantoms in daylight.

Klytaimnêstra,
queen,
daughter of Tyndareos,
what have you heard,
what news that makes you order sacrifice
throughout all Argos?
The altars of the city's gods
are ablaze with offerings,
gods above and below the earth,
gods of the marketplace.
Torches everywhere leap
heaven-high with flames
fed by holy oils from the inner store.
Tell me,
tell me what you can,
what is allowed,
tell me
and end this fear I suffer,
this anxiety,
this pain that
one minute fills me with dread,
and with hope and relief the next.
Am I to see in these victims slaughtered,
these flames that answer on all sides,
the hope that will release me
from the fear that eats at my heart?

FIRST OLD MAN: *(Sings.)*
> I sing a song of power,
> power seasoned by age,
> age that knows decline
> but also depth of sight,
> the power of inspiration
> breathed on me by gods.
> I sing a song of heroes
> and days of glory in the sun,
> of men marching in majesty.

OLD MEN OF ARGOS: *(Sing.)*
> I sing how the twin-throned
> kings of the Greeks and their
> host of young warriors raised anchor for Troy,
> heroes united in
> arm and vengeance,
> and saw two eagles,
> twin kings of the skies,
> appear to the twin-throned
> kings of the ships,
> on the right of the palace,
> the side of the spear arm,
> one black-tailed,
> one white,
> and there from on high they
> swooped to the earth and
> tore with their claws
> a hare,
> pregnant,
> whose womb teemed with young,
> and feasted their fill
> on her unborn brood.
>
> Sing sorrow,
> sing sorrow,
> but let good prevail.

FIRST OLD MAN: *(Sings.)*
>When Kalchas, the army's loyal prophet,
>saw the happy omen,
>he knew the proud twin eagles
>to be the twin sons of Atreus,
>Agamemnon and Menelaos,
>and up he rose to speak.

OLD MEN OF ARGOS: *(Sing.)*
>"The meaning is this!
>The meaning is victory!
>Time and your spears will capture Priam's city;
>in time it will fall;
>in time its herds,
>its hordes of people,
>its riches and crops,
>will be ravaged beneath its walls,
>its towering walls.
>It cannot be otherwise.
>But beware of heaven,
>beware the envy of the gods,
>let nothing check this huge iron bit,
>the army encamped,
>forged to curb the spirit of arrogant Troy.
>For holy Artemis,
>in pity,
>is angered
>at her father's sky-hounds that slaughtered the hare
>and her unborn young.
>She detests the eagles' feast!"

>Sing sorrow,
>sing sorrow,
>but let good prevail.

>"Fair Artemis,
>goddess kind to the cubs of fierce lions,
>and the young of all wild beasts
>of the fields and forests,

hear our prayer and fulfill these omens,
and let what is evil in them be made good,
for not all the signs are favorable.

And you,
Apollo,
god,
healer,
let her not send gale winds to thwart us,
to prevent the Achaian fleet from sailing,
to delay us in port,
a long delay,
to force another sacrifice,
another!
One not suitable to feasting or song,
unlawful,
vicious,
the victim a child,
a child of the palace,
and source of bitterness
between husband and wife,
a wife's lost faith.
And Wrath will rule there,
in the royal house,
unforgetting,
unforgiving,
unmerciful,
treacherous,
Wrath demanding blood
for the blood of a child."

FIRST OLD MAN: *(Chants.)*
Thus Kalchas shrieked omens of evil,
but also omens of good,
seen on the march,
a fate foretold by the royal birds,
omens to the royal house;
in harmony with which:

OLD MEN OF ARGOS: *(Sing.)*

Sing sorrow,
sing sorrow,
but let good prevail.

Zeus,
whoever he is,
if this is the name pleases him,
this is the name I am pleased to call him.
I know nothing,
nothing to compare him with,
no greater power,
nothing but Zeus,
nothing if this burden of anxiety
is to be lifted from my heart.

Ouranos once,
swollen with power,
sky-god,
first of gods,
reigned and is no more.
And he who followed,
Kronos,
met his match,
was thrown,
and is no more.
And so it is to Zeus I pray,
to Zeus who threw him in a triple fall,
Zeus the victor,
for in Zeus I find wisdom.

He set us on the path of understanding,
and gave this law to man,
that knowledge comes through suffering.
Not even in sleep are we free of pain,
of memory,
of recollection;
for care drips and stains the heart,

reminding us of our wounds.
Discretion comes against the will.
God's course is stern.

And so Agamemnon,
elder of the kings,
and lord of the fleet,
lay no blame on the prophet for his words,
but bent with the winds of fortune,
there,
at Aulis,
on the shore opposite Chalkis.
And no ship sailed,
long delay,
fierce winds from the Strymon,
hunger,
deprivation,
impatience,
boredom,
that drove men near to madness
in that cruel harbor where cables snapped
and hulls rotted,
unattended.
And the sullen,
angry flower of the Argives
grew more desperate and wasted away
as the tides roared to and fro with no end.

FIRST OLD MAN: *(Chants.)*
Then up stood the prophet,
up stood Kalchas,
shrieking above the gale,
shrieking a cure worse than the illness.
"Artemis demands sacrifice," cried Kalchas.

OLD MEN OF ARGOS: *(Sing.)*
And the eyes of the twin kings flooded with tears
and they beat the earth with their royal staves.

FIRST OLD MAN: *(Chants.)*
> And Agamemnon, the elder king,
> rose and spoke.

OLD MEN OF ARGOS: *(Sing.)*
> "I have a duty,
> and that duty is obedience,
> and that obedience is my doom,
> obedience to the gods!
> But obedience to myself and my love,
> what of that?
> If I massacre my daughter,
> the ships sail
> and we reach Troy.
> But if I massacre my daughter,
> the pride of my house,
> my joy,
> my love,
> what am I to myself but a monster,
> and a monster to all the world?
> It is a heavy price either way.
> How am I to desert my ships,
> my fleet,
> desert my allies,
> when they have every right to demand the sacrifice?
> The blood of a virgin for the winds to cease,
> the ships to sail,
> to reach Troy.
> And it is right in the eyes of the gods.
> Their anger is just,
> the rage of my men,
> and am I not bound?
> But how am I to kill my child,
> stain my hands,
> a father's hands,
> make them stream with a virgin's blood,
> a daughter's blood,
> make an altar run with her blood,
> for the gods to see?

That is not right in the eyes of the gods.
But so be it."

Sing sorrow,
sing sorrow,
but let good prevail.

FIRST OLD MAN: *(Chants.)*
With this,
Agamemnon bent low,
and Necessity strapped on him her yoke.
Madness took hold.
His mind changed course in the evil blast
and reeled in its utter ruthlessness.
From that moment he could stop at nothing.
His mind, sickened by Necessity,
grew bold with evil.
Only then did he have the heart
to seek his daughter's death,
first sacrifice to a war to win back a whore,
the life of a child for a fair wind.

OLD MEN OF ARGOS: *(Sing.)*
Nothing moved them,
those battle-hungry war-chiefs,
neither prayers,
nor cries,
nor her fragile youth,
nothing.
They would have their war.
And so it began.
First the prayer,
her father's prayer;
then the order,
her father's order,
to lift her high,
high above the altar
where her blood would flow,
high like a goat,

face downward.
She fell to his knees,
her father's knees,
grasping his robes in supplication,
imploring mercy.
Then a gag to her mouth,
the gentle mouth,
the lovely lips,
like a horse,
bridled,
to arrest a cry
that would curse the royal house,
her house once.

Her saffron robe,
a bridal dress,
drops from her shoulders,
pale skin,
fair,
shivering in the windblast,
behold the bride,
a gross deception.
And up they lift her,
above the altar,
struggling,
high, high,
tough hands roughing
her virgin flesh.
And gagged,
silent,
she darts piteous arrows,
shafts of grief,
at her sacrificers,
but as in a painting
unable to speak.
She knows them all,
sang for them often at her father's banquets,
in her father's halls,
her voice,

pure,
chaste,
the voice of a virgin,
in celebration of her father's prayer
as he poured the god's wine.

What followed the sacrifice
I did not see,
nor can I tell it.
But Kalchas' prophecies never fail.
And Justice teaches that
knowledge comes only through suffering.
The future you'll know when it comes.
Forget it till then.
Grief comes soon enough.
All will come clear at the break of day.
For what is to come,
let good prevail,
for that is our wish,
we,
old men,
remnants of men,
left alone to defend the kingless throne,
the only defenders of Argos.

(The ritual concluded, KLYTAIMNÊSTRA comes forward.)
(Music out.)

FIRST OLD MAN:
Majesty—

queen—

Klytaimnêstra—
we come here in respect of your
power and authority.
For when the king is away
and the throne empty of the male,
it is only right that the
honor that we owe to him
should fall to his woman—

his wife—

                our queen.

Majesty.

May I ask the reason for these flaming altars
            here and throughout the city?
Is there news?
            Good or bad?
                        Or is it rumor?
Another empty hope that brings this sacrifice?
I long to know, lady.
            Loyal as I am.
                        But if not—
we respect your silence.

KLYTAIMNÊSTRA:
    As the proverb has it:
                            "May Dawn,
            coming from her mother Night,
                        bring glad tidings."
    The news I bring beggars all hope.
                                Troy has fallen.
    Priam's citadel is taken.
    The Greeks are in Troy.

FIRST OLD MAN:
    Troy taken? I can scarcely believe it.

KLYTAIMNÊSTRA:
    Yes, Troy taken. I say what I mean.

FIRST OLD MAN:
    The joy of this news—my eyes—my tears—

KLYTAIMNÊSTRA:
    The tears of a loyal servant, yes.

FIRST OLD MAN:
    But Troy fallen? Have you proof?

KLYTAIMNÊSTRA:

    I have; unless some god has deceived me.

FIRST OLD MAN:

    Perhaps some dream you dreamed deceived you.

KLYTAIMNÊSTRA:

    I believe in dreams no more than you.

FIRST OLD MAN:

    Rumor, then, some unfounded report.

KLYTAIMNÊSTRA:

    I'm not a young girl! I won't be insulted!

FIRST OLD MAN:

    Yes, well. And Troy was taken *when?*

KLYTAIMNÊSTRA:

    Last night, I told you!
        Last night that gave birth to this
            burst of light.

FIRST OLD MAN:

    Was the news winged to arrive so fast?

KLYTAIMNÊSTRA:

                        Winged?
    No, better yet, and faster.
                Fire.
      A courier of fire,
          from peak to peak,
             from Troy to Argos,
               beacon signals from fire-god Hêphaistos.
    In the flash of an eye,
        it sped from Ida to Hermês Crag on Lêmnos,
    then leapt to Athos, where the Rock of Zeus
                  took flame in the night,
    and rising high above the sea's back,

a speeding torch,
              a second sun,
it brought its dazzling news to the heights of Makistos.
The watchers, awake,
                waste no time in feeding the flame
                and speeding it across the waters of Euripos
                        to the sentinels waiting on Messapion.
There they kindle an answering flame
        with heather and dry brush,
        till it blazes to the shame of its predecessor,
then leaps like a brilliant moon,
                    across the Plains of Asopos
            to light on the peaks of Kithairon,
                igniting fire after fire
                        that flashes the news on its course.
And the distant flame is not rejected by the watch,
        but urged onward beyond the Swamp of the Gorgon
                to the Mountain of Roving Goats,
                where the watch does itself proud.
                                    Sparing nothing,
they set blazing a mountain of kindling
                that shakes its great head of flaming hair
and soars out across the headland
                that looks down upon the Gulf of Saron,
            then down and down to Spider Peak,
                the watchpost nearest our city—

                                        and,

        in one final leap,
                plunges to the roof of this palace
                of the sons of Atreus.

This is my proof!
This my certainty!
                    Fire upon fire upon fire,
                        a relay race of flame,
sent me by my king from the blaze at Troy,
        my husband,
                            Agamemnon.

FIRST OLD MAN:
>The gods will have their thanks in time, lady,
>>but first, because what you say is such a marvel,
>>>I'd be grateful to hear your fable told again.

KLYTAIMNÊSTRA:
>What is it you don't grasp?
>>>>>Troy is taken.
>>>It's as simple as that.
>>>Taken today.
>>>By the Greeks.
>And Troy is today a city of cries,
>>cries that refuse to blend,
>>>like vinegar and oil,
>>eternal contestants:
>>>>>Greek and Trojan,
>>>victor and vanquished,
>>cries as different as their fortunes differ.
>Trojans mourn husbands and brothers,
>>parents,
>>>children;
>>>>a keening lament
>>from throats no longer free,
>>mourning the loss of loved ones.
>Mourning themselves,
>>>>soon to be slaves.

And the Greeks?
>>Exhausted from battle,
>>>>>starving,
>>>all night scavenging what little they can find,
>>they eat their scraps and
>>sleep an untroubled sleep,
>>>free of frost for once and an open sky,
>>in houses their spears captured,
>>>sleep unguarded and rise refreshed
>>>>like men blessed by the gods.

But the gods,

the city's gods,
the gods of the vanquished city,
what of them?

If tomorrow the conquering Greeks
honor those gods,
their altars,
their temples and shrines,
they themselves will not be conquered.
But let them—
and this I fear gravely—
let them succumb to greed and avarice,
let them lust for spoils
and blaspheme against the gods,
and their homeward lap will be troubled.
But even if they appease the gods
and come safely home,
the agony of the dead may be wakened
and demand payment;
and if not that,
then some unexpected calamity.

So.

This is my tale, my fable, as you say.
A woman's words.
Nothing more.
But let good prevail for all to see.
And let it end here,
the murders, the evils.
We have much to hope for.
And I have much hope.

FIRST OLD MAN:
Spoken wisely and like a man, to be sure.
Armed with such "proofs" and "certainty,"
let us now give thanks to the gods,
for the joy we feel is worth all the pain suffered.

(Music. Song. Dance.)

FIRST OLD MAN: *(Chants.)*

> Zeus, lord, master, king,
> and gentle Night, radiant in all of your splendors,
> Night that cast over sleeping Troy
> a net of slavery that none could escape,
> trawling old and young to their doom.
> It is Zeus I praise,
> Zeus I revere,
> Zeus, great lord of host and guest,
> Zeus who has accomplished this.
> It was Zeus who aimed his bow at Paris
> that took ten years to hit its mark.

OLD MEN OF ARGOS: *(Sing.)*

> And hit it did.
> That arrow struck.
> Pinning Paris to the black earth.
> That much can be proven.
> What Zeus decreed,
> Zeus did.

> And what of the gods?
> What of them?
> What?
> Are they blind?
> What!
> Are they careless of men who mock holy things?
> Men who trample,
> who destroy what is sacred,
> who scorn heaven?
> How wrong they are.
> Such men are evil.

> I see it now,
> see it revealed,
> point to it,
> there,
> see it like a beacon:
> Ruin!

Ruin!

Men of conceit,
who dare the undareable;
men of pride,
who prize wealth over honor,
whose houses heave with treasure past knowing,
past what is best:
their end is ruin to many generations,
and we see that now!

Let me be moderate,
give me good sense,
let that be enough,
and the gods will be happy.
The man with too much is his own destruction,
he drowns in surfeit,
for he has kicked the altar of Justice
into obscurity.

Persuasion lures him,
tempts him,
seduces;
Persuasion,
irresistible child of Destruction,
Destruction that connives his fate beforehand.
And no escape,
no remedy for the evil Destruction planted,
no hiding place;
it glares like a lurid beacon in the night.

As bad bronze,
as counterfeit coinage,
turns black in the handling,
in the tear,
in the battering,
the guilty is blackened when he comes to judgment,
and no escape.
Does the boy catch a bird in flight with bare hands?

The evil he has spread,
this victim of Destruction,
pollutes his whole city beyond redemption.
When he prays,
the gods turn away,
ears made of stone,
and he is destroyed.

So with Paris,
Paris who came to his hosts' table,
came to the palace of the sons of Atreus,
received in honor,
and repaid that honor with the theft of a wife.

What of Helen?
What does she leave behind for her country?
Hammers pounding,
metals hissing,
shields clashing,
the rattle of spears,
men arming,
ships outfitted,
armadas launched.
And lightly she passes between Troy's gates,
armed with the dowry she brings to Troy,
Troy's ruin,
Troy's destruction,
daring a deed that goes beyond daring.

And the prophets groan,
the house's wise men,
groan for the house,
and the house's princes,
Menelaos,
Agamemnon,
cry for the bed,
IOOOO!
IOOOO!
the bed that Helen once shared with her husband,

the bed where Paris and Helen lay laughing,
empty now,
polluted with passion.
A new bed now,
a new bed in Troy,
new husband in Ilion,
and Paris laughing.

So mused Menelaos,
silent,
apart,
no word said against her,
dishonored,
shamed,
seeking no vengeance,
that was for others.

He throws himself down,
twisting, turning,
the bed that was theirs once,
the bed that held Paris,
and then they're there,
there beside him,
laughing Paris,
Helen sighing,
and dream apparitions,
visions swarm in,
Helen-shaped,
no Paris now,
pleasure comes,
momentary,
fleeting,
deceitful,
counterfeit,
pleasures that fade,
slip through his arms,
and he wakes with a shout.
And now her statues,

OLD MEN OF ARGOS: *(Sing.)*
Murmur begins,
words are muttered,
complaints,
grievances,
sharp-voiced resentment,
against the sons of Atreus,
Menelaos and Agamemnon,
war-chiefs who tore their men from their beds,
leading them on in their battle for justice.

And their sons,
their husbands,
now lie at Troy's walls,
beneath her tall towers,
now toppled,
their husbands,
their sons,
their boys,
in the glory of youth,
their radiant flesh now mottled with earth:
broken towers their tombs at Troy.

All Argos mourns the death of its men.
A curse hovers like a gathering storm.
Something to fear,
a burden to bear.

Citizens' talk is angered,
dangerous.
Rulers should quake at the rage of the people.
A debt must be paid for men slaughtered,
for hardships endured.

I wait,
I wait,
anxiously wait,
for something,
something,

hidden in darkness,
shrouded in gloom,
not yet seen,
something,
something.

I am afraid.
Payment will come.
Leaders who lead off hordes of men
into glorious death will pay the price.

The gods see,
the gods keep watch
while those who slaughter
sleep in peace.
But Spirits of Vengeance,
dark Erinyës,
will swoop on those who win without justice,
cut them down,
reverse their fortune,
wear them away,
and lead them down to the land of the vanished,
lost forever.

Ambition is fraught with great danger;
rise too high and
Zeus will strike you into oblivion
with his eye-sped thunderbolt.

Prosperity is best that brings no envy.
I have no wish to sack cities,
nor to be a captive and live my life
in the hard palm of a conqueror.

OLD MAN 1: *(Chants.)*
Rumor runs wild through the streets!
Who knows if it's true?
Are the gods making fools of us?

OLD MAN 2: *(Chants.)*
>Rumor is all it is!
>The flames lie!
>I'm not so childish!

OLD MAN 3: *(Chants.)*
>Woman's rule!
>Only a woman acts on no facts!

OLD MAN 4: *(Chants.)*
>Credulous creatures!
>They believe anything that suits them!
>Gossip that moves fast and dies as fast!

>*(KLYTAIMNÊSTRA approaches from the altar.)*
>*(Music out.)*

KLYTAIMNÊSTRA:
>We will know soon
>>the meaning of those beacons and bonfires.
>Did they speak the truth,
>>or, like dreams,
>>>the fanciful delusion of women,
>>>>bring counterfeit joy?

>But look, here's a herald rushing from the shore,
>>his clothes ragged and mud-caked,
>>an olive wreath on his head—
>>>>one good sign, perhaps—
>>>>>and, yes,
>I think we can count on him to find a voice,
>>one that speaks facts as opposed to rumor and
>>>lying flames,
>>>the domain of credulous women.
>He'll light no fires to speak for him,
>>no mountain brushwood,
>>bright semaphores in the night.
>His words will be welcome, and confirm our joy,
>>>>>or—well,

but I choose to reject the alternative.
Let the news we have so far
    be fair in his confirmation.
And if anyone prays to the contrary,
    let him reap what he deserves.

(Enter the HERALD from the side.)

HERALD:
My home at last.
    My Argos.
        Ten years in the wishing.
Here at last,
    the least I hoped to see.
Death will find me happy now.
    To lie in my native soil,
        my motherland.

Earth.
Sun.
Sun's light.
Sun and earth.
Sunlight on the earth of Argos.

Zeus.
And lord Apollo,
    whose arrows cut us down once at Troy,
        at Skamander's banks,
    be our healer now,
        we've had enough of illness.
And all the gods,
    and Hermês above all,
        guardian god,
            master herald,
the master of all heralds,
    whom heralds revere,
and heroes whose spirits marched out with us into battle:
    receive us now,
those who survived the thrust of the bronze spearshaft.

Palace,
halls,
thrones,
altars,
seats of the gods,
 and gods whose eyes sparkle in the rising sun,
  welcome him after so long a time,
 the man who out of darkness brings us a new dawn,
welcome him as kindly as once you wished us farewell,
 Agamemnon,
 your king,
  master of us all.

He deserves your praise,
 warlord Agamemnon.
He has uprooted Troy,
 turned her topside under,
 smashed her palaces,
 cracked her grand towers,
  now rubble,
 and destroyed her holy temples and altars,
  the seats of the gods.
Gutted,
scattered,
laid waste,
 he has made of her land
 a desolate, futureless plain,
  its seed of generations thrown to the wind.
A feat he made with the point of Zeus' pickaxe,
 a feat he was commanded to by Zeus.

This was the yoke of slavery he fastened on Troy,
 your king, firstborn of Atreus,
  a man loved of the gods,
most worthy of praise of all men living:

       Agamemnon.
And neither Paris nor his accomplice city
 can boast that the crime was greater than the punishment.
Rapist and thief,

he has lost what he won and brought
   ruin on his father's house and his people.
      Priam's sons have paid a double price.

FIRST OLD MAN:
   Welcome, Herald,
      and welcome to the Greeks to come.

HERALD:
   To die now would be the greatest happiness.

FIRST OLD MAN:
   You were homesick, then?

HERALD:
   My tears will answer that.

FIRST OLD MAN:
   A sweet sickness, then.

HERALD:
   I don't understand.

FIRST OLD MAN:
   You longed for us as we longed for you.

HERALD:
   For us? I don't—

FIRST OLD MAN:
   So much, it made us groan in our misery.

HERALD:
   For us, or for yourselves?

FIRST OLD MAN:
   Better to say nothing.

HERALD:
   What threatened you while your kings were away?

Who can hear such words
and not praise our city and her generals?
And Zeus who did this,
Zeus who urged us on and brought us victory,
will be honored and praised beyond believing.

I've said what I came to say.

FIRST OLD MAN:
Your words prove me mistaken,
and I'm happy to be corrected.
One should never be too old to learn.
But your message is more for
Klytaimnêstra and the house,
though I'm glad I heard and
share the wealth of this news.

KLYTAIMNÊSTRA:
I first cried out my joy
when the night sky blazed with the news
over leagues of land and sea:
Troy taken.
Troy defeated.
Troy is no more.
And they laughed.
Yes, laughed,
called me fool, and—o yes,
credulous creature, was it?
Mumbling in their beards:
"Just like a woman.
Believe anything, they will.
Get carried away.
A spark in the night,
a shepherd's fire on a hillside,
and Troy has fallen!"
You'd have thought I'd lost my wits.

But I went on with my sacrifice,
and then one voice and then another,

women's voices, you can be certain,
     cried out here and there around the city,
and soon the whole population had turned "womanish"
     and voiced their joy,
          crying praise in every temple,
               at every altar,
          heaping incense on the flames
          to raise clouds of smoke.

But why tell me anything more?
I'll hear it all from my husband when he comes.
And that's what we must prepare for now,
     for there is no joy sweeter for a wife
     than to throw wide the gates to her husband
     brought back safely from the war.

                              Take him this message.
Tell my husband
     to come at the soonest possible,
          the city's darling!
Tell him:
     the wife he left behind when he sailed,
          awaits him in his house,
          faithful as ever,
          watchdog at his door,
          loyalty itself,
          an enemy to his enemies.

Nothing has changed,
     no lock opened,
     no seal broken.
Untouched by any man,
I have known no pleasure of men,
     and scandal has no more fingered me
     than I have been disloyal
     to my husband's interests.

This is what I've come to say,
     a boast, to be sure,

but bolstered by truth,
no shame for a queen to utter.

HERALD:

A boast it may be,
but so heavy with truth
that it would become any noble lady.

FIRST OLD MAN:

Innocent words to innocent ears.

So.

But tell us.
Menelaos?
Has he returned with you?
Is he back safe?
He's very dear to this land.

HERALD:

I could lie to please you,
but the gift would soon rot.

FIRST OLD MAN:

If only good and true were the same.

HERALD:

Menelaos has vanished from sight,
and his fleet with him.

FIRST OLD MAN:

He sailed with you from Troy,
and was what?
Lost in a storm?

HERALD:

You're a good marksman.
Our fears exactly.

FIRST OLD MAN:

>Dead or alive? Tell me.
>Is there anyone who knows?

HERALD:

>Only the sun that sees all.

FIRST OLD MAN:

>Tell me about the storm.
>Were gods involved?
>Were they angered?
>Out to destroy us?
>Some grudge, some hostility?

HERALD:

>Grudge, anger, hostility?
>There are gods and then there are gods!
>The gods I choose to avoid,
>>the gods of the dark world,
>>>avenging Furies,
>>I'd sooner forget.
>But the gods keep these things separate.

>This is a day of homecoming.
>It should also be a day of rejoicing.
>Not right to spoil it with news of disaster.
>When a messenger arrives,
>>tears flowing,
>>his face pained,
>>eyes heavy with his message
>>>that the city's worst fear has taken shape,
>>its army destroyed,
>>its young men routed,
>>>slaughtered,
>>piled high on the field,
>>rotting corpses, stench,
>>flies so thick they blot out the sun—
>the work of butcher Arês and his double meat-hook—
>>when no house of the city is free of loss,

but all reel with the same anguish,
    and the city,
  the city totters in its desolation—

                then—
that's the time to sing battle hymns to the Furies.

But when he comes,
    when the herald comes, with news
      that sings of salvation,
of deliverance for the city,
    of victory,
      and the city dances and shouts
    its good fortune,
      how am I to pollute such joy
        with news of evil?
How am I to tell of the gods' wrath
    that sent tragedy down on the Greeks
    when those two bitter enemies,
      fire and water,
    conspired an alliance
      to annihilate us?

Suddenly,
    in the black of night,
    as every living thing slumbered,
the sea rose up beneath us, mountainous
      shoulders of waves heaving as blasts from
    Thrace collide with seafoam, and
    spray whitens the air with a deadly glow as
    fire falls from the sky with a thunderous roar.
Hulls gash ragged holes in hulls,
    sterns rise and plunge and
    mount each other,
      crashing,
      splintering,
        down, down,
dislodging masts that fall like cracked pillars
    in the heavy surge,
prows tear into prows like raging bulls

butting wildly in the boiling sea,
        and hurricane blasts and pelting rain
swirl our ships like toys on the waves,
        a shepherd gone mad,
        scattering his sheep,
        driving them off a mountain edge
                into the abyss.

And then silence.

Dawn.

Then sunrise.

And we saw.

The Aegean, like a grizzly garden,
        bloomed with the remains of men and of ships.

By some miracle, some god's guidance,
        some god begging us off,
                our ship was spared.
Fortune had taken her seat at our helm and,
                                hand on the tiller,
        kept us from being swamped in the gale or
        dashed onto the rocky coast.

Our death in a watery grave behind us,
        we sat stunned in the morning light,
we who had suffered a terrible pounding sat there,
        unbelieving,
        brooding on our near-misfortune,
                and taking stock of our situation.

If any of those others survived,
        they think of us as dead,
                as is only natural;
        and we think the same of them.
All we can do is hope it turns out well.
                        As for Menelaos,

let's hope he came through it.
And if he did,
and he's out there somewhere in the light of the sun,
he'll make it back.
Unless Zeus intends to wipe out his whole bloodline,
which I doubt he has in mind just yet.

(Music. Song. Dance.)

OLD MEN OF ARGOS: *(Sing.)*
Helen.
Helen.
Who was it?
Who named her?
Who was it named her?
Some unseen spirit?
Prophetic.
Inspired.
A name steeped in Destiny.
Who guided his choice?
Who led his tongue?
Led his tongue rightly?
Spear-bride Helen.
Plague-bride Helen.
Helen hell to men,
Helen that means Death,
Helen who held two nations' destiny.
Helen, true to her name.
Helen.
Destroyer.
Destroyer of men,
destroyer,
destroyer of cities,
of races.

Helen slipped off,
soft as a breeze,
from golden Mykênê,
from her perfumed bed,

As god would have it,
a Priest of Ruin was raised in that house.

I think there first came to Troy
what seemed a spirit of unruffled,
windless calm,
a delicate ornament of wealth,
a precious jewel,
seductive darts from the eyes,
a flower of passion that pierces the heart.
But then it swerved from its course,
and made of the marriage a bitter thing,
for Zeus Protector of Guests
had sent as escort of Helen
an evil spirit to the sons of Priam,
one who brings tears to the eyes of brides:
Erinys,
Wrath,
Vengeance,
Fury!

Men have said since ancient times
that wealth never dies childless,
that at its height it breeds trouble in the house,
children that turn to evil,
that happiness always gives birth to misery.
But I see it otherwise.
I see now that it is evil,
the evil deed,
that breeds other evil deeds,
like itself.
A house that is decent,
that deals in justice and righteousness,
that house will have children
that are decent and be always blessed.

But in men of evil arrogance breeds,
old arrogance gives birth to young arrogance,
and in its wake comes Ruin,

irresistible,
unconquerable,
an unholy thing,
black Ruin for the house and its progeny.
But Justice lives in poverty,
in humble houses.
She honors the decent life,
shuns palaces of gold and
men whose hands are foul.
She loves men who honor the gods,
and scorns the power of wealth
made counterfeit with praise.
She guides all things to their proper end.

(Enter from the side in a chariot AGAMEMNON and KASSANDRA, accompanied by a GUARD.)
(Music out.)

FIRST OLD MAN:

King!
Great conqueror of Troy!
True son of Atreus!
How am I to greet you?
How am I to do you proper honor,
neither too much nor too little,
but what you deserve?

There are many who are not honest
who play at seeming,
to whom appearance is all,
reality nothing.
And these transgress against Justice.
When one man groans with another in pain,
but feels nothing,
he hides behind seeming,
his heart is unmoved—
tears may be shed, but they are false tears.
Or he pretends to join in another's triumph
by forcing his face into layers of smiles.

But you can see through that, Majesty.
The alert shepherd always can.
That look in the eye that betrays itself.
What seems the product of a loyal mind
    ends up fawning with watery friendship.

And so with me.
I can't deny it.

Ten years ago,
    when you marshaled the armies
    to repossess that worthless whore,
    you threw all Greece into a panic,
        we thought you evil,
            a man gone mad with power,
sending so many young lives to their graves.

And then that sacrifice
    to save your demoralized men
        from desertion and mutiny.
Horrible, we said,
    a mad man's desperate decision!

But times change, and so do minds.
And I welcome you now in friendship,
    and praise you for this victory you have brought us.

You will learn soon enough
    which of us stay-behinds
    have been loyal to your cause,
        and which have not.

AGAMEMNON:

                                                    Argos,

    it is right and just that I turn first to you
        and to your gods, for it is you
            who share with me in my safe homecoming,
    you who were partners in my triumph over Troy
        and the vengeance I took on Priam and his house.
    Without hearing charge and counter-charge,

the gods, as one,
    cast their vote in the urn of blood,
    demanding the death and destruction
        of Troy and of Troy's men.
Only the hope of a hand
    hovered over the urn of Mercy,
        and left it empty.

The city that once stood proud in its arrogance,
    now lies a mass of smoking rubble,
        hard in the dying,
        breathing its last,
    exuding the stench of its Asian wealth
        and luxurious living.
The gods who did this deserve eternal thanks.
Troy raped our woman.
    We destroyed Troy.
Ground it to dust.
    Troy is no more.

                  The Argive beast,
    our shield-bearing army,
burst from the belly of the horse as the Pleiades set,
        cleared the ramparts,
    and in a grand leap over the great wall
    the lion of Argos fed ravenously
        on the royal blood of kings.

This much for the gods:
    our thanks in never-ending gratitude.

                  As for what you say,
    I haven't forgotten.
And I agree. It's a rare man
    who's not envious of a friend's success.
Envy eats at the heart;
    it nurtures hatred;
    and he suffers twofold:
        his own lack and his friend's good fortune.
I know what I'm saying;
    I've been through it.

I've known false friendship up close.
Like a mirror.
                    And as deep.
Appearance.
                    Not the reality.

                              Only Odysseus,
        bull-headed Odysseus,
                so reluctant at first,
                        fought against joining,
        once convinced and in harness beside me,
                was faithful to the end.
We worked, we fought together, side by side.

Is he alive or dead?
I don't know.

As for the rest,
        for matters of state and religion,
        we will call a general assembly
        in sight of the city and the gods,
                and be advised.
What has been done well is well done,
        and we will see it remain so.
But where there is sickness,
        where disease has rotted the body politic,
        like the good surgeon we will cut deep,
                to the cancer's core,
                cut or burn, but remove
        what is detrimental to our health.

But I will go into the palace now,
        to greet the gods of my house.
They sent me to Troy
        and have brought me back safely.
                              I won the victory.
May victory be with me forever.

KLYTAIMNÊSTRA:
Citizens,

honored men of Argos gathered here,
I shall feel no shame in speaking openly before you
     of my love for my husband.
Once, perhaps, it may have seemed unseemly,
          but time overcomes timidity,
          and I have known time in superflux.
What I know, I know from experience,
               not from stories,
          not from reports from the front,
          but from pain, ten years of pain,
          sitting alone in my house,
          my man gone to war,
          a terrible grief,
          the victim of legions of rumors,
          of lines of messengers,
each with news more malignant than the other,
               each doling out new sorrow for the house.
If he, my man, had suffered as many wounds
          as Rumor channeled to me,
          he would be riddled with more holes than a fisherman's net.
If he had died as many deaths as Rumor told of,
          he would be another Geryon
          and claim three deaths and three burials.
The number of nooses I knotted and hung from the rafters
          I can scarcely count,
               and would have used had interfering hands
          not interrupted my resolve.
It would all have been so much easier.

Your son, my lord,
          yours and mine,
          the first blood-pledge of our love,
                    Orestês,
          is not here today to stand beside me,
               as he should,
          but don't be disturbed.
Our friend and kindly ally Strophios of Phokis
          warned me of two dangers:
               the threat to your life at Troy,

and the prospect of civil revolt here in Argos.
When a great man is down, it is the nature
       of men to kick him even farther.
There is no deceit or guile in this;
                                        have no fear.
He's safe, our son,
in the caring hands of Strophios.

                                        As for me,
I once gushed fountains of tears,
       but now they're dry.
Night after night I kept vigil,
       my eyes raw with weeping,
              waiting for the beacon to be lighted,
                     but it never was.
And when I slept,
                     when,
       the wailing scream of a gnat
       would wake me in terror from my dream.
I dreamt of you,
       of you being butchered,
       of you being slaughtered—
ten years of dangers hounded into a nod.

All this I suffered.
                            But now,
       my mind freed of anxiety and mourning,
       I can say to my man:
              welcome,
              welcome to his house,
              to his home,
       watchdog of the fold,
       mainstay of the vessel,
       supporting pillar of the palace's lofty roofs,
       a father's one true son,
       first sight of land when all hope is dashed,
       sunlight after storm,
              water to the parched traveler!
How sweet, how sweet it is

to rip off the yoke of Necessity.

These are the titles of which I deem him worthy.
But let envy be absent,
> for we have suffered our share,
> we have paid for our joy.

Now, my lord, my dearest love,
> step down from your war-chariot.

> > No, wait,
> the foot that trampled Troy
> mustn't walk on the lowly earth.

You!
Slaves!
What's this delay?
You have your orders!
Spread out for his feet the tapestries of many colors!
Prostrate before him
> the crimson,
> purple,
> the vermilion riches
> > fit for the feet of the gods!
Let Justice lead him to the home
> he never thought to see!

As for the rest, I will see to that.
My unsleeping mind,
> with the gods' help,
> will set all things right.

AGAMEMNON:
> Guardian of my house, of my palace,
> > queen,
> > > daughter of Lêda—
> your speech was like my absence:
> > > > long.
> And you will never praise me like this again.

That will come from others,
  and more properly,
    and it will.
Do not pamper me as though I were a woman,
    an effete barbarian,
  hailed with wide-mouthed acclaim and groveling,
you there, prostrate at my feet,
    as though I were some effeminate eastern potentate.

And what's this?
What can you be thinking,
    if you thought at all?
To strew my path with purple tapestries,
    exposing me to envy!
A fitting reception for the gods perhaps,
    for the feet of gods,
      not of men,
    to walk on woven finery.
I would do so only with the greatest fear.

So if you choose to honor me,
    then honor me with honors proper to men
      and not to gods.
I have no need of footwipes and tapestries;
    my fame speaks aloud,
    speaks for itself,
      without the aid of such crutches.

Good sense, proper judgment,
    is the gods' greatest gift to man.
Nor is a man happy until death comes
    and takes him without disaster.
If I live my life like this in all ways,
then I live my life with confidence.

KLYTAIMNÊSTRA:
  Tell me something, my lord, tell me honestly.

AGAMEMNON:

Honestly? Why should I not? Am I ever not honest?

KLYTAIMNÊSTRA:

If the gods had ordered this, would you have done it?

AGAMEMNON:

Yes, if a priest had commanded, I would have done it.

KLYTAIMNÊSTRA:

And what of Priam? If he had won, would he do it?

AGAMEMNON:

He'd have walked your tapestried path without question.

KLYTAIMNÊSTRA:

Then why be so afraid of what people think?

AGAMEMNON:

The voice of the people is a harsh and powerful weapon.

KLYTAIMNÊSTRA:

And people envy great men. What else *is* greatness?

AGAMEMNON:

This lust for conquest of yours is most unwomanlike.

KLYTAIMNÊSTRA:

Still, a conqueror can concede without disgrace.

AGAMEMNON:

Is it so important to you, this conquest?

KLYTAIMNÊSTRA:

Concede of your own free will and you lose nothing.

AGAMEMNON:

Well, if this is your pleasure.

Slave,

help me off with these boots!
They've served me well.
Constant companions that trod down Troy.

Well, then.

One step from my chariot
   onto these sea-red vestments of the gods,
and I trust no envious god will see from afar.

Purple of the sea!

What reluctance I feel so to waste my house's wealth,
      ruining with my unwashed feet
      these woven riches bought for silver.

(He steps from the chariot onto the tapestries.)

So much for that.

(Indicating KASSANDRA in the chariot.)

As for her,
take her into the house.
         And be kind.
The gods favor the conqueror who is kind.
And no one willingly bows to the yoke of slavery.
Pick of the lot from fallen Troy.
They gave her to me,
         the men,
      for my own,
         the army's gift,
from all the wealth of Troy.

But now,

since I am the conquered, and you the conqueror,
I will do as you say and
      tread your purple path into my palace.

(AGAMEMNON begins a slow progress into the palace through the central doors.)

KLYTAIMNÊSTRA:
                              The sea.
There is the sea.
          Who can drain it dry?
Endless store,
          endless gush of purple
                    to dye our vestments.
Crimson rich as silver.
          Inexhaustible.

And we have many such stuffs, my lord,
                                        many,
          and silver to buy more. This house
                    has never known want.
The gods have seen to that.
I would with my feet willingly have walked
          upon many wealths of such woven splendors, had some
          oracle ordered, if from that deed
          this man's life had been saved
          to bring him back safely home to me.
                              When the root survives,
new leaves will come shading the house
          against the searing heat of the dog-star.
Your coming, my lord, to the hearth of your house,
          is like the sun in winter, bringing warmth,
          or in summer,
                    when Zeus treads the grape,
and wine flows,
          a coolness blows through the house,
          as the master moves through his domain.

*(AGAMEMNON crosses the threshold and exits into the palace through
the central doors. Immediately the SLAVES gather up the tapestries and
exit.)*

O Zeus, Great Zeus Fulfiller of Prayers,
          fulfill my prayers, and bring to pass
                    what is your will!

(Music. Song. Dance.)

OLD MEN OF ARGOS: *(Sing.)*
What is this fear?
This terror,
this horror that haunts me,
makes my heart tremble?
Hovering, hovering,
always the fear.
Why can I not wipe it away?
Why has it come?
Like an evil dream that will not fade,
prophetic vision,
dreadful foreboding.
Long time has passed since they set sail,
long time since the cables were cut,
long time since they landed at Troy.

And now he is here,
now he is back,
now my eyes see him,
my own witness.
But still no hope,
no joy, no certainty.
My heart sings its heavy lament.
Erinys sings her dirge in my heart.
I have no hope.
I have no trust.
My heart reels with frenzied foreboding
of things to come,
of deeds to be done,
things that Fate has in hand.
Let them not come.
Let my fears be unfounded.
My sad heart deceived.

(Music out.)

KLYTAIMNÊSTRA:
> Kassandra, you, too.
>> Come inside, dear. Yes, you,
>>> I mean you.
> Think of how kind Zeus has been
>> to make you part of our house,
>>> part of our worship.
> Come inside, wash yourself.
> We have many slaves, many,
>> just like you, and you will
>>> join us and them round our altar.
>>>> Come, dear,
>> now is not the time for pride.
> Why, they say that even Heraklês once
>> broke the bread of servitude.
> So there you are.
>>> Come down from the car now.
>>> Fate is fate:
>> one has only to endure it.
> Consider your good fortune:
>> you're enslaved to an ancient house.
>>> The newly-rich
>> have no class, they're cruel,
>>> insensitive to slaves.
> But not here. Not in our house.
>> Here we respect custom.
>>> You will be treated accordingly.

FIRST OLD MAN:
> It's you she's speaking to, you know.
> Don't you hear?
> Considering you have little choice in your fate,
>> it would be best to obey.
> But, then, perhaps you won't.

KLYTAIMNÊSTRA:
> What's this?
>>> Is she an idiot?
> I don't understand?

Has she no more Greek than some
   bird of the air?
My words are plain.
  I insist she obey.

FIRST OLD MAN:
  It's best to go with her, you know.
   You haven't a choice.
    Come down now,
  and do as she says.

KLYTAIMNÊSTRA:
  I don't have time for this,
   outside here with this girl.
  The victims are ready.
    Inside. At the fire. At the altar.
    Ready for sacrifice.
  O! A joy I never hoped to see.

      You.

  Will you obey?
   Will you join us at the altar?
   The sacrifice?
  If so, then hurry.

       Very well.
  If you don't understand, you at least
   know what I want. Make some gesture,
   yes or no.
      Even a Barbarian can do that.

FIRST OLD MAN:
  She's foreign.
  She needs an interpreter.
  Look at her—
   like a wild thing caught in a net.

KLYTAIMNÊSTRA:
  She's mad is what she is. Her mind

as wild as her actions.
Her father's city only now destroyed,
    her mind went with it.
        She's new to the bridle.
She'll chomp at the chain-bit first
    till her madness foams her spirit away in blood.

I won't be insulted like this.
I have no time to waste.

(Exit KLYTAIMNÊSTRA into the palace through the central doors.)

FIRST OLD MAN:
    At least I have pity for you, poor woman.
        Come, now,
    let's get you down and out of that wagon.
        Necessity isn't a pretty mistress.
    It's best to bend your neck to the yoke.

(Music. Song. Dance.)

KASSANDRA: *(Sings.)*
    OTOTOTOI POPOI DA!
                Apollo!
    Apollo!

FIRST OLD MAN: *(Chants.)*
    Not right, no, not Apollo.
    Apollo turns from grief.

KASSANDRA: *(Sings.)*
    OTOTOTOI POPOI DA!
        Apollo!
             Apollo!

FIRST OLD MAN: *(Chants.)*
    Again. Again.
    That cry. A cry not
    fit for the god.

KASSANDRA: *(Sings.)*
>> Apollo!

>>>>>> Apollo!

>>>> Apollo Agyeios!
>>>>>>> God of the Ways!

>>> Destroyer god!
>>>>> You destroy me,

>>>> destroy me,

>>>>>> so easily,

>>>>> again.

FIRST OLD MAN: *(Chants.)*
>> She'll prophesy now her own miseries.
>> The god is in her. Even enslaved
>> the god is in her.

KASSANDRA: *(Sings.)*

>>>>>>> Apollo!

>>>>> Apollo!

>>>> God of the Ways!
>>>>>>> Destroyer!
>>>>> What is this house of horror?

FIRST OLD MAN: *(Chants.)*
>> The house of Atreus.
>> The house of the sons of Atreus.
>> That much is true.

KASSANDRA: *(Sings.)*
>>>>> No!

>>>> A house of hatred!
>>>>> House that hates the gods!
>>>>>>>> God hater!

>>>>> Murder!

>>>> Slaughter!
>>>>> Kindred slain!

>>>>>>>> Men butchered!
>>>>> Floors run bloody!

FIRST OLD MAN: *(Chants.)*
    With the scent of a hound
    she'll search out the blood.

KASSANDRA: *(Sings.)*
                 In there,
            I know,
    my evidence,
                there,
       behind,
                      behind doors!
            I hear them,
    screaming,
             children slaughtered,
                sons,
                    torn,
           ripped,
                       their flesh,
       roasted,
                dished up,
    for their father to feast on!

FIRST OLD MAN: *(Chants.)*
    We need no prophet to tell us our story.

KASSANDRA: *(Sings.)*
            IO POPOI POPOI!
    What—
        what is she—
          what new plot,
          what new horror—
      horror, horror!
              Agony, new agony!
    Evil in the house!
      Pain without cure!
              And help so far away!

FIRST OLD MAN: *(Chants.)*
    What is she saying?

I know of the children,
all Argos knows;
but this, what is this?
What are these riddles?

KASSANDRA: *(Sings.)*

IOOOOO!

IOOOOO!

IO TALAINA!

Evil woman!

Evil! Evil!

In the house!

You!

He shared your bed—
your man, your husband—

you bathed him—

his body naked,
you tended,

o,

o,

slick with firelight—

o then—

o then—

o how do I end—

do I end?

It will come,
it will be,

soon, soon,

come,

will be!

Her hand,

stretching,

hand stretching out,

first one,

then the other, then—

o, o, then—

o, then, reaching out—

FIRST OLD MAN: *(Chants.)*
Her prophecies, confusion,
obscure riddles,
shadowy sayings.

KASSANDRA: *(Sings.)*
                                É!
        É!
                PAPAI!
                                PAPAIIIIIII!
        I see—
                        I see—
                so clear, so clear now—
        there—
                        a net—
                a net from Hell—
                        a snare,
                        snare, no,
                she is the snare,
                                she is the net,
        she the snare-net,
                        shares the guilt shares the bed the
                                woman the wife evil evil and they
                come come they come flooding the
                                house evil come
                                        DISCORD
        WRATH
                                RETRIBUTION
        FURY
                        raise a SHOUT to the heavens
                                SCREAM to the gods
                                        RAGE
                RAGE over the sacrifice
                                sacrifice sacrifice
        that death only death that death death death
        only death only death by stoning death by stoning
        alone death by stoning can avenge—

FIRST OLD MAN: *(Chants.)*
> What Fury is this
> you cry to howl through the house?
> I hear you and hope deserts me.

OLD MEN OF ARGOS: *(Sing.)*
>   Look,
>   her face,
>   white as a ghost when
>   blood flows to the heart,
>   drop by drop,
>   the saffron dye,
>   and life ebbs away like a dying warrior
>   at the setting of his sun.
>   Deadly visions conjure up death.

KASSANDRA: *(Sings.)*
>   É!
>   É!
>   There!
>   Look there! Drag her,
>   drag the bull from the cow!
>   She has him,
>   look,
>   wrapped-trapped,
>   robe,
>   robe-net,
>   wrapping,
>   grappling,
>   lunging,
>   stumbling,
>   totters,
>   bull horn gores,
>   black horn gouges,
>   into flesh,
>   flesh receiving,
>   manflesh-husbandflesh,
>   striking,
>   plunging, bull's horn gory,
>   falling,

                              tumbling,
         down,
                 down,
                     falling,
                              turning,
         writhing,
                                   ecstatic—
                              bath blood-crimson—

    It is the cauldron of cunning murder!

OLD MEN OF ARGOS: *(Chant.)*
                              I know nothing of
                         prophets and prophecies,
                              but there is evil here.
                    When, when is it ever not evil,
                         the words of prophets
                         that lead men into terror?

KASSANDRA: *(Sings)*
    IOOOOOO!
                              IOOOOOO!
             IO TALAINA!
    With him,
                 with him,
         not my own pain now,
                         not alone, his and mine,
                         one cup, one pain!
                                   Apollo,
             Apollo, why have you brought me?

    (Speaks.)

    To share a death, one pain with his,
                         I know this now.

OLD MEN OF ARGOS: *(Chant.)*
                         Frenzied mind,
                         frenzied soul,
                         the god is in her,

she sings for herself her tuneless song,
her shrill lament,
her bitter fate,
Itys! Itys!
Like the tawny bird,
she laments her pain,
the nightingale trilling her sorrow's song,
forever mourning,
no end, no end.

KASSANDRA: *(Sings.)*
IOOOOOO!

IOOOOOO!

Not pain, not lament.
The gods gave her freedom,
feathered flight,
no pain, no lament.
Her life is sweetness.

(Speaks.)

Mine will be broken by a bloodied axe.

OLD MEN OF ARGOS: *(Chant.)*
What god,
what power,
forces you to this?
Where is it from?
Cries,
shrieks,
tuneless melodies
of terror and horror.
What set you on this path of evil?

KASSANDRA: *(Sings.)*
O Paris, Paris, I sing of you now,
and your marriage that destroyed us!
You killed,
killed all you loved!

And you, Skamander, blessèd stream,
I sing of you.
I grew up beside you, I was happy there.
But soon I will sing beside the Kokytos,
prophesy beside the Acheron's banks.

(Speaks.)

Rivers, rivers of the dead.

OLD MEN OF ARGOS: *(Chant.)*
I see.
Now I see.
So clear a child would know.
And I'm struck again,
again with your pain,
like a serpent's sting,
and your deadly fate.
Your pain tears me in two just to listen.

KASSANDRA: *(Sings.)*
IOOOOOO!
IOOOOOO!
My city destroyed!
No sacrifice enough to save your towers!
Fields emptied,
cattle slain,
never enough, never,
never!
Troy is dead.
The city fallen.
And I, too, must die,
must fall, like Troy's towers,
my mind aflame,
my heart on fire,

(Speaks.)

down, down,
to the bitter earth.

OLD MEN OF ARGOS: *(Chant.)*
>   What evil,
>   what spirit of evil
>   makes you sing of sorrow,
>   sorrow,
>   of tears and death?
>   But where will it end?
>   Is there an end?
>   I don't know.

(Music out.)

KASSANDRA:
> No hiding now,
>   no bride behind the veil.
> No riddles now,
> but searing truth,
>   like mountainous waves blown by a sea-squall
>   into the sun's flaming cauldron,
> a monstrous truth far greater than what you know.
> Bear me witness, hunt as I hunt,
> hard on the scent of ancient evils
>   done in this sad house.

>   Listen.

> On the roof.
> A choir that will not depart.
> Hovering, hovering,
>   they sing in concert a deadly hymn,
>   a deadly text.
> Bloated on blood of generations,
>   they drink the house's lifeblood dry.
> And sbolder, too, they grow on blood, these
>   Furies bred up with the house's brood.
> More boldly they range the house's halls,
>   this band of ancient, fiendish debauchers
>   that will not be dismissed,
>   that infects the rooms with its evil song,
>   a song of destruction,

the song of the original evil,
a brother's bed defiled by a brother,
a bed they spit on in disgust.

Have I hit it?
Hit the mark? Or like a bad archer,
missed it? A false prophet
peddling her lies?

Bear me witness: swear.
I know this house.
I know its crimes.
I know its curses.

FIRST OLD MAN:
How could an oath make it easier for you?
But how do you know this?
A foreigner from across the sea.
And yet you speak of a city foreign to you
as if you'd been there.

KASSANDRA:
Prophet Apollo gave me this power.

FIRST OLD MAN:
A bribe to bring you to his lusty bed?

KASSANDRA:
Yes. I can say so now, not before.

FIRST OLD MAN:
Modesty is always a luxury for the rich.

KASSANDRA:
He took me like a wrestler, his body on mine.

FIRST OLD MAN:
And you bore his child?

KASSANDRA:
At first I consented, then—cheated him.

FIRST OLD MAN:
You had the gift of prophecy beforehand?

KASSANDRA:
I had already foretold Troy's fall.

FIRST OLD MAN:
And Apollo took no revenge?

KASSANDRA:
No revenge? No one believed me again.

FIRST OLD MAN:
But we believed every word you spoke.

KASSANDRA:
AIIIIIIIII!
AIIIIIIIII!
Again,
again!
The pain,
the agony,
the horror of prophecy!
The whirlwind in my mind,
storm waves
crashing, breaking,
swirling!
AIIIIII!
Evil coming,
evil, evil!
O, o there!
There!
By the door!
By the palace!
Children, the children,
dream-children,
house's children!
Horror, horror!
AIIIIIII!

Killed by kin,
by kin killed,
flesh in hands,
children's flesh,
their flesh,
offering,
holding up,
serving handfuls,
hearts,
livers, innards,
guts for father to taste,
father to gnaw,
eating, tearing flesh,
sons' flesh,
devouring!

AIIIIIII!

The debt will be paid.
I know.
I see.
The avenger
lurks, the cowardly
beast, waiting,
plotting,
in the house,
in the bed, the master's
bed, the great king's
couch where he has
lolled for years,
loitered, tumbled, crouching,
waiting the master's
return.

But he who commanded the great fleet,
he who lay waste the proud city of Priam,
cannot see the treachery that
lurks in the smile of the hell-bitch,
who with guile and cunning

licks his hand, who with
flattering tongue draws out long
welcomes, bowing and
scraping the earth before him,
whose evil-intended stroke will
bring his ruin.

Incarnation of evil!
The female slays the male!
How does she dare!
What do I call the fiendish
beast with a Fury in her blood?
Monster snake,
hated of the gods,
rock-dwelling Skylla, ruin of sailors,
raging hell-mother, merciless war-maker
on those she loves!

And how she howled, the brazen bitch,
ecstatic shouts of joy in seeming
welcome, but in truth
shouts of the evil victory to come.

You who refused to believe will see.
For now it doesn't matter.
What will come will come.
One day in pity you'll
see that the words I spoke
are true.

FIRST OLD MAN:
Thyestes eating his children's flesh I know,
and I shudder with terror
at hearing it told so plainly.
But the rest I don't understand,
what do I make of it?

KASSANDRA:
The body of Agamemnon dead.

FIRST OLD MAN:

    Quiet! You mustn't say such things.

KASSANDRA:

    Too late for that. Silence can't help.

FIRST OLD MAN:

    If that's true, then I pray the gods prevent it.

KASSANDRA:

    While you pray, they slit his throat.

FIRST OLD MAN:

    What man would dare to do such a thing?

KASSANDRA:

    Man? You didn't understand a word.

FIRST OLD MAN:

    But how would anyone plan such a plot?

KASSANDRA:

    I spoke clearly. I spoke clear Greek.

FIRST OLD MAN:

    So do the oracles that we don't understand.

KASSANDRA:

PAPAIIIII!

    Again, again,

the fire,

        the fire,

  burns me,

        burns,

searing,

    blinding!

AIIIII!

Apollo!
Lykeian Apollo!
AIIII!
AIIII!
The pain,
the pain!

The two-legged lion-bitch fucks with the wolf.
Her lion lord gone,
she whets her sharp sword,
meant for his back in a welcoming gesture.
For me she brews poison in the cave of her heart.
He will die, she boasts, for the bringing of me.
I will die with him, the source of her outrage.
Together we came,
together we die.
Husband-corpse.
Concubine-corpse.

Why do I wear these things that mock me?
The curse,
the plague,
of Apollo's privilege.
Staff and fillets of prophecy that bind me!
Off with you,
down,
down in the dust,
on the trash-heap with you,
and I stomp you,
stomp you,
you brought me pain,
you bring me death.
Die, die, die, die!
And with that I pay you back, Apollo.
But you die first.
You die before me in this final ritual.
Give them to some other fool to suffer.

My hands?

My hands?

Tearing at me?

At my prophetic robes?

Not mine, not mine!

No!

Apollo's!

Apollo's hands!

Tearing,

ripping,

stripping me of my raiment!

Apollo who made me a fool in these

robes,

who saw me

mocked, who made

friends into enemies who

reviled me with their

laughter, who

made me a beggar,

wandering, homeless,

in misery, starving,

skin and bones,

and I endured it,

bore it for the god,

his prophet, to serve

his glory; the same god who

undoes me now,

who drags me off to my deadly fate.

My father's altar no longer awaits me,

but a butcher's block where my

blood will flow hot as the knife slips in.

But the gods keep stern watch on these matters.

My death will be avenged.

There is one coming with justice in his sword,

a son of the house,

who will slay his mother to avenge his father.

An exile now,

a stranger to his land,

he wanders far from his father's

home.

But the gods have sworn a mighty oath:
>> his father's mutilated corpse will
>>> summon him home, and he will come,
>> a delivering prince,
>>> to crown the achievement of his family's
>>>> destruction.

>>> Why should I weep?
I have witnessed the destruction of Troy,
>> and have seen her captors receive their reward.
> The gods have acted.
>> Fate took its course.

I will go now and do what I must do.
>> Endure to die.

These gates I name The Gates of Hell.

And I ask one thing only.
>> A swift stroke, a swift death.
>>> No struggle.

> Eyes close.
> Blood flows.
> An end.

(KASSANDRA descends from the chariot.)

FIRST OLD MAN:
> So much suffering and pain, poor child,
>> and so much wisdom.
> But if you know your death,
>> if you've seen it, as you say,
>> then why go to it so calmly,
>> like a beast led to the slaughter?

KASSANDRA:
> There's no escape.

FIRST OLD MAN:
> There's always hope.

KASSANDRA:

  No. The time is now.

FIRST OLD MAN:

  How strong you are.

KASSANDRA:

  Praise for the doomed.

FIRST OLD MAN:

  A brave death is everything.

KASSANDRA:

  Like my father's and brothers'?

  (KASSANDRA starts for the palace, but recoils.)

FIRST OLD MAN:

  What is it? Fear?

KASSANDRA:

  FÉU! FÉU!

FIRST OLD MAN:

  What do you see?

KASSANDRA:

  Death. I smell it. Blood in the house.

FIRST OLD MAN:

  Only the smell of the sacrifice.

KASSANDRA:

  Corpses. An open tomb. I smell.

FIRST OLD MAN:

  No, the scent of Syrian incense.

KASSANDRA:

  Well.

I'll go in now.
I have my fate and Agamemnon's to lament.
                    I've had enough of life.
I'm no bird startled by a quivering leaf.

        Bear me witness, friends.
When a woman dies in return for my death,
        and a man for another man,
        one who was married to a monster—
                remember me and my dying prophecy.

FIRST OLD MAN:
        I pity you for the death you've foreseen.

KASSANDRA:
        I have one more word to say,
                this one perhaps a dirge,
                                my own.
                I pray to the last light of the sun I will see,
        that when the avengers come to pay back the murderers,
                they avenge my murder as well,
                though I was only a slave,
                        an easy conquest.

        I weep for man and his destiny.
                Success, good fortune,
                is only a shadow,
        and man's grief the scribble of chalk on a board,
                cancelled by a wet
                                sponge.

(Exit KASSANDRA into the palace through the central doors.)
(Music. Song. Dance.)

FIRST OLD MAN: *(Sings.)*
        No man is ever rich enough,
        no man ever has too much wealth.
        His house may be the envy of all,
        but he will never bar Prosperity

from his door, saying:
"Enter no more!"

To this man they gave Priam's city;
the gods gave Agamemnon Troy;
and the gods honored his coming home.
But now if he must pay in blood
for blood spilled in ages past,
and if his own death must be atoned for
by others whose death must pay the penalty:
what man, what mortal, may boast himself born
to a life that is safe from the slings of Fate?

(AGAMEMNON's voice is heard from inside the palace.)
(Music out.)

AGAMEMNON:
AIIIIIIIIIII!

FIRST OLD MAN:
Whose voice was that?

AGAMEMNON:
AIIIIIIIIIII!

FIRST OLD MAN:
Agamemnon.
His voice.
It's done.
The deed.
What do we do?

OLD MAN 1:
Raise an alarm,
every man to the palace.

OLD MAN 2:
No, we break in,
catch them in the act
with the bloody sword.

OLD MAN 3:
>And now.
>>Whatever we do,
>>do it now.

OLD MAN 4:
>It couldn't be clearer:
>>Kill a king,
>>start a tyranny.

OLD MAN 5:
>We're wasting time,
>>while they're acting.

OLD MAN 6:
>What do we do?
>>We need a plan.

OLD MAN 7:
>Talking never brought a
>>dead man to life.

OLD MAN 8:
>Do we save our own skins
>>and bow to the murderers?

OLD MAN 9:
>Not me!
>>I'll take death before tyranny!

OLD MAN 10:
>First, do we know
>>the king's even dead?

OLD MAN 11:
>Certainty is everything.
>>We must know before we act.

OLD MAN 12:
>   Let's find out what's
>   happened to Agamemnon.

(The central doors open and enter SLAVES with the corpses of AGAMEMNON and KASSANDRA, which they toss to the ground. KLYTAIMNÊSTRA enters close behind and stands triumphantly above them with bloodied sword.)

KLYTAIMNÊSTRA:
>   Words.
>   Many.
>   Many, many words have I
>   spoken, words to suit the
>   moment, cautious
>   words, but here's an
>   end,
>   an end without
>   shame.

>   I've paid my debt.
>   Blood with blood.
>   Hate with hate.
>   How else could I have
>   strung my nets of doom high enough
>   to prevent overleaping? How else
>   have trapped an enemy who pretended loving
>   friendship?
>   And now it's done.
>   And I have won.
>   And I stand here where I struck to end the agony
>   of my long planning, this ancient
>   curse, years-long in the fermenting,
>   and he never knew,
>   there was no escape, no way
>   to ward off death. And I deny
>   none of it,
>   none.

I catch him then like a fish,
in a mesh of rich
webbing, and I strike, I
strike, strike twice,
twice, once,
then again,
again, and he cries twice,
twice to the heavens, and then he's
limp, his legs give way, his
tendons slacken, and he
falls,
down,
down into the crimson swirl,
and then another, another
strike, a third, three
blows, the last for Zeus beneath the earth,
Zeus Keeper of Corpses, a third
strike to keep the ritual proper.

He falls, his huge body,
and a sharp jet of blood spurting,
falling on me, spattering, like a
dark shower of crimson
dew, and I revel in it,
revel like a field of
flowers revels in spring in the sweet rain
of Zeus' heaven.

I rest my case, noble gentlemen of Argos.
Rejoice if it's your will;
as for me,
I exult in my triumph.

If I had poured the libation this corpse deserves,
no wine could have matched the
deserving curse of my words.
He filled every bowl in this house
with a multitude of evil,
and now comes home to drain it to the
dregs.

FIRST OLD MAN:

> I'm stunned with disbelief, woman,
> at your arrogance—over the body
> of the husband you've just murdered.

KLYTAIMNÊSTRA:

> Don't treat me like some witless girl.
> I'm not on trial here.
> Praise or blame me,
> > it's all one to me.
> This is Agamemnon.
> > And this is my husband.
> > > And that husband is now a corpse.
> The work of this right hand that killed him justly.

(Music. Song. Dance.)

FIRST OLD MAN: *(Sings.)*

> What root from the earth,
> what drug from the sea have you taken
> to make you do such a thing?
> You murdered your husband.
> The people curse you for your deed.
> You cut him down, you cast him away,
> and now you, too, will be cast away,
> an exile, condemned,
> thrown from the city,
> an object of hatred and revulsion.

KLYTAIMNÊSTRA: *(Speaks.)*

> > My, how pious we are,
> > so suddenly!
> Judge and jury all in place.
> Passing judgment.
> > Curses,
> > > hatred,
> > > > condemnation,
> > > > > exile!
> Where were you then,

where were *they,*
these citizens,
when *this* man,
at Aulis,
raised the knife to his daughter's throat,
Iphigeneia,
his daughter and mine,
caring not an iota that this was his child—
she was no more to him than a goat
from a flock of thousands!—
this sacrificial creature torn from my womb,
and for what?
To charm away the cutting winds of Thrace
and make some sailors happy!

Why not have exiled *him,*
driven *him* from the land,
for his vicious, polluting act that soiled us all?
No, you never gave it even a *first* thought,
let alone a second.
But of me and my *just* actions
you are a cruel and exacting judge.
All right.
But let me warn you.
Menace me all you want,
but know that our scores are even.
Prove yourself the stronger,
and I'll be your slave,
and the throne is yours.
But if the gods decide otherwise and give *me* the victory,
and the throne remains mine,
you,
all of you,
old as you are,
will finally learn wisdom and where discretion lies.

FIRST OLD MAN: *(Sings.)*
You're mad, with ambition,
with pride, with arrogance.

This bloody murder has fired your mind.
I see it in your eyes flecked with blood.
But I tell you this:
the day will come,
the time for payment,
when blow for blow,
stripped of honor,
no friend in sight,
Vengeance will take her reward.

KLYTAIMNÊSTRA: *(Speaks.)*
I, too, have the solemn power to swear an oath.
Witness for me, then.

I swear by Justice that brought justice
    to bear for my child;
I swear by Ruin and by the Fury
    to whom I sacrificed the blood of this man:
I will know no fear as long as my hearth is
    shared by my loyal partner,
    my defense,
        my shield of confidence,
                        Aigisthos.

                    Look at him,
        the beast who wronged me, the rapist
            of all Troy's nubile sweet young things,
                how low he lies.
                    And she,
        his captive prophetess, his soothsaying
            concubine, who made the trip from Troy
            less a burden in his bed,
public whore for rowdy sailors.
            Both now have the honor due them.
                        Here he lies,
        and she beside him, as is only proper,
        her swan song sung, his belovèd Kassandra:
            side-dish for his bed,
                grand satisfaction for mine!

OLD MEN OF ARGOS: *(Sing.)*
Let me die,
let me die swiftly,
let my death come fast and painless
and without lingering illness.
Now he is gone,
my spearshaft,
my defender,
my shield of defense,
give me sleep that will never end,
eternal rest.
For a woman he suffered,
by a woman he died.

Helen,
mad, raging Helen,
you who destroyed those thousands at Troy,
you are crowned with your final victory in this.
But the blood remains.
The blood is forever.
Ruin and Destruction thrive in this house,
an agony so deep it cannot be sounded.

KLYTAIMNÊSTRA: *(Speaks.)*
Why pray for death?
Why surrender to grief?
And don't turn your wrath against Helen.
Did she alone drag Greeks to their ruin?
Did she alone cause the Greeks anguish?

OLD MEN OF ARGOS: *(Sing.)*
Spirit,
Daimon,
god of Ruin,
that trampled the twin sons of Atreus,
spirit that works its way through women,
spirit of evil tearing my heart,
I see you in the face of Klytaimnêstra,
a hateful raven poised above his body,
exultant in your discordant song.

KLYTAIMNÊSTRA: *(Speaks.)*
    Now you have it right.
    Now you blame the Spirit,
        the curse that has gorged on this family
            for three generations.
    Slaughter, feud, vengeance,
        each wrong paid in full.
            And with each payment,
        a new thirst,
        for new blood.
    Always new pus before the old wound heals.

FIRST OLD MAN: *(Sings.)*
    His power is mighty.
    His grip unrelenting.
    His wrath unforgiving.
    An evil tale,
    a tale of destruction,
    insatiable lust.
    And it comes from Zeus,
    Zeus the source of all,
    Zeus in whom all things are done.

OLD MEN OF ARGOS: *(Sing.)*
        IOOOO!
        IOOOO!
        My king!
        Agamemnon!
      How shall I mourn you?
      How should I weep?
   No words can tell of the love in my heart.
     A spider's web caught you up,
        and here you lie,
      victim of a shameful death,
      at the hand of your wife.

KLYTAIMNÊSTRA: *(Speaks.)*
    I killed him, you say.
    I am his wife, you say.

No.

But you said better when you saw in me
        the destructive Fury raging through this house,
    the Spirit of Vengeance, ancient avenger
of Atreus' cruel banquet.
                That Fury killed him, not me.
I was the instrument of Justice that
    slew this victim as payment for
        children slaughtered.

FIRST OLD MAN: *(Chants.)*
    Guiltless? You?
    Guiltless?
    Where is your witness?
    Yes, the ancient Spirit of Vengeance
    may have given you strength in your insanity,
    but it was you who did it, you.

    Arês, black wargod,
    Spirit of Slaughter,
    Spirit of Hatred in brothers' hearts,
    forges forward
    through seas of royal kindred blood,
    seeking,
    seeking atonement, seeking
    satisfaction for the blood of children butchered,
    dried gore of children devoured.

OLD MEN OF ARGOS: *(Sing.)*
        IOOOO!
        IOOOO!
        My king!
        Agamemnon!
      How shall I mourn you?
        How should I weep?
  No words can tell of the love in my heart.
      A spider's web caught you up,
        and here you lie,
      victim of a shameful death,
      at the hand of your wife.

KLYTAIMNÊSTRA: *(Speaks)*
    And how was his death shameful?
    What of the treachery,
        the guile,
            the lies he brought to this house,
      and with it the house's destruction?
                    What of that?
    What of my child, my Iphigeneia,
        his child, too,
        what he did to her,
        evil what he did to her,
      and he suffered evil justly in return,
            blow for blow.

    Let him not boast of anything in Hell-house;
      he paid for what he did,
        for what he began,
      death for death.

OLD MEN OF ARGOS: *(Sing.)*
          What do I do?
          Where do I turn?
         I'm at my wits' end.
        No time for thought,
      no time for meditation now.
        The house is falling.
      The shower of blood is over,
  for now a bloodstorm beats at the roofs,
      torrent upon torrent,
  and Destiny sharpens the sword of Justice
     for another round of ruin.

          O earth,
          o Argos,
        o earth of Argos,
     why didn't you take me,
     wrap me in your folds,
    before I saw my king dead,
    laid low in a silver bath?

Who will bury him?
Who will mourn him?
You?
Will you bury him?
Will you mourn him?
Will you dare?
First slay, then mourn?
You?
Your husband?
Unkindly kindness for his great deeds?
Who will sing praise at his tomb
with honor and truth,
with greatness of heart?

KLYTAIMNÊSTRA: *(Speaks.)*
His burial is no concern of yours.
My hand killed him,
my hand will bury him.
And there will be no mourning in this house.

But his daughter,
his dear,
his Iphigeneia, will
meet him at Hellgate,
by the swift-running ferry of sorrows,
and tossing her arms about his neck,
kiss her beloved father in greeting.

OLD MEN OF ARGOS: *(Sing.)*
Reproach is met with reproach,
taunt with taunt,
malice with malice.
And how difficult to judge between them.
The plunderer is plundered, the spoiler spoiled,
and the slayer slain.
And it is as certain as Zeus keeps his throne,
that he who does evil will have evil in return.
That is the law.
But who can cast the seed of curse from the blood?
The brood of this house is nailed to its doom.

KLYTAIMNÊSTRA: *(Speaks.)*
    Finally you begin to understand.
        The future,
            the truth of all this.
    I am ready,
                ready here and now,
    to swear a pact with the Fury that haunts this house.
    What is done is done, never to be undone,
    and I will accept that, hard as it may be.

    Let him go, this house's Fury,
            somewhere else, some other
            house, some other family,
    and through killing of kin by kin wear it away
            to despair and destruction as he has us.
                I need little,
                I can live modestly,
    I will give all my wealth and riches
            if only this house is purged of this
                            frenzy of killing.

(Enter AIGISTHOS through the central doors of the palace with a mass of ARMED GUARDS.)
(Music out.)

AIGISTHOS:
    O blessèd, blessèd day, to see justice done!
    I know now that there are gods
            who watch over man, who
                punish his crimes.
    Here lies Agamemnon, dead,
            caught up in a crimson robe-net
                woven by Furies—now, finally,
            here at my feet.
    And he has paid. He has paid
                dearly for his father's evil
                            doings.

    King Atreus,
            the dead man's father,

clashed with his brother,
  my father, Thyestes, and
      drove him into exile. My father
had challenged Atreus for his throne.
      But Thyestes in time made his way back
  home, a broken man,
      on his last legs, despondent,
          defeated,
  and threw himself as a suppliant
    at his brother Atreus' feet.

                              Atreus then,

this man's father,
    godless Atreus, showed his brother

                              mercy.

Instead of spilling his blood as retribution,
      he kissed him,
          welcomed him into his
    house, the rescuer of his starving brother's life.
In celebration, he called for a feast.
Atreus feasted my father Thyestes,
    his own brother. A feast to
    cancel recriminations,
      to wipe out bad blood, so to speak,
    a feast of reconciliation.

And seating him in the seat of honor,
      apart from all others,
    he served him up with his own hands
      a feast of steaming stewed flesh.
His sons' flesh.
The flesh of Thyestes' own children.
My brothers.
      He had invited them,
        slit their throats,
          bled them, and chopped them up
    beyond recognition.
Meat stripped from the bone,
    filets, steaks, kidneys, livers,
    brains, cleverly chopped.

But at the bottom of the dish
       he placed feet and toes,
     hands and fingers, to avoid too early
            detection.

Thyestes ate heartily of this
     extravagant feast of friendship.
          Innocently.
    Suspecting nothing. But then
dipping into the dish at its bottom,
    he raises up, ready to chew,
    a recognizable fragment, and he
       understands the enormity of the
    horror, the abomination.
Retching, he throws himself backward
    with a howl, spewing, vomiting onto the floor
      his butchered children.
Table overturned, sent clattering,
    testimony to the justice of his curse, he
       condemns unto all eternity the present and future
             of Pelops' line,
  born and unborn,
  children and fathers, all—
    a house destroyed.

It is by that curse this man has fallen.
I wove this web of Justice, I
    nurtured it into being.
          I! I!
    And saw it to fulfillment.
He drove us out then, Atreus,
      into exile, my father and I,
        the last of his sons,
    a baby,
      too insignificant for Atreus to be concerned.
But I grew,
   and Justice grew in me,
     and Justice led me back to my bloody home.
I reached out from a great distance

and put my mark on this man.
I stitched it together, piece by piece,
this plot, this scheme of the
fatal plan.
And here he lies.
Trammeled up like some monster of the
deep.

I can die happy.
Justice has been served.

FIRST OLD MAN:
I have no respect, Aigisthos,
for a man who gloats over others' pain.
You say you alone planned this piteous murder.
Then I say that when the day of Justice arrives,
you will be stoned to death by every
man and woman of this city.

AIGISTHOS:
What's this?
Murmur and muttering of mutiny below the decks?
Make no mistake,
we have the tiller in hand,
we guide the ship.
For such old cockers to learn new
tricks can't be easy. But you'll learn.
Starvation and chains
are apt at teaching manners.
Can you have eyes and not see?
Kick at the pricks and you will be
pricked.

FIRST OLD MAN:
Woman!
For that's what you are!
You skulked behind while
others went to war! You

wallowed in his bed, you
plowed his wife, our king,
our general,
planning his death!

AIGISTHOS:
Words can lead to tears.
Beware yours.
Orpheus singing tamed wild beasts;
your raucous song only
infuriates me. It will take
stronger tactics to tame you.

FIRST OLD MAN:
Hail the conquering tyrant, eh?
You?
You who planned the deed,
and then hadn't the balls to carry it through?

AIGISTHOS:
Not true!
Deception was for the woman.
It was her role.
Given our history,
his and mine, I would have been
smelled out at the start. We were
blood enemies. He would have seen
right through it.

I now take the reins here in Argos,
and with his wealth I will
attempt to rule this city. And the man who
balks will have a heavy yoke to wear.
No pampered, corn-fed
trace-horses in my state.
Chains, darkness, hunger will break you.
Break you or kill you.

FIRST OLD MAN:

        Coward!
  Not to kill him yourself!
 But let a woman do it, and in the
     doing pollute the gods and all
         Argos!
  If Orestês is alive to hear,
 let him return one day—return with fair
 fortune blowing him on—to kill these two
   vultures feeding on his house,
     and killing, avenge with his sword
   the death of his father,
 Agamemnon!

AIGISTHOS:

 Eager to start our lessons, are we?

FIRST OLD MAN:

 Friends, old friends, be ready, your sticks will defend you!

AIGISTHOS:

 Guards! Draw your swords!

FIRST OLD MAN:

 I'm ready! I'm not afraid to die!

AIGISTHOS:

 Then I'll see you're not disappointed!

KLYTAIMNÊSTRA:

        No! Stop!
 Stop! You mustn't!
  Beloved Aigisthos, we've had
  enough of killing. We've reaped
   too much death already,
     a sad harvest.
 Let us shed no more blood.

Old men, elders of Argos, go home.
Go now, before you regret what will come.
What's done is done.
Accept.
Pray that the evil that gorges on Argive death
has had his fill. He has held us in his talons
far too long.

A woman says this—if anyone will
condescend to hear.

AIGISTHOS:
But you can't!
Listen to them!
Their foul mouths spitting out
flowers of evil! Testing their luck—
how far they can go!
I'm in charge here!
The new leader!
Master!

FIRST OLD MAN:
No real Argive grovels to murderers.

AIGISTHOS:
Then real Argives will have to be taught.

FIRST OLD MAN:
Not if Orestês comes home first.

AIGISTHOS:
Exiles feed on hope. I know.

FIRST OLD MAN:
Grow fat, while you can! Pollute Justice!

AIGISTHOS:
Fool! You'll pay for this one day!

FIRST OLD MAN:
>   Cock of the walk! Strut for your hen!

KLYTAIMNÊSTRA:
>   Ignore them. They're nothing.
>   >   Idle barkers.
>   >   >   We rule here now.
>   >   >   We have the power.
>   Together you and I will set all things
>   >   >   >   >   >   right.

(KLYTAIMNÊSTRA takes the hand of AIGISTHOS and together they enter the palace, the doors thudding shut behind them. The OLD MEN OF ARGOS wander off in diverse directions.)

LIBATION BEARERS

(ΧΟΗΦΟΡΟΙ)

CAST OF CHARACTERS

ORESTÊS *son of Agamemnon and Klytaimnêstra*

PYLADES *friend of Orestês*

ÊLEKTRA *sister of Orestês*

KLYTAIMNÊSTRA *queen of Argos*

AIGISTHOS *king of Argos*

KILISSA *old nurse of Orestês, a slave*

CHORUS OF LIBATION BEARERS *captive slave women*

FIRST LIBATION BEARER *chorus leader*

GATEKEEPER *slave*

SLAVE *to Aigisthos and Klytaimnêstra*

MALE AND FEMALE SLAVES

LIBATION BEARERS

Seven years later
Dawn.
Mykenê, in Argos.
Outside Agamemnon's palace.
Agamemnon's tomb and grave mound downstage.
Enter ORESTÊS and PYLADÊS in traveling clothes.

ORESTÊS:
    I'm home, Pyladês.
    Home at last.
    So many years.
    Away from my country, my land.
    My kingdom—
        not yet my kingdom.
    Home from exile, here at my father's grave.

                    I'll pray.

    Hermês, earth-god,
        guide to the world of the dead,
            son of Zeus;
    Hermês, guardian of my father's rights,
        help me in my struggle, my need is great,
        hear my prayer, for I am returned.
    Hermês, hear me.
    Hear me, father.

    I honor now first Inachos,
        river-god of our Argive Plain,
            for raising me, for nurture.
    With this lock of my hair
        I lay aside my childhood
            and am a man.
    And to the dead, dear father,
        this second lock, for mourning.

An exile,

    I wasn't here to weep your death,
    to defend you, father, from your enemies,
    from the butchers who slaughtered you.
I wasn't here to reach out to you my hand in farewell
    as your corpse was borne away for burial.

(Enter from the side door to the women's quarters ÊLEKTRA and the
CHORUS OF LIBATION BEARERS carrying jars with libations.)
(Music. Song. Dance.)

                Pyladês! Look!

There!

    Who are they?
What do they want?
A procession of women in black.
Has someone died?
Some new disaster for the house?
        No,
they're headed here, with grave offerings,
    libations for my father, to appease the dead.
        What else could it be?
                    O god!

Look there!
    Êlektra! My sister!
      I know her by her grief.

I pray to you, Zeus, let me avenge him,
    let me avenge my father's spirit,
    fight beside me now!
        Zeus, be gracious!

        Hurry, Pyladês!
    We mustn't be seen!
Out of the way, hurry!
I want to know the meaning of these rites.

(ORESTÊS and PYLADÊS retreat to a distance.)

LIBATION BEARERS: *(Sing.)*

I come,
I come from the hated palace,
not willingly in this cold dawnlight,
bearing libations to ease his spirit,
Agamemnon,
once lord of all Argos,
drink-offerings to placate the dead.
My hands, my fists,
beat at my breast with pain-piercing strokes.
My cheeks are torn,
nail-torn and ragged,
crimson flesh newly gouged,
furrows of pain for my grieving heart
that feeds on unending groans.
My clothes are in shreds,
torn in my grief,
ripped in my anguish as I beat my breast
for a life that knows no laughter.

A cry,
piercing,
terror-striking,
shrilled through the house from the depths of the dark,
from troubled sleep,
ominous dream,
nightmare-making,
hair-on-end-standing.
Terror woke screaming,
and women trembled in their chambers.
Dream-readers,
armed with god's meaning,
told that in earth dead men were stirring,
raging anger against the killers.

That evil woman,
hounded by guilt,
sends me here with graceless gifts,
gifts to offer to Mother Earth,

empty gifts to keep away ghosts.
But how can I pray,
how can I mouth her foul prayers?
What can wash away blood spilt on earth?
This house is doomed,
this house of misery,
house destroyed by men's hatred.
Hated gloom covers it now,
no light in its heart,
its master dead,
sunless gloom,
anxious despair.

Where once awe for Majesty ruled,
now Discontent sits waiting.
Where Respect once reigned in people's hearts,
now Hatred sits brooding,
now Loathing crouches,
and my evil masters live in terror of Justice.
Success is god and more than god,
but success for my rulers sits on thin ice.
Justice seeks evil late or soon.
Justice waits and turns her scales.
For some the blow comes swift at dawn;
for others at dusk, and the waiting is agony;
the last are borne off by devouring night.

Earth has drunk deep of blood,
but the gore of blood-spill clots
and will not wash away.
And Ruin will hound the guilty mind,
and frenzy never loosen its grip,
till the maggots of madness have eaten through.

Lost virginity knows no remedy,
and the bloody hand can never be washed clean,
not if all the earth's currents
flowed in one stream.

The gods deserted my city,
the enemy destroyed my land,
the yoke of Necessity compelled me,
ripped me from my father's house,
dragged me from my burning city,
to a fate of evil servitude.
I have no choice,
I do what I must,
submission to just and unjust alike,
choke down hatred for evils endured.
But still I weep,
weep for my poor mistress,
hiding my tears behind my sleeve,
for her sad fate.
Sorrow chills the heart to its core.

(Music out.)

ÊLEKTRA:
Dear women,
slaves of the palace—
you have come here with me to my
father's grave to help me in this ritual,
and I need your advice.
Tell me what to say.
I know I pour the offerings on his grave,
yes, and I will,
I know that,
but what words can I say to
cheer my father's spirit?
What prayer do I make
to the gods? Do I say these
gifts are from a loving wife
to a loved husband?
How can I do that?
She's my mother.
I would be lying.
Or do I repeat the usual words men say:
to give in return to the giver—yes, a gift

worthy of their crimes.
Or shall I do it in silence,
    as silently as when my father
    died, and in that silence
             disgrace him?
Do I pour it out for the earth to drink
    as it drank his blood? Do I
    leave the scene as one who has just
    emptied the polluted remains of a sacrifice,
        tossing the vessel behind her with
    averted eyes?
                Please,
        please help me, my dears.
Share with me in this decision.
Share as surely as we share
    a hatred in this house.
               Tell me.
Don't be afraid,
    not afraid to speak.
        Not of anyone.
We're all of us slaves, slaves and
    freemen alike. Fate pays his visit
        to us all.
              But tell me what you think.
If you have anything better than this to say.
    Tell me, please.

FIRST LIBATION BEARER:
    I honor your father's grave
        as if it were an altar. And that honor
        makes me open my heart to you.

ÊLEKTRA:
    Yes, speak out of honor for his grave.

FIRST LIBATION BEARER:
    As you pour, pray for those who are loyal.

ÊLEKTRA:

But which of my friends, or his, are loyal any longer?

FIRST LIBATION BEARER:

You, for one, and whoever hates Aigisthos.

ÊLEKTRA:

Pray for you and me, then—for all of us here?

FIRST LIBATION BEARER:

You know the answer to that. You must ask yourself.

ÊLEKTRA:

Who else can I add? Who else is loyal to us?

FIRST LIBATION BEARER:

Orestês. Orestês is loyal. Even in exile.

ÊLEKTRA:

Orestês! Yes, Orestês! How could I forget!

FIRST LIBATION BEARER:

As for those you can't trust—the killers, pray that—

ÊLEKTRA:

The killers! Yes! What do I pray for them?

FIRST LIBATION BEARER:

Pray that some god may come, or some man—

ÊLEKTRA:

Yes, to do what, sit in judgment, punish them?

FIRST LIBATION BEARER:

Punish? No. Kill. A life for a life.

ÊLEKTRA:

Kill? Can I ask such a thing of the gods?

FIRST LIBATION BEARER:
>   Justice! Death for death! Justice is holy!

ÊLEKTRA:
>   I'll pray.

Hermês, earth-god,
>   guide to the world of the dead,
>   help me.
Call up for me the gods below
>   to hear my prayers.
>   Come, daimon,
>   infernal spirit,
>   spirit of this house
>   who witnessed my father's murder!
And call to me Great Earth,
>   Great Mother,
>   fountain of life who takes all
>   back in its fullness
>   when the course is run!
Pouring these lustral offerings for the dead,
>   I call to my father:
>   Father—
>   father, have pity!
Kindle in our house the light that is Orestês!
>   The dearest of lights, our beacon!
For we are children sold in the market by our mother
>   in return for a man,
>   a mate,
>   a husband,
>   Aigisthos,
>   who murdered you.
>   As for me,
>   I am a slave, no better,
>   live the life of a slave.
And Orestês—Orestês has nothing,
>   an outcast, penniless, an exile,
>   while they wallow in the luxury your
>   labor brought them. But Orestês,

father, I beg you, I pray you,
>> let him come home,
>> let him be happy in his fortune.
And for myself
>> I ask that I never be like my mother,
>> in mind, in body, in act.

So much for us; for us this prayer.

>> For our enemies I pray:
Let an avenger come with a mighty sword
>> and in justice cut them down,
>> death for death,
>> blood for blood,
>>> as they cut down you!

Enough of this prayer for evil
>> that interrupts my prayer for good.
>> I speak it against *them*.

Bring us your blessings,
>> to us here above—
>> in the gods' name,
>> in the name of Earth,
>> in the name of Justice,
>>> Justice triumphant.

>> These are my prayers.
And after them, this last of libations.
Now make my words flower with your songs of lament.

(ÊLEKTRA pours onto the grave mound the last of the jars while the LIBATION BEARERS sing.)
(Music. Song. Dance.)

LIBATION BEARERS: *(Sing.)*
>> Come,
>> come,
>> let the tear fall,

the tear of care for our lost master,
our master dead,
let it fall on this grave,
this bulwark of blessings,
this tear that keeps pollution at bay,
now the gifts,
the libations to the dead,
have been poured.

OTOTOTOTOTOTOTOI!
Where is he,
where is the man,
the spear-wielding man,
the man, like Arês Wargod,
to deliver this house,
the man with Scythian weapons
in close combat?

(Music out.)

ÊLEKTRA:
He has our libations now.
The earth has drunk them.

But this. What is this? Something new.

FIRST LIBATION BEARER:
My heart danced with fear when you picked that up.

ÊLEKTRA:
A lock of hair laid here on the tomb.

FIRST LIBATION BEARER:
Whose? Man's or woman's? A young girl's?

ÊLEKTRA:
That's easy enough to see. No guessing here.

FIRST LIBATION BEARER:
>   Well, then? Tell us. We're old, you're young. Teach us.

ÊLEKTRA:
>   No one in Argos could have left this here but me.

FIRST LIBATION BEARER:
>   Who else? Those who should have are his enemies.

ÊLEKTRA:
>   Yes, and yet it looks very like—

FIRST LIBATION BEARER:
>   Like what?

ÊLEKTRA:
>   My own.

FIRST LIBATION BEARER:
>   What are you saying? Orestês?

ÊLEKTRA:
>   Nothing looks more like.

FIRST LIBATION BEARER:
>   But how would he dare to come here?

ÊLEKTRA:
>   He sent it, this—*this,* to honor his father.

FIRST LIBATION BEARER:
>   Sent! Yes!
>   All the more reason to weep.
>   He'll never again set foot on Argive soil.

ÊLEKTRA:
>   I can't, I can't—

it overwhelms me, my tears,
a wave of bitterness rising against me,
        sword ripping my heart,
                my anguish!
My tears flow like floods of winter
                rain beating down the
        gates of my eyes when I see this
                            lock!

Who else in Argos,
        in this city, could
        own this hair, could
                share it with me?
My mother,
        my whore-mother, his
                murderer?
                            No,
she'd never have clipped it from her *precious* head,
        never have offered it!

No!

My mother who can't bear the
        sight of me, my mother who is
                no mother,
        my mother who hates her children,
                            hates!

But how, how can I say,
        how can I even think, that this was
        left here by Orestês,
                the dearest of men to me, when—
o Orestês!
        Hope is making a fool of me!

If only it had words and
        sense and could speak. If only it could
        tell me it *is* Orestês, then I would

know and not be tossed so
cruelly from hope to despair and
back again. Or it would
tell me it was cut from some enemy head and I could
hate it, because it came from no kinsman
to adorn and honor his tomb, a kinsman
who could share with me my mourning.

Perhaps the gods know how we're tossed like
sailors in a tempest; but are they ready to
help, we can never know.
And yet if Hope smiles on us,
if we're meant to survive,
safety may come and,
like a mighty tree, grow from the
tiniest seed.

O god, I don't know what to—
what to think—I'm so
confused, I—

(ORESTÊS comes forward, followed at a distance by PYLADÊS.)

ORESTÊS:
Your prayers are answered, my dear.
May the gods treat you as well in the future.

ÊLEKTRA:
What have the gods ever given me?

ORESTÊS:
The sight of someone you most long for.

ÊLEKTRA:
And who would that be, I wonder?

ORESTÊS:
Orestês. I know him. I know how you love him.

ÊLEKTRA:

And how does that answer my prayer?

ORESTÊS:

I am Orestês.

ÊLEKTRA:

Is this some trap?

ORESTÊS:

If it is, then I'm trapping myself.

ÊLEKTRA:

Don't mock my pain, stranger.

ORESTÊS:

Your pain and mine are one.

ÊLEKTRA:

Yes, well—then I'm to call you Orestês, is that it?

ORESTÊS:

So slow to see the truth when it
stands in front of you.
How is that possible?
And yet when you saw the
hair I cut in mourning, your heart
soared as if there could be no question.
Here.
Match the lock to my hair.
It's no different.
It's mine.
It's your brother's.
And how like it is to yours.
And look. My cloak.
The animals woven into it.
This is your weaving. You wove it for me
when I was taken to safety,
years ago.

(ÊLEKTRA runs to embrace him.)

Dear, dear Êlektra!
But control yourself.
          You must. It's too soon for joy,
                    and those who should love us
          most are our mortal enemies.

ÊLEKTRA:
          O dearest, dearest darling of your father's
                                        house!
          How much I've hoped, how much I've
                    wept,
                    the seed to renew this house!
          You'll win it back, you will,
                    your father's house! Your
                    strength will win it back!
          Orestês bright light of this house,
                    I have four loves to give you!
          The love for a father,
                    for that's what you are to me now;
          the love I should have for my mother—
                    the woman I so justly hate,
                                        despise;
          the love I had for my sister, ruthlessly
                    slaughtered; and the love that's only your own,
                    the love for a brother,
                    mine, my own,
                    who loved and honored me!
                              O Orestês!

ORESTÊS:
                                        Zeus!
          Zeus, hear us!
Be faithful to our cause,
                    two fledglings, the eagle's brood,
                    orphans of the father eagle dead,
                    netted in the viper's vicious
                              coils, starving, weak, too young yet to

lift to their nest their father's prey!
See in us these fugitives,
        fatherless, robbed of our home!
                Agamemnon,
     who revered you, offered you countless
        sacrifices, rich banquets in your
                           honor.

Who will do so now, Great Zeus,
     who in all of Argos,
        if you bring us to perdition?

ÊLEKTRA:
    Destroy the eagle's brood,
        and there dies with it
      omens sent to men, signs
        to win men's belief, and who will
      again believe your word, Zeus?
    But destroy the royal stock of Argos,
      let it wither, and there will be
        no more parades of bulls to the land's altars,
      no more sacrifice.
                Hear us, Zeus,

     hear our plea!
Our house lies humbled in the dust:
      raise it again to greatness.

FIRST LIBATION BEARER:
           O my dears, no,
     not so loud. Even the air has
     ears, all Argos is alive with
          ears.
To save your father's house,
     you must be careful. A word overheard
       and idly passed on to our rulers
       could bring disaster.
How I long to see them wrapped in pitch
     and lighted as living torches!

ORESTÊS:
Apollo will never betray me,
    not the oracle of Great Pythia.
He charges me to endure the coming
    trial, whatever the danger, and
        threatens with calamities that
    freeze my heart's blood if I
        fail to obey.
He shrieked so his voice
        shrilled through the temple, to
kill them as they killed my father,
        by deceit and duplicity.
He said like a bull I should rage,
    charge in my fury, gore them
        for having stolen my birthright.
    And if I refuse him, if I
        disobey the god,
I pay with a life of unspeakable misery.

He told of malignant powers beneath the
    earth that turn against men who
    fail to honor revenge. He spoke of
        plagues and diseases they impose
    on those they hate, of leprous
ulcers, cancers in the flesh that
    gnaw forever at the source of
        creation, scabrous sores that
    sprout white hairs, pus-filled
                pockets.

The Fury Avengers will come,
    springing from my father's blood.
    I will see them, glaring at me
    through the gloom, their brows
        knotted, scowling
    faces. Their arrows will
        fly through darkness like
pitch and pierce me as my father's blood
        cries out for revenge. I will be

tormented by madness and
empty fears that will drive me from the city,
my body jabbed with bronze goads.
    No cups of friendship will welcome me, no
        thank-offerings to the gods,
    my father's unseen
        wrath will bar me from
sharing in the altar's service.
    I will never again find
shelter under another roof, but die
    cruelly, shriveled by a wasting
    death, alone and
            uncared for.

These are Apollo's oracles,
    and how can I not believe them?
But believe or not, the deed is there to do,
    and must be done. And there's
        nothing in the world that I want
            more.
Many motives meet and
        drive me on.
    Apollo's command,
    my grief for my father,
    my desperate need for my
        inheritance; and then my
    people, those citizens of the greatest
city on earth who overthrew
    Troy with the hearts of heroes,
        they must no longer be slaves,
    to grovel at the feet of a pair of
women—
        for in his heart he is a woman,
    Aigisthos.
        And if he isn't,
        we'll soon see.

(Music. Song. Dance.)

FIRST LIBATION BEARER: *(Sings.)*
　　Come, Great Destiny,
　　come, almighty
　　　　　　　　Fates,
　　Powers that with
　　Zeus guide man's
　　　　　　　　mortality!
　　Hear us,
　　hear our prayers!
　　Let Justice lift her
　　　　　　　scales,
　　let Justice turn her
　　wheel of
　　　　　vengeance,
　　and bring all things
　　to
　　　balance.
　　Let hateful word pay
　　hateful
　　　　　word!
　　Let murderous
　　deed pay murderous
　　deed!
　　Let blood pay
　　　　　　blood and
　　outrage outrage!
　　Justice,
　　demand your
　　　　　　due!
　　The doer must suffer.
　　Such is the wisdom of
　　ancient
　　　　origin.

ORESTÊS: *(Sings.)*
　　O father,
　　unhappy father,
　　　　　　　father
　　who fathered our

grief,
what word of
love
I can speak,
what deed of
love
I can do,
will reach you
in your
dark grave,
will make its way to your
world of
darkness?
What will bring
light to you
and
light to us?
I will lament in
hope you can
hear,
lament for a dear dead
father,
lament to
bring you gladness,
lament,
lament
to bring you to us,
you who lie here
beneath this
stone,
you who must give us
hope.

FIRST LIBATION BEARER: *(Sings.)*
O child,
dear son,
no fire that
tears with its
jaws

at a dead man's
                    flesh
can ever burn away
his
        anger;
his will for
                    vengeance
lives on in death;
his spirit of revenge
never
        dies,
but grows ever stronger.
What once was
                    bitter
is more bitter still.
Hatred seethes
for the murderer's
                    deed.
And then come the children,
to weep,
to mourn,
to lament the
                    dead father.
And he hears,
he hears the
            song
for the dead,
and light bright as
fire
sailing the
            sky
shines down on the
doer,
hunts down the
killer.
Let us raise our
voices to
waken the
            dead

and the guilty
will be
            hunted,
the guilty will
                pay.

ÊLEKTRA: *(Sings.)*
    Hear me, father,
    hear your children!
    Here at your
    grave we
                sing
    our lament,
    our song for
    the dead,
    for a
            dead father.
    Your grave is our
    love,
    your grave is our
    house.
    We have nothing else.
    Exiled and suppliants,
    we beg at
                your tomb,
    we cry for
    protection,
    sing our
    lament,
    pour out our
                    sorrow.
    But what is
    good here?
    What is not
                evil?
    Rise, dear father,
    rise from your
                    grave,
    rise and be

                    with us.
For all we know
now is
          ruin
and
      despair.

LIBATION BEARERS: *(Sing.)*
                    God, if he wills,
                can wrest good from evil,
                 can change our song
                  from dirge to joy.
                 A triumphant song
               can ring out in the palace
                 to welcome the son
               returned to his kingdom.

ORESTÊS: *(Sings.)*
     O father,
     why didn't you
     die at
           Troy,
     there under
     Troy's walls,
     slain in
     battle by a Lykian
                      spear?
     Your halls would now
     resound in
                  glory,
     your fame soar
     high in its
     majesty
     by all who
     remember
               Troy,
     and your children
     honored.
     Your tomb would

tower on
Troy's coast,
a landmark for
     sailors.

LIBATION BEARERS: *(Sing.)*
     Dear to all who fell at Troy,
     brave men,
     honorable warriors,
     you would now be honored by heroes,
     a king of majesty
     who ministers only
     to the Powers below that rule the dead,
     a lord and master of
     endless renown.

ÊLEKTRA: *(Sings.)*
No,
he should not have
died at Troy,
or be
     buried beside
Skamander's banks
with the legions who
lie there in
     death!
Those who killed him
should have
     died as he did,
died at the hands of
those they
     loved,
the hands of kin,
and be
     rotting now
in dark earth.
And men in far off
lands would have
learned of their

                        deadly
    fate.

FIRST LIBATION BEARER: *(Sings.)*
    You're dreaming, my dears,
    golden dreams,
    dreams better than
                        gold,
    more blest even than the
    most Blest
    who dwell beyond the
    wild North Wind.
    Dreams come easy,
    had for the
                        wishing,
    but the double
    scourge is heard in the
    land.
    Our champions
    beneath the
                        earth
    are stirring,
    and those in power
    here in Argos,
    those who
                        murdered,
    those we hate,
    have dirty hands
    stained with
                        evil.
    The time to act is now.
    The house's
    children
    have won the
                        day!

ORESTÊS: *(Sings.)*
    The arrow hits
    home!

We hear!
Have we roused you,
sleeping Vengeance?
Zeus,
Zeus of the world of the
                              dead,
send up Vengeance
from the world below,
Vengeance,
though late,
bringing
        Justice,
and smite with
evil the
        evil
heart,
        smite with
evil the
        evil hand!
The parents will be
avenged!

LIBATION BEARERS: *(Sing.)*
                        Let me cry,
                    cry out,
              the first to cry out,
          the song of triumph,
          the song of victory,
     when that man is hacked down
       by the hand of Vengeance,
       and the woman down,
          fallen in death!
Why stifle the rage that blows me on,
        the hatred that blows
      before my heart's prow?

ÊLEKTRA: *(Sings.)*
Zeus!
        Zeus!

Give us our rights!
Smash them,
crush,
break in their
                    skulls!
Kill!
        Kill!
Show us your power!
Let the land
believe once more.
I demand
justice from
                injustice.
Great Earth,
Great Mother,
hear me,
and hear me,
lords of the
                Earth below!

FIRST LIBATION BEARER: *(Sings.)*
There is a law.
Blood will have blood.
Blood spilt
demands more
                blood.
Murder
shrieks in the
night,
Murder
calls for the
                Furies.
"Furies, come!
Aid the long dead!
Demand blood for blood!"
Ruin demands ruin!
Destruction, destruction!

ORESTÊS: *(Sings.)*
>   Lords of the underworld,
>   infernal gods,
> > > hear us!
>   O hear us,
> > >   exalted
>   Curses of the dead!
>   Behold in us the
>   end of the race of
>   Atreus,
>   helpless,
>   dishonored,
>   despairing,
>   shamed,
>   with only bare
>   life to cling to,
>   adrift on a
>   shoreless sea.
>   Where can we
> > >   turn,
>   Great Zeus?
>   Where?

LIBATION BEARERS: *(Sing.)*
> > To hear such grief, my king,
> > makes me tremble with fear.
> > My eyes turn inward,
> > I see black despair.
> > But when confidence wakens
> > and hope stands firm,
> > my heart's pain fades and
> > hope appears in all her beauty.

ÊLEKTRA: *(Sings.)*
>   What must we do
>   to rouse you, brother?
>   Recite our
> > >   agonies,
>   the pain we've

suffered?
Let her fawn.
Let her try.
Let the wolf-mother
smile and smile!
She bore us,
she bore
      two wolves,
and we will
not be
softened,
not appeased
by the
      savage
she-wolf!

FIRST LIBATION BEARER: *(Sings.)*
Dead,
      o dead,
when he lay
        dead,
Agamemnon,
my head, my breast,
I beat them,
beat them,
like a Persian
        mourner,
my arms stretched high,
beat,
     beat down,
my hands clutched,
tearing hair, fists
pounding,
spattering blood,
blows
     resounding
on my battered and
wretched head.

ÊLEKTRA: *(Sings.)*
IOOO!

IOOO!

Cruel mother!

Reckless mother!

Evil wife!

You buried him,
buried,
but a savage
farewell,
savage,
no eyes to
weep,
no people to
mourn,
no lamentation for the
slain warrior!

FIRST LIBATION BEARER: *(Sings.)*
Listen, son,
hear me,
Orestês.
You must know this.
The she-wolf
who
murdered also
mutilated.
Hands, feet,
ears,
manhood,
lopped away,
tied to his neck,
slung through the
armpits!
A crime to make his
death
unbearable to you.
You know now your
father's

suffering,
his grave
   dishonor.

ÊLEKTRA: *(Sings.)*
 You've heard how he
 died, what they
 did to his
   body.
 They did the same
 to my
   life.
 They shut me away,
 no funeral mourning for me.
 Locked me in a room
 deep in the
   house,
 like a rabid bitch
 chained in a kennel.
 Laughter died in me
 that day, and
 tears ran
   channels
 in my cheeks.
 A secret
   mourning,
 a private
   lament.
 You know now, brother,
 you know now,
   Orestês.
 Carve it in your
 heart
  forever.

LIBATION BEARERS: *(Sing.)*
   Hear her, Orestês!
  Let her words ring in your ears!
   Remember.

The past is past.
The future is all!
Raise up your heart now in rage
and enter the battle!

ORESTÊS: *(Sings.)*
Your tale is a tale of
dishonor!
                His,
yours,
        the people!
My father's body,
naked,
mangled!
And her hands did it!
Dishonored his body,
dishonored his
                memory!
She'll pay!
By god she'll pay!
The gods are with us!
And my hands with them!
And when I have
                slain her,
I can die happy!

Come, father,
come,
join us in battle!

ÊLEKTRA: *(Sings.)*
Bathed in tears, I call on you, father!

FIRST LIBATION BEARER: *(Sings.)*
Together,
        as one,
in a single
        cry,
we call to you,

Master,
to come to the
                    light!
Join our battle
against the hated!

ORESTÊS: *(Sings.)*
Let force battle
                    force,
let Justice battle
Justice!

ÊLEKTRA: *(Sings.)*
Bring Retribution in a way that is just!

FIRST LIBATION BEARER: *(Sings.)*
I shudder to hear
these
        prayers.
The hour of doom has
long been waiting.
And prayer will
surely bring it.

LIBATION BEARERS: *(Sing.)*
Deadly curse bred in the race,
evil, bloody, discordant stroke,
the rage of Ruin,
unspeakable grief,
unending pain!

There is no cure but one;
no outside hand can set it right,
only the children,
only their hands.
Strife,
savage, brutal strife.
The only cure: blood for blood.
To the gods below we sing this hymn!

Hear us, blest Powers beneath the earth!
Give us your aid,
send us help!
Bless these children!
Give them victory!

(Music out.)

ORESTÊS:

Father, who died an unkingly death,
answer my prayer:
give me your throne.

ÊLEKTRA:

I ask, too, father: let me escape
when I have brought ruin
down on Aigisthos.

ORESTÊS:

For then when men feast the dead
you will get your share of honor.
If not, and I fail,
you will lose both feast and honor.

ÊLEKTRA:

And on my wedding day I will bring you
the best my father's house has to offer.
But first, father,
I will honor this tomb.

ORESTÊS:

Earth, send up my father to witness my battle.

ÊLEKTRA:

Persephonê, Queen of the Underworld, give him victory.

ORESTÊS:

Remember the bath, father, that robbed you of life.

ÊLEKTRA:

Remember the net they fashioned to catch you up.

ORESTÊS:

The fetters that caught you up were made in no smithy.

ÊLEKTRA:

They plotted to trap you in a web of shame.

ORESTÊS:

Father, how can you sleep through these taunts?

ÊLEKTRA:

Lift your head, come up to us, father.

ORESTÊS:

Either send Justice to fight on our side,
the side of those you love and
        who love you, or let us kill them
by their own means,
        grip for grip,
        cunning for cunning.
They threw you, won't you help
        us throw them?

ÊLEKTRA:

This is our last cry to you, father,
        your eagle's brood,
        your fledglings,
            here at your tomb.
Pity us,
            Orestês,
                Êlektra,
        pity your children.

ORESTÊS:

Don't blot out the race of Pelops.
While we live, you live,
        even in death.

ÊLEKTRA:

> Listen, father, it's for your sake we do this.
>> Honor our prayer.
>>> Save your name.

FIRST LIBATION BEARER:

> Your words are without
>> fault, my dears. They have never
> mourned with libations this
>> tomb or his fate.
> But now you're set,
>> your minds made up,
>> only the act awaits you.
> The time is come.
>> Do the deed.
>>> Test your fortune.

ORESTÊS:

>>> And we will.
>> But first a question.
> Why has she sent these libations
>> now, after so long, after
>>> years,
>> and too late?
>>> What was she thinking?
> A futile gift to heal a wound past curing,
>> to a man who's dead and hates her?
> What sense does it make? And so
>> paltry an offering as that? A mockery
> to the enormity of her offence! No act,
>> however great, can ever atone
>> for the taking of a life.
> Why did she do this? Why?
>> What's her reason?

FIRST LIBATION BEARER:

> I can tell you that, son.
>> I was there.
> Dreams.

Terrible dreams.
                    Roaming the night.
Haunting her. Making her wander,
    distracted, in unspeakable
                                fear.
And so she sent these
    gifts, these libations—
            the godless woman.

ORESTÊS:
    What was this dream? Tell me.

FIRST LIBATION BEARER:
    She dreamt she gave birth to a snake.

ORESTÊS:
    And?

FIRST LIBATION BEARER:
    She wrapped it. In swaddling clothes. Like a child.

ORESTÊS:
    Did this monster cry for food?

FIRST LIBATION BEARER:
    She fed it at her breast.

ORESTÊS:
    Surely it didn't bite her?

FIRST LIBATION BEARER:
    No, but it sucked a clot of blood in the milk.

ORESTÊS:
    This is no empty dream. This was a man.

FIRST LIBATION BEARER:
    She screamed out in her sleep in terror
        and ran wildly through the house.

Lamps were lighted everywhere
          till the palace glowed with light.
               She then sent these. Libations,
     funeral libations. And us to bring them
     to the dead to make a cure and
               end her distress.

ORESTÊS:
     I pray to Earth, and the infernal Powers below,
          and to you spirits that summon up
          dreams to men, and my father's
                         tomb!
     Let this dream be made flesh in me!
               This is all of a piece.
     I see it now. Born from the same place
          I was born, wrapped in the same
          cloths I was wrapped in, fed by the same
          breast that fed me, and drew from that breast
          milk with clots of
               blood; and then she shrieks out in
                    terror—what can it be,
          that horrendous portent,
     but that the woman who nursed a monstrous
               vision, must also die a
          monstrous death!
               I am that snake.
               My sword is my sting.
               The dream is true.

FIRST LIBATION BEARER:
     I believe you. Yes.
          You're right. But tell us, now,
               we're friends, what do we do.
     We're with you, all of us.

ORESTÊS:
                         It's simple.
          Êlektra,
               you go inside. And say nothing.

All of you.
You know nothing of what's
    happened here. Not a word.
They who killed by cunning will die by
    cunning, one noose for both.
How can it not be so if Apollo said it,
        and who calls Apollo a liar?

Pretending to be a stranger,
        I'll approach the gates of the courtyard
            with Pyladês, a stranger and
    spear-friend to this house.
We'll pretend we're from Parnassos,
    and speak like Phokians.
But if a sentry turns us away and
    denies us—after all,
an evil Curse lives in that house—
        we'll wait till someone
    comes by and sees, and says:

    "What is this? If Aigisthos is home
    and knows these men are here,
    why is he shutting out suppliants?
    It's unheard of!"

But once I'm inside those gates, once I
    cross that threshold and find him
        idling on my father's throne, or if he's
    out and returns and meets me
        face-to-face, before he can lift and then
    lower his eyes and ask where this
    stranger is from, he'll be
meat for my sword. I'll strike him,
    and run him through with a single thrust.
And the Fury that haunts this
    house, and has suffered no lack of our
    blood, will drink deeply
        a third goblet of unmixed gore.

It's up to you, Êlektra.
          Keep close watch.
                    We'll work together.
Women, guard your tongues.
               Say nothing.
          Or if you do, be careful.

Stand by me, Pyladês,
I need your help.
You've led me right so far, now
               lead me home.

(Exit ÊLEKTRA into the door to the women's quarters.)
(Music. Song. Dance.)

LIBATION BEARERS: *(Sing.)*
                    Many are the horrors
               the earth gives birth to,
          dreadful, appalling creatures,
                    devouring beasts;
          and the sea in its wide embrace
               teems in its dark waters with
                    monsters hostile to mortals;
          and the heavens flare and flash with dangers;
          and who does not know the whirlwind's wrath?

          But what of man and his high conceit,
                    what do we know of that,
                    does it have an end?
                    And worse is woman
                    and her reckless passions,
          unscrupled woman crazed for man's destruction,
               the female perverting marriage
                    with her shameless lust,
          uniting man and beast in their loveless ways!

               Let any man of sound mind
               learn from that cruel mother,
                    Althaia.

She burned the torch
her son's life was tied to,
her own son,
when he killed her brothers.
He expired with the expiring flame.

And here is another to hate in the tales,
the ancient fables:
murderous Skylla.
She killed her father for Krêtan gold,
golden necklace,
gift of Minos,
clipped while he slept
his lock of life,
and father died unsuspecting.

Now I have called up wounds that won't heal,
let me sing of the hateful marriage,
the house's ruin,
an abomination,
and the brazen treachery of this woman's mind.
She attacks her husband,
her master and warlord;
he falls, her enemy,
to whom once all bowed.
Give me a hearth not heated by woman's passions,
a hearth not guarded by a cowardly spear.

Of all tales,
the worst, most evil of crimes is
Lemnos!
Men tremble to hear it and gods are appalled.
They killed them,
their men,
the women of Lemnos,
in one short hour.
All the men of Lemnos, dead.
Give no honor to what gods detest.
Which of these tales should I not have told?

The sword strikes deep,
Justice strikes,
straight through the lungs:
right has been wronged;
they trampled the law,
destroyed the good,
dishonored the sacred majesty of Zeus.

Justice has planted her anvil firmly,
and Fate has forged her keen bronze blade,
and the son is brought home to the house of his fathers,
home to the halls of ancient murders,
a son to atone for the fathers' crimes,
led by the house's age-old Fury,
a prince,
to pay the debt in blood.

(ORESTÊS and PYLADÊS approach the palace. ORESTÊS knocks at the central doors, waits, knocks again.)
(Music out.)

ORESTÊS:
Hello in there!
Is there anyone there?
Anyone at the gates?
Boy! Slave! Anyone!
How long do I have to knock?
Boy!
Here's a third time! Or has Aigisthos
forgotten the meaning of hospitality?

GATEKEEPER: *(From inside.)*
All right, all right, I hear you!
Don't knock down the door!

(The GATEKEEPER's head appears in a small hatch in the central door.)

Now.

I have to ask
        where are you from, stranger,
        and what's your business?

ORESTÊS:
        Tell the masters of the house
                there are strangers come with news.
                                Hurry.
        Night's chariot is racing
                westward, and for travelers it's
                        time to drop anchor at a friendly inn.
        Bring someone in authority.
                Your mistress, or better
                        yet, your master.
        A woman takes tact to speak to;
                with a man you can say what you
                mean and not mince words.

(The hatch closes, the central doors open, and KLYTAIMNÊSTRA enters, followed by a female SLAVE.)

KLYTAIMNÊSTRA:
        Strangers, you are welcome.
        Whatever you want is yours;
                you have only to ask.
        This is a house friendly to strangers.
        Hot baths to sooth tired bodies,
                beds to charm away the pains of travel,
                and honest, caring eyes that Justice herself
                        would be proud of.
        But if more weighty matters
                concern you, some action better
                dealt with by men,
        I can bring you to them without delay.

ORESTÊS:
        I'm a foreigner, madam,

from Daulia, in Phokis.
On my way here to Argos—I'm here on
    business—I met a man who
walked a distance with me, and in
talking I learned he also came from Phokis.

Well, as these things happen,
    he told me his name. "Strophios," he said,
    "Strophios of Phokis." And once he'd
        learned my destination was Argos,
    "Stranger," he asked, "would you be so
kind as to deliver a message for me?
But be certain you don't forget.
        It's most important.
Tell his parents that Orestês is dead.
You won't forget, will you? And inquire
        whether those who loved him
want his remains brought back to Argos for burial,
        or to bury him in the land of his exile,
a stranger forever in a foreign land."

I'm to bring the decision back to him.
For now, I'm told, his ashes
        rest in a bronze urn, and he's been
much lamented and properly mourned.

So much for this message.
        I've told you all I know.

Am I speaking to someone in authority,
    I don't know—someone, I should say,
        to whom this matters.
But it's only proper
        his parents know the truth of the matter.

KLYTAIMNÊSTRA:

                    OI'GOOOOOOO!
Now our house is ruined to its roots!
O Curse upon this house that we

wrestle in vain, how you
search us out, how you
shoot your cunning arrows at
even what is hidden!
You pick us off from afar,
laying low those we love, leaving me
naked in my misery!
And now Orestês—Orestês who showed
good sense.
He kept himself out of the mire of
ruin that is this house.
Safe!
And now he is dead, our only hope.
No end now to the Furies' evil revelry.
The physic is spilled that was to be our cure.

ORESTÊS:
I regret I haven't come with better news.
With a house so prosperous in its good fortune,
a guest does well to deliver good news
and be entertained for his troubles.
For what is better than good humor between
host and guest?
But I thought it wrong not to do as I
did for Orestês' friends.
I had promised them, and am also
bound to this house by the rules of hospitality.

KLYTAIMNÊSTRA:
You will receive your due
no matter what.
Good news or bad, anyone could have
brought it. And you are no
less a friend to this house for that.

But it's evening now, and you have a
long road behind you. You need food,
rest, and your just
reward.

(To the SLAVE.)

Show him into the men's quarters,
    his friend, too, and anyone else
    who may be with them.
Let them know the welcome this
    house is famous for.
               As I say,
treat them well. You'll be held to
    strict account.

I'll see the house's ruler has your message.
    We have no lack of friends to take
    counsel touching this matter.

*(Exit the SLAVE leading PYLADÊS and ORESTÊS in through the door
to the men's quarters; then exit KLYTAIMNÊSTRA into the palace
through the central doors.)*
(Music. Song. Dance.)

FIRST LIBATION BEARER: *(Chants.)*
    Women of this house,
    dear friends, when, when will we
    raise our voices in strength
    in honor, in praise, of Orestês?

LIBATION BEARERS: *(Sing.)*
               Earth Mother,
               Great Earth,
           sacred, holy name,
    here by the grave-mound of Agamemnon,
           lord of the fleet,
    hear us now and give us your aid.

               The time,
          the time is now,
    the time for cunning Persuasion
    to stand beside him in battle,
and for Hermês god of Death and Night

to guide the deadly
thrust of his sword.

(Enter KILISSA from the palace.)
(Music out.)

FIRST LIBATION BEARER:
Our stranger must be about his mischief.
Look, the old nanny of Orestês,
in tears.

Where are you off to, Kilissa?
Why are you crying?

KILISSA:
I'm to bring Aigisthos for the strangers.
Mistress' orders.
Fast as I can. He's to face
the strangers man to man and
hear the news, she says.
Her face is all
tears—all for the
slaves—but I saw it there, I
saw it, the smile she
hides beneath her pain-mask, her
eyes, her mouth, smiling
inside for how well it has all worked
out for her.
But not well for the house where
everything is evil now with the
strangers' news. And how overjoyed
with the news he'll be.

O TALAIN' EGO!

How can I bear it! All the ancient
evils this house has suffered
joined as one, are not so terrible as
this that tears my heart.

He's dead!
Orestês is dead!
         My baby, my boy!

All other sorrows I bore
         patiently—but this,
                  this—I wore my life away for him.
I helped him from his mother's
         womb, I raised him,
         a mother to him, the nights I
sat up with him, bawling away in my
         arms—could I let him cry and do
                  nothing? And all the troubles he
         brought me, and what
         good did it do me,
                  what?

They're like animals, babies,
         do what they want, no
         tongue to tell what's wrong.
                           Is he
hungry, is he thirsty, does he
         want his potty—how do I
                  know, no way to know—and a
baby's belly will have its own
         way, a terror at both ends.

Was I a prophet to know?
         So I guessed, guessed and
         guessed, sometimes right,
                  sometimes—well—and so I was
washerwoman, too, don't you know.
Nanny and washerwoman in one,
         the day Agamemnon
                  handed him over to me to raise,
         Orestês—and now I hear he's
                  dead—and I'm to go fetch
         the king—that man who brought this
                  ruin on our house.

I'll tell him.

I'll watch him smile.

FIRST LIBATION BEARER:
How is he to come to the queen?

KILISSA:
How? Come to her? I don't understand.

FIRST LIBATION BEARER:
With or without a bodyguard?

KILISSA:
With, the bodyguard always with him.

FIRST LIBATION BEARER:
No.

Tell him nothing.
Nothing if you hate our detested
tyrant. Nothing of the
news. And that he's to come
alone, nothing to
fear, that the news is
good and will make his heart
dance.
The good messenger knows how to twist facts.

KILISSA:
What? This news pleases you?

FIRST LIBATION BEARER:
What if Zeus were changing a foul wind to fair?

KILISSA:
But how? Orestês is dead. The hope of the house.

FIRST LIBATION BEARER:
Don't be too sure. You said you were no prophet.

KILISSA:

    What is it? You have other news?

FIRST LIBATION BEARER:

    Go. Take this message.
    The one I gave you.
    The gods look after whatever they look after.

KILISSA:

    I'll go and do as you say.
    The gods willing,
        all may turn out well.

    (Exit KILISSA to the side.)
    (Music. Song. Dance.)

LIBATION BEARERS: *(Sing.)*

            Zeus, hear me,
            hear my prayer,
           Lord of Olympos,
          Zeus Great Father!
        Make a new house here,
          found it anew,
        and let all who will
        see Justice restored.
     These words I sing for Justice
        and Zeus Protector.

         He is in his halls,
        home in his house,
        the house's prince,
         its rightful ruler.
   Place him face-to-face with his enemies;
        let him win, Zeus,
        make him strong,
      and in double measure,
        no, in triple,
    he will pay you with heartfelt thanks.

The orphaned colt
of the father you loved
is yoked to a chariot of danger.
Hold him steady,
give him purpose,
guide him storming to a swift conclusion!

And you,
gods of this house,
gods who dwell in rooms of gold,
hear us, join us,
and with your will
wash clean this house of its ancient stain
in the new blood that Justice spills.
Cut off Death!
Let him breed no more!

Apollo,
lord of the deep cavern,
lord of light,
give us light,
lead us from this night of darkness,
let this house lift its head once more!
Give us freedom's light!
Tear from our eyes this veil of doom.

And Hermês help,
bring winds to blow us to a swift end,
belly our sails to a happy conclusion.
God of deception,
god of cunning,
guide Orestês' tongue and design,
help him net the tyrants with words.

For then, o then,
we will shout, rejoicing,
our song of triumph, free from fear,
shrill shouts to praise the wind in our sails!
Our ship of state once more on course,

the city is safe and my loved ones set free
of disaster's grip.

Steel yourself, son!
When the moment comes,
and she cries "Son!"
you must shout back,
"Never! No!
My father's son!"
Then do the deed that none can blame,
an act of horror.

For those you love,
living and dead,
raise in your breast the heart of Perseus,
turn your eyes and slay the Gorgon,
conquer love with hate,
destroy the guilty.

(Enter AIGISTHOS from the side, followed at a distance by KILISSA.)
(Music out.)

AIGISTHOS:
I was brought a message to come.
For what I don't know; for some
unfortunate news, I take it.
Strangers, I hear? The death of Orestês?
Something. Another blood-stained
burden for this house to bear.
Aren't there enough festering wounds of
disasters?

Anyone? Is it so? Is it true?
Or some far-fetched fantasy of women
that dies in the speaking?
Who can tell me?
Anyone!
Who can shed light on this mystery?

FIRST LIBATION BEARER:
>Yes, we've heard.
>>But go inside.
>>Question them.
>Question them yourself.
>>It's the only way to know.

AIGISTHOS:
>I will, yes. The only way.
>Did he see the death himself,
>>Orestês? Or is he mouthing some
>>>vague hearsay?
>>One thing's for certain.
>No one deceives a man whose eyes are open.

(Exit AIGISTHOS into the palace through the central doors.)
(Music. Song. Dance.)

LIBATION BEARERS: *(Sing.)*
>Zeus! Zeus!
>What do I say?
>How begin?
>How pray the gods?
>How find words
>to match the deed?
>The blade rises!
>Now! Now!
>Bloody! Bloody!
>Fall of the house!
>Annihilation!
>Or freedom comes!
>Freedom's torch!
>Lighted!
>Flaming!
>Son of the house!
>Godlike Orestês!
>Possess your fate!
>Embrace your throne!
>Father's rule!

King of Argos!
Orestês!
Lord!
The match is made!
Wrestle the foe!
Two against one!.
And god give you victory!

(The death-cry of AIGISTHOS is heard from the palace.)

AIGISTHOS:
É! É! OTOTOTOIIIIIIII!

LIBATION BEARERS: *(Chant.)*
ÉA! ÉA! MÁLA!
There! There!
Whose voice?
Whose?
The house?
What has happened?

FIRST LIBATION BEARER: *(Speaks.)*
Shhh!
Say nothing.
Stand back.
Away from the house.
We must look guiltless.
Our fate is decided.
Which will it be?

(A SLAVE cries out from inside the palace.)

SLAVE:
OIMOI PANOIMOIIIIIII!
He's dead!
He's dead!
The master's dead!
Killed!
Aigisthos!

(He enters from the palace and runs to the door of the women's quarters, pounding on it.)

Open! Open!
Open in there!
Open!
Unbar the door to the women's quarters!
Hurry! A strong arm's need!
Not for him, not for Aigisthos,
          he's dead!
Are you deaf in there?
Asleep? Open! Open!
Call Klytaimnêstra!
Hurry!
Where is she?

FIRST LIBATION BEARER:
Her head's next on the butcher's block!
And Justice raises the axe!

(Enter KLYTAIMNÊSTRA through the door to the women's quarters.)
(Music out.)

KLYTAIMNÊSTRA:
What's this shouting?
What's the matter here?

SLAVE:
The dead—the dead are living!
The dead!
          Killing!

KLYTAIMNÊSTRA:
          OI 'GOOOOO!
                    I know this riddle.
By treachery we killed,
          by treachery we are killed.
Give me an axe!
          Quickly!

(Exit SLAVE through the door to the women's quarters.)

Win or lose. The game's soon up.
We'll see soon enough who's master here.

(KLYTAIMNÊSTRA is about to enter the palace through the central doors, when they open and enter ORESTÊS and PYLADÊS with blood-ied swords drawn.)

ORESTÊS:
> Your turn now. The one in there
> > had all he could handle.

KLYTAIMNÊSTRA:
> O dear Aigisthos! Dead, dead!

ORESTÊS:
> You loved him in life?
> Now lie beside him in death.
> > Never to part.

KLYTAIMNÊSTRA:
> O son, have pity!
> These breasts cradled you asleep,
> > These breasts nursed you—

ORESTÊS:
> > > Pyladês!
> She's my mother!
> > Do I kill my mother—?

PYLADÊS:
> Remember Apollo. You swore
> > oaths at Delphi.
> It's better to have no friends
> > than the gods hate you.

ORESTÊS:
> I accept your words, my friend.

You!
Inside!
I'll kill you beside your "man"!
Your Aigisthos!
You preferred him to my father once,
a greater man than Agamemnon!
You loved him, and
hated the man you should have loved.
Sleep with him now in death!

KLYTAIMNÊSTRA:

I raised you, Orestês; take care of me in my age.

ORESTÊS:

You kill my father, and now you want to live with me?

KLYTAIMNÊSTRA:

No, son, no. Fate must share the blame for this.

ORESTÊS:

Yes, and that same Fate sends you your death.

KLYTAIMNÊSTRA:

Are you so uncaring of a mother's curse?

ORESTÊS:

Mother? You gave me birth, then flung me out

KLYTAIMNÊSTRA:

Flung you out? I sent you to an ally.

ORESTÊS:

I was born free, and you sold me for a price.

KLYTAIMNÊSTRA:

Price? What price? Tell me what price I got!

ORESTÊS:

I can't. I won't. It shames me to taunt you with it.

KLYTAIMNÊSTRA:
  You think your father was a paragon of fidelity?

ORESTÊS:
  While he was away at war, you dangled your manikin.

KLYTAIMNÊSTRA:
  Life is cruel on a woman with her man gone.

ORESTÊS:
  Cruel? While the man fights? And you dawdle at home?

KLYTAIMNÊSTRA:
  Orestês, son, you're murdering your own mother.

ORESTÊS:
  You're murdering yourself, mother, with your own guilt.

KLYTAIMNÊSTRA:
  Remember the hellhounds of a mother's curse.

ORESTÊS:
  And forget my father's hounds if I fail in this?

KLYTAIMNÊSTRA:
  I see my words falling on deaf ears.

ORESTÊS:
  You began to bleed when you murdered my father.

KLYTAIMNÊSTRA:
  OI 'GOOOOO!
  This was the snake I bore and gave my breast!

ORESTÊS:
  The terror you dreamed prophesied the truth.
  Your murder was wrong, now suffer a wrongful murder.

(ORESTÊS and PYLADÊS drive KLYTAIMNÊSTRA into the palace through the central doors.)

FIRST LIBATION BEARER:
>I pity even the fate
>>of these two in their fall.
>King and queen,
>>>then nothing.
>But I choose Orestês, our prince,
>>who has scaled this mountain of bloody
>>>>>>deeds.
>The eye of this house must never be extinguished.

(Music. Song. Dance.)

LIBATION BEARERS: *(Sing.)*
>>>>Justice came late to the sons of Priam,
>>>>>but Justice came,
>>>>>Justice prevailed.
>>>>Conquering Justice brought
>>>>>Retribution.
>>Twin lions came to the house of Agamemnon.
>>>Twin lions slew a double quarry,
>>>>a double war to bring
>>>>>Retribution.
>>>>Sped on by god,
>>>>>by Delphi's decree,
>>>>>the exile came,
>>>>>the exile conquered.

>>>Sing Triumph! Sing Triumph!
>>>>The house is free!
>>>Our master's house has shed its grief !
>>The wicked are dead who wasted its wealth!
>>>Our twin polluters have paid their debt!
>>>>Murder for murder,
>>>>>blood for blood!

Hermês came in stealth to lead by stealth,
cunning Hermês, crafty god,
Zeus' daughter guiding his hand,
Zeus' daughter whom we name Justice.
Together they struck,
together they won,
breathing destructive wrath of her enemies.

Sing Triumph! Sing Triumph!
The house is free!
Our master's house has shed its grief!
The wicked are dead who wasted its wealth!
Our twin polluters have paid!
Murder for murder,
blood for blood!

And Apollo cried out from his deep-cleft cavern:
"By guile will guile be overthrown!"
And down he came,
the pure god,
down to us and healed our wounds,
our ancient, grievous wrong.
And god is right!
And god is just!
May the will of the gods prevail,
and wickedness never be served!

Raise high the newly kindled beacon!
The yoke that curbed this house is lifted!
House of Atreus, rise in glory!
Your sour humiliation is done!

Time,
great Time that fulfills all things,
will roar through the halls,
a purifying flood,
scouring evil and fetid pollution.
Then will Humiliation be banished,

Disaster and Ruin and Vengeance exiled,
and the house's age-old unwelcome guests
will shriek in headlong flight,
the scourging Furies!
Fortune's dice have fallen out well!
Fortune has thrown us triple sixes!
The house is free at last!

Raise high the newly kindled beacon!
The yoke that curbed this house is lifted!
House of Atreus, rise in glory!
Your sour humiliation is done!

*(Enter SLAVES through the central doors with the corpses of
KLYTAIMNÊSTRA and AIGISTHOS that they throw to the ground.
They are followed by ORESTÊS who stands over them with drawn
sword. Behind him enter SLAVES displaying aloft on long poles the
monstrous bloodied tapestry used in the murder of Agamemnon.)*

ORESTÊS:
Behold the land's tyrants!
Behold the double tyranny of Argos!
The demons who raped my house,
who plundered my rights, and murdered my father!

What majesties they once were,
high on their thrones,
loving partners then,
loving partners now,
as their fate must show,
loving partners in suffering.
They swore an oath once to catch-up my father,
to slaughter him, kill him in his bath,
both together, as one, united.
And now another oath comes true,
to die as one,
to die together,
lovers united even in death,
their lofty bed now a lowly grave.

(Indicates the tapestry held aloft.)

Look, everyone who will, on this sad work,
    the trap they wove to catch him,
    to fetter him, my helpless father,
to manacle his hands, his feet!

                        Slaves!
    Throw it down!
Down where he once walked to his death!
    Let everyone see!
Let everyone look at this woman's devious
    device for trapping her husband.
Let the father see—not mine, but the father
    of the skies that sees all—Hêlios, Sun-god!
Let him see the godless work of my
        mother's hands.
Let him witness on the day of judgment
    that my hand acted in league with
        Justice to do this bloody
            deed,
my mother's death.

           As for him, this,
    this animal, this Aigisthos,
        what's he to me!
He died the just death of an adulterer,
    as the law provides.

But what of her?
    What of her who plotted this monstrous
        deed against her husband, who carried his
        children in her womb?
Once there was love,
    I loved her once. But what is there
        now but hatred,
    as this sight shows?

What do we make of her?

Look at her.
Sea-snake, serpent, viper that needs no
fangs, no sting, but poisons by
touch, infects, rots a
mate with a single swipe of the evil
pride that festers in her heart!

And this—this snare, this trap for beasts?
Or is it a drape for a dead man's feet?
A coffin's cover? A robe-net-shroud
to catch-up a king in death?

No.
No, a net. A net.
A hunting-net, would you say?
A highwayman's trick?
A snare to drop on travelers, steal them
blind, then run them through
till his heart bursts with
good fellowship?

Gods, protect me from such a mate as this!
Even death is better!
Death without an heir!

FIRST LIBATION BEARER: *(Chants.)*
AI! AI!
The queen is dead!
A dreadful death!
É! É!
Grief blossoms now
for the son who remains.

ORESTÊS:
Did she do it? *Did* she?
She *did* it!
Did it!
My proof is *here!*
This robe!

Crimsoned with his blood,
blood drawn by this woman with the sword of Aigisthos!
Did it!
She did it!

Look, here,
        the blood, and
here, here, where the
                blade dipped in, again,
                again, darkened with
        time, with time the colors
mottled, the grand
        embroidery of this robe netted for
                                kings.

                Now he is here.

Now I speak who was not here.

Now, father, over you,
        I lament a long-delayed lament.
Grieving over this death-net,
        I mourn for what is done,
                for what is suffered,
for what suffering will come,
                for all our race, and for the evil
        pollution my victory now brings.

FIRST LIBATION BEARER: *(Chants.)*
        No man is happy all of his days.
        É! É!
        Sorrow not here today
        will come tomorrow.

ORESTÊS:
                        I feel it.
        Coming, coming.
                I know.
        Where does it end?

Pulled, dragged, no reins,
    storm, confusion,
      reins whirling, team, wild,
          off course, dragging,
heart racing, pounding,
      pounding, terror beating,
beating down, chariot plunging, horses,
    wild, mind, frothing, fear, mind, terror, horses,
      terror close, close to heart, singing, dancing, anger
        rising, anger, charioteer, no
            reins!

        Listen!
Listen! Time,
    while there's time—time—
  listen—o listen.
What I did, I did with Justice,
    Justice at my side,
      my mother's murder.
She killed my father, hands bloody, polluted, foul,
    mother hated of heaven. My guide
      was Apollo, prophet Pythia,
        tongue of Loxias.
"Do this deed and be free of guilt!"
So said Apollo.
    But if I failed, if I refused, if terror gripped me and
      crippled me, there would be horrors no
        mind could conceive.
Behold me now,
    behold me here, armed with this olive
    branch and a flock of wool.

I will go to Delphi, Apollo's shrine,
    the earth's navel and the flame called everlasting,
      I who shed kindred blood.
"Approach no other hearth," cried Apollo,
    "no hearth but mine!"
          And so I do,
I who have no shelter but Apollo's

shelter, I who have no protection but Apollo's
protection, Apollo who will free me of
pollution from my deed, I, exiled,
I, Orestês, who killed my mother,
my hands
stained.

Witness for me, men of Argos.
Remember how these evils came about,
and tell this to Menelaos when he comes.

I wander now, an exile from Argos,
banished from my native land, a man
who leaves behind, in life and death,
a name no man will forget for what I did.

FIRST LIBATION BEARER:
What you did was noble.
Don't cripple yourself with slander.
You've liberated us,
liberated Argos.
Killed two serpents in one grand stroke.

ORESTÊS:
AIIII! AIIII!
Coming!
Coming!
There! There!
Look!
Gorgons! Black,
all black, in
black! Women of
Argos,
look! Serpents,
twining, hair, faces!
I can't!
Can't stay!

FIRST LIBATION BEARER:
Ah, son, dearest
son of your father!
What is this madness?
What are these sights
whirl you in such a
frenzy? Don't fear!
You've turned a great
victory!

ORESTÊS:
No!
No fantasies!
I know them! See them!
My mother's! My mother's
hellhounds!
After me!

FIRST LIBATION BEARER:
For the blood on your hands,
still fresh.
Why else would your mind
reel with such pain?

ORESTÊS:
Apollo!
Help me!
More!
There!
More! More!
Around me! Closing!
Eyes dripping
blood! Help!
Apollo!

FIRST LIBATION BEARER:
Apollo is your only help.
One touch of Loxias and your
mind is free.

ORESTÊS:

No!

You can't
see them!
I see them!
Hellhounds! Hounding!
I can't—can't
stay!

FIRST LIBATION BEARER:
Luck go with you! And may the god
protect and guard you in
kindness!
May good prevail!

(Exit ORESTÊS.)

LIBATION BEARERS: *(Sing.)*
Three storm blasts have shaken this house.
The first, when children's flesh was eaten;
the second, warlord Agamemnon, slaughtered,
king, father, husband, in a bloody bath;
and now, the third: a deliverer comes.
Or do I call him doom?

Where will it end,
this power of destruction?
When will it rest,
this spirit of Ruin?
When will it sleep?

EUMENIDES

(ΕΥΜΕΝΙΔΕΣ)

CAST OF CHARACTERS

PYTHIA *priestess of Apollo*

APOLLO *son of Zeus*

ATHÊNA *patron goddess of Athens*

ORESTÊS *son of Agamemnon and Klytaimnêstra*

KLYTAIMNÊSTRA'S GHOST

CHORUS OF FURIES *daughters of Night*

FIRST FURY *chorus leader*

JURY *twelve male Athenian citizens*

HERALD OF THE COUNCIL OF THE AREOPAGOS

TRUMPETER

ESCORT OF ATHENIAN WOMEN

ATHENIAN CITIZENS

EUMENIDES

Sunrise.
Delphi.
The sanctuary of Pythian Apollo.
PYTHIA, dressed in white, stands at the central door.

PYTHIA:

>   To Mother Earth
> I give pride of place in my prayer,
> > Gaia,
> > > prophet,
> > > > first of gods;
> then to Themis, her daughter,
> > protector of Law and
> > Tradition, the second, as legend
> > > tells, to hold her mother's
> > prophetic seat;
> and third in line is Phoibê,
> > Bright One, Titaness and
> > > daughter of Earth,
> a seat given in peace and
> >   calm.
> And she in turn gave it, a birthday
> > gift, to Apollo, along with her
> > name:
> Phoibos Apollo he is,
> > god of prophecy and light.

> Leaving the lake and rocky ridge of
> > Dêlos, he came to Athêna's ship-thronged
> > shores, and then to this
> > > land, and took his prophetic
> > seat here on
> > > > Parnassos.
> His escort? The sons of Hêphaistos,
> > god of fire, road-builders,

men of Athens, who tamed the
          wilds and civilized our savage
                    country.

And the people honored him,
          Apollo,
     lining the roads on his way, and
Delphos, our king and
     steersman of our state, praised him
               greatly, and Zeus breathed
inspiration into his mind, the art of
          divination, and set him,
               his son,
fourth in line of
     prophets, here on this
               throne, he who sees, and
     he who speaks.
And it is for Zeus he
     speaks; for none but
          Father Zeus.

These gods I honor first in my prayers.
               But Athêna of the
     Precinct I honor
               most. And I revere the
Nymphs in the Korykan Cavern,
          the haunt of wheeling birds and
               gods. And Bromios, too,
Dionysos, Roaring God, and
     not to be forgotten, rules here, too.
Dionysos who, at the head of his
     army of Bakkhai, hunted down
     Pentheus, netting him like a
          hare in flight and ripping him
     in pieces.

I honor also the sweet waters of
     Pleistos, and Poseidon I honor,
          mighty Poseidon, and

Zeus Fulfiller,
Zeus Most High.

I will now take my seat on the
        throne as prophet, and pray the gods
        for a consultation far better than
                        any before.

If any Greeks are present,
        they may enter, as custom
        allows, in the order chosen by
                lot, for my prophecy comes
whatever way the god leads me.

*(Exit PYTHIA into the temple by the central door. After a silence her
screams of terror are heard from inside, and a moment later she emerges
crawling on all fours in a state of hysteria.)*

                        Horror!
                Horror!
                        Horror for any eyes, what I saw!
Horrible!
Too weak to stand with my
        fright! I scramble on
                hands and knees! A feeble old
        woman—a nothing—a babbling
                baby with what I've
                                seen!
                        Foul!
                Foul!
In the temple—there in the
        temple—there—

(She rises slowly to her feet.)

On my way to the inner shrine,
        garlanded everywhere with
                green wreaths, there at the
Navelstone, I saw him,

a man, horrible sight,
                    horrible,
        polluted, an abomination to the
            gods, there, sitting where
suppliants sit, hands
        bloody, bloody
                sword drawn, dripping,
        bloody, and a tall branch of
                    olive twined with bright
                wool, a silvery
        fleece.

And around him,
        everywhere, sprawled on stone
        benches, asleep, a ghastly
                crew of women—women?—no,
                    women they are not, not
                women,
Gorgons—but no, not even Gorgons.

I saw once in a painting the
        figures of creatures that
                carried off the feast of Phineus.
But these have no wings,
            all black, loathsome,
                    hateful. When they
        breathe they snort, and their
        mouths and noses drip and
                bubble, too terrible to
        approach.
                            Their eyes,
                ulcerated,
        run with blood and pus.
Unclean!
Abominable sight!
Unfit for the statues of gods or
        human dwelling!
Where they are from I don't know.
What country could have bred them and not

regretted their evil error?
But this must be mighty Apollo's concern.
Apollo seer, Apollo great
    healer.
Apollo, Apollo, come, purify your
        halls!

(Exit PYTHIA.)

(The inner shrine of the temple is revealed. ORESTÊS, at the Navelstone, is surrounded by the sleeping CHORUS OF FURIES. APOLLO appears from nowhere, first a voice, then a form.)

APOLLO:
    I'm with you, Orestês,
        now and to the end of your
          suffering, no matter where, near or
            far, I'm at your side to protect you.
    Nor will I be gentle with your enemies.
    You see them here. Savage,
        despicable creatures,
    loathsome to god, man, and beast. Who would
        touch them? Ancient virgin maidens, senile
            children.
    As you see, I've overcome them with
        sleep, these maddened females
        who exist for one reason only,
        ruin and destruction.
    Evil darkness is their home, Tartaros,
        Earth's bowels, that they range at
          will, hated both by men and the
            gods of Olympos.

    Never rest in your flight, Orestês,
        for they will chase you through lands and
        continents, across seas, past water-lapped
          islands, from city to city, their feet
        pounding, pounding in pursuit.
    But you must never resign your will,

never weary of coping with your task.
Endure at any cost!
                    And come at last to Athens.
        There is your sanctuary.
Sit as a suppliant in the temple, and
        embrace Athêna's ancient image.
We will find judges there and
        justice, for with Persuasion we will
        weave magic spells with words to
                release you forever from your suffering.
It was I who persuaded you to kill your mother.

ORESTÊS:

                        Apollo, my lord,
    you and Justice go hand in hand.
    Therefore find compassion in your
        heart, compassion for me, and
                never neglect me.
    You have the power to do good.
                        Save me.

APOLLO:

                    And remember.
    You must never allow fear to destroy you.
                    Go.

(Exit ORESTÊS running.)

And, Hermês, brother,
        son of Zeus, blood of my
        blood, guard him, be with him
                always, near or far.
True to your title, be his escort,
        shepherd him, his guide, for he is my
                        suppliant.
            This outlaw is sacred to Zeus.
Guide him safely on his return to the world of men.

(APOLLO's image fades and disappears. KLYTAIMNÊSTRA'S GHOST emerges from the dream of the sleeping FURIES.)
(Music.)

KLYTAIMNÊSTRA's GHOST:
                                 Asleep?
              Asleep?
                   What use are you asleep?
          Why am I forgotten?
                                 AIIII!
          You forget me, forget me!
                                 AIIII!
          Dishonored!
                   You have dishonored me.
                   Dishonored among the dead.
          Murderess, they cry, and pursue me.
          Murderess!
                   The dead!
                        Scorn me, every one, for my bloody
          deeds among the living.
                   I wander, wander, disgraced, among the
                        dead. I who suffered so,
                                      suffered,
          treated so heartlessly by my most loved.
                   Cut down, slaughtered, butchered by my
                        own turned evil
                   serpent. And none among the
                        gods, none, to take my side.
          Killed his mother, and gods are
                   silent. Here, here the stab went through.
          Straight to the heart. A mother's heart.
                   And still you sleep! You who have
                        lapped up so many an offering,
          so many libations, water and honey,
                   no wine among them, sober
                   appeasements for you who drink no wine.
          And majestic midnight banquets I made you
                   at fiery hearths, an hour not shared by
                        other gods.

I see them now,
                    trampled on,
my offerings, my libations,
        while like a fawn in one light leap
he speeds away, out of your net,
            making a mockery of you as he goes!

Furies!
Hear me!
Goddesses of Night and Dark!
I am a dream who speaks!
I! Klytaimnêstra!
Dream Klytaimnêstra invokes you now!

(The FURIES begin to stir in their sleep, making snorting sounds.)

Snort all you like!
But he's gone, fled,
        your man! He has friends to defend him,
                not like me.

(Further stirring and snorting from the FURIES.)

Still asleep?
            Still?
        No pity for me? None?
                None? Killed his mother
and the murderer's fled!

(The FURIES begin to moan.)

                        Up, get up!
                Up, do you hear?
There's evil's work to do!

(Moaning and whimpering from the FURIES.)

Has so much toil made you
        tired, draining the mighty
                mother dragon of her force?

(A sharp moan, then snorting and whimpering grow louder, and the FURIES' movements more agitated as words begin to emerge.)

FURIES:

        Hunt!

    Hunt him!

           Hunt him!

Hunt!

KLYTAIMNÊSTRA:

        Dreamers!

      Fools!

         In dreams you

chase him! On, on,

    never off the scent!

        Awake, you idlers!

   My pain is great!

My disgrace! Remember!

         Feel it, my

   pain! Feel it! Let my

      pain sting you! Sting in your

          heart!

Don't be undone by

   weariness! My goad is

     just!

Blast him with your gory

     breath, char him, shrivel him with the

fire of your womb!

   After him! Run—

      run him—

   run him down!

         Run—

(KLYTAIMNÊSTRA'S GHOST disappears as the FIRST FURY wakens and rouses the FURY beside her.)
(Song. Dance.)

FIRST FURY: *(Chants.)*
Wake!

Wake up!
Wake her next to you!
Asleep?
Still asleep?
Kick off sleep!
Shake off stupor!
Now!
Let's see if this dream
has any truth?

(The FURIES come awake, some rise, look around for ORESTÊS; see him missing. Pandemonium. All rise and swarm out of the central door of the temple.)

FURIES: *(Sing.)*

IOOOOOOO!
IOOOOOOOOO!
IOOOOOOOOOOO!
Betrayed! Betrayed!
All our work, our suffering, in vain!
Unbearable pain!
IOOOO POPOIIIIIIIII!
Out of the net!
Vanished!
My prey!
Drugged by sleep, I've lost my quarry!

Apollo!
God Apollo!
Thievish Apollo!
You're young,
you're a man,
you owe us respect,
ancient powers,
but you ride us down!
You saved him,
saved the matricide,
the suppliant,
the godless man who spat on the gods!

And you stole him from us,
and call this justice!
Guilty, both of you!
Guilty! Guilty!
A god who steals from gods!

AIIIIII!
A dream,
a dream came,
a dream scourged me like a charioteer,
deep in my heart,
her goad in my vitals,
under my ribs!
The pain! The pain!
The hard goad sticks!

These are their doings,
the young gods!
Seize power and rule beyond justice!
Their throne drips blood,
bloody feet, bloody heads,
their altars run blood!
Omphalos,
Earth Navel,
stained with pollution,
evil blood from evil men,
evil deeds,
evil, evil!

You,
god of prophets,
you,
god Apollo,
defiled your own temple,
polluted your altar!
Your own hands did it!
Honored man more than Law allows!
Guarded one man from age-old divinities!
Struck down Destiny's Laws old as Time!

And all for one man!

You, god Apollo,
you are Fate's enemy,
as you are mine,
my enemy for ever!
You will never protect him,
not the criminal,
not his mother's murderer,
never!
Let him flee beneath the Earth,
he will never be free!
We'll find him!
We will!
Vengeance will have him!
Another of his blood will crush his skull!

(Enter APOLLO, enraged, from the central door with bow and arrows.)
(Music out.)

APOLLO:
Out of this temple,
out of this precinct,
away from here, all of you,
this ground is a place of prophecy!
Out!
Get out!
Now!
Or my winged arrows will
sting you like snakes and fire your
bowels to disgorge black curds of
blood that you suck from your victims!
This is no place for you,
filthy, unfit for this
house of holiness! You belong where
men are slaughtered, heads
chopped, sentences passed, where
eyes are gouged, a place of
murders where screams of castrated boys and

mutilations pollute the air,
                    hands, feet, ears, noses tossed to
            yapping hounds and bitches, death by
            stoning, and the endless groans of
                    men skewered naked onto spikes,
                        their quivering flesh ripped by nails,
            hung high for all to behold their
                    long, humiliating agonies!
Blood, gore, screams are your delight!
This is your feast,
            your kitchen,
                        your dining table!
This is what you love, and
            this is why the gods detest you!
Even the sight of you shows your evil!
The den of a blood-lapping lion is your haunt!
                                            Out!
                    Get out!
And never come here again to rub off
            pollution onto those near you!
You're a flock with no shepherd!
No god could love such a herd!

FIRST FURY:

It's for you, now, to listen to us, Lord Apollo.
The blame for all this is yours,
            yours alone. Everything that has happened
is your responsibility.

APOLLO:

I presume you can explain that?

FIRST FURY:

You commanded him to kill his mother.

APOLLO:

As vengeance for his father's death.

FIRST FURY:

And with blood still fresh on his hands you gave him shelter.

APOLLO:

I ordered him here to be purified.

FIRST FURY:

And we escorted him here. And you revile us?

APOLLO:

You're not fit to approach this temple.

FIRST FURY:

But this is our duty, our right.

APOLLO:

Right? What right? Tell me this precious right of yours!

FIRST FURY:

To run matricides from their homes.

APOLLO:

And the wife who kills her husband?

FIRST FURY:

Where there's no blood-kinship, there's no blood-guilt.

APOLLO:

Ah, well!
So much, then, for Hera and Zeus!
So much for the sacredness of
marriage, and Hera the protector of that
bond!
And you in your bargain dishonor
Aphroditê herself, the giver of
life's greatest pleasure!
No oath is more
sacred than the bond between
man and woman; it's loyalty

itself, and has Justice herself to
                    guard it.
And yet you close your eyes, you
            refuse to punish with wrath and
            vengeance a mate who murders a
                                mate?
Well, then, I say to
            you, your pursuit of Orestês is
                    unjust.
How can you be so rabid about
            one crime, as you are in this, and
disregard another, done in open
            daylight, murder plain and simple?
Only the goddess Athêna can decide this case.

FIRST FURY:

This man will never go free, never!

APOLLO:

Then pursue to your heart's content—but it will cost you.

FIRST FURY:

No words of yours will ever destroy my privilege!

APOLLO:

Privilege? I wouldn't have it as a gift.

FIRST FURY:

Yes, well, you don't need it, I dare say.
Such an important god!
            Throned beside Zeus, I suppose!
But I'll sniff out this Orestês wherever he is.
His mother's blood leaves a long trail,
            and the hounds of vengeance will
                    hunt down their man.

(Exeunt the FURIES howling in pursuit of ORESTÊS.)

APOLLO:

> And I'll protect and save him.
> He came as a suppliant, and the
> > wrath of a suppliant
> > > rejected is a terror for both
> men and gods.

(Exit APOLLO into the temple.)

(The scene changes to Athens. ORESTÊS enters in flight and kneels at Athêna's statue.)

ORESTÊS:

> > Athêna,
> > great goddess, hear me!
> On Apollo's instruction, I made my
> > way here to Athens and your temple.
> > > Be kind.
> I'm no longer a suppliant. My hands are
> > cleansed of my mother's blood, my guilt
> > > blunted and worn away at other
> > shrines and by dealings with
> > > > men.
> I have fled across continents and
> > seas as Apollo decreed, and so I come to your
> > shrine, great goddess, and your
> > > statue.
> I will wait here the outcome of my trial.

(Enter the FURIES in pursuit of ORESTÊS concealed by the altar and statue.)

FIRST FURY:

> > He's here!
> > We have him!
> > > Somewhere!
> Look, his tracks! Silent witnesses!
> > Like hounds, we track the wounded fawn,
> > hot on the trail of spilt

blood! Ah,
the labor I've endured!
                        Man-killing! My lungs
            about to burst! I've ranged
                every region of
earth, and pursued him in
            wingless flight across
                seas, faster than

                                    ships!

But he's here!
Here! I'll find him!
He's crouching!
        Somewhere!
                I smell it!
Human blood!
And I smile.

(Music. Song. Dance.)

FURIES: *(Sing.)*

                    Look! Look!
                    Everywhere!
                    Look again!
                Don't let him escape!
                The mother-killer!
                    Find him!
                    There he is!
                    There!
            Arms around her statue!
                The goddess!
                Waiting to stand trial!
                    Never!
                That will never be!
                Her blood is spilled,
            the earth has drunk it,
                    too late,
                    never!
            Blood for blood is my demand.
            Living blood licked from your limbs,

sucked from your flesh,
clotted blood drunk from your veins,
a cruel drink,
a vile draft!
I'll drain you dry,
I'll shrivel your body and drag you down,
down,
drag you living down,
down where you will pay your debt,
agony for agony,
for a mother's death.
And you'll see them there,
see them all,
the violators of gods, of guests, of parents,
paying their debts to Justice.
And Hades is a strict accountant,
a mighty corrector of men,
whom nothing escapes.

ORESTÊS: *(Speaks.)*
I've suffered much,
and in suffering I've learned much,
and I know the many ways of purification.
I've learned when and when not to speak,
and now a wise teacher commands me
to speak of this.
The blood on my hand falls asleep, and the
guilt for my mother's death has faded.
The stain is washed clean.
Apollo at his shrine cleansed me of matricide
with the blood of a slaughtered swine.

My story is a long one.
I won't tell of every man I've met,
of every house that gave me shelter;
but not one was ever polluted by my company.
Time purifies all things that age with time.

So now with pure lips and reverent tongue,
    I call on this land's queen,
        glorious Athêna,
    to come to my aid. I call her to come
    without troops or arms,
for with me come also my country and people,
Argos and the Argives,
    in eternal peace and friendship,
        a true alliance.
I call her now to come, whether from the scorching
    deserts of Libya and the banks of the
        Triton where she was born,
whether at rest or marching to the aid of allies,
    or overlooking the Giants' Plain
        like a bold commander.
                Come, Athêna,
for gods can hear from afar,
    come and save me in my present plight!

FIRST FURY: *(Speaks.)*
    No one can save you.
    Not Apollo, not mighty Athêna
        have the power. Down you'll
    go to perdition, to ruin, destruction,
    to pain, abandoned. No joy in your
        soul, a bloodless shade among
    shades, bled white, a thing for
        spirits to gnaw at, a husk,
        an empty nothing.

            Nothing to say?
You spit back my words, you who were
    fatted for me? I'll feed on your
        living flesh. No throat cut on the
    altar, no easy death.

Now hear my song,
    the spell that binds you fast.

(Chants.)

Come, Furies, come!
Let us link hands!
Link hands in the dance,
the weaving dance,
the dance that
binds!

Let us show him our
evil art,
our right to power over the
lives of men,
our right to steer men's
lives to
life or death.
We who are honest,
we who are just.

The guiltless man
never knows us;
he lives a life unscathed
and joyous.
But the man who hides his
bloody hands,
the criminal,
this man here,
who offends Justice,
we rear up in anger and
strike.
We witness for the dead,
loyal defenders of those killed,
avengers of blood,
blood for blood, and we
never end till we
have our prey.

FURIES: *(Sing.)*

Hear me, Great Mother!

Hear me, Mother who bore me!
Mother Night, hear me!
You bore me to avenge the living and the dead,
the sighted, the blind,
those in darkness and in light!
God Apollo, now, Leto's son,
dishonors us.
He steals our prey,
this cowering hare,
the mother-murderer
who must pay with his blood.

Over the victim we sing,
we sing,
we sing a song to wither the mind,
a song of madness,
song of delirium,
song that chains the mind to frenzy,
the Furies' song that binds the brain,
a song that drains him dry as hay,
a song,
a song sung to no lyre.

By Fate assigned,
by Destiny given,
we hold as right our inalienable trust:
to pursue to the death
below the earth
the man who knowingly spills kindred blood.
And not even in death is he free.

Over the victim we sing,
we sing,
we sing a song to wither the mind,
a song of madness,
song of delirium,
song that chains the mind to frenzy,
the Furies' song that binds the brain,
a song that drains him dry as hay,

a song,
a song sung to no lyre.

From birth we have it,
from birth decreed,
by Destiny given,
by Fate assigned,
no god of Olympos may intrude on our right.
We share nothing,
no feast, no festival.
We wear no white,
and Fate made us free.

Mine is the ruin of houses when War-lust,
raised in the house like a harmless lion-cub,
turns and savages a loved one,
a blood-kin.
Him we pursue,
as we pursue him,
the slayer we descend on,
however mighty,
we drag him to darkness,
hands dripping, fresh with blood.

And we will have him,
no god is our judge,
no god has the power,
no god has authority,
he's ours,
the slayer,
there will be no trial!
Zeus may scorn us,
blood-stained,
hateful,
and we may not approach his halls.
But judgment is ours,
there will be no trial!
There is no appeal!

Mine is the ruin of houses when War-lust,
raised in the house like a harmless lion-cub,
turns and savages a loved one,
a blood-kin.
Him we pursue,
as we pursue him,
the slayer we descend on,
however mighty,
we drag him to darkness,
hands dripping, fresh with blood.

Great though his pretensions may be,
dreams of grandeur the proud man dreams,
they melt,
they waste away,
dishonored,
when we,
daughters of Night and Darkness,
approach with vengeance pounding in our dance.

I leap from the heights with a crushing footfall,
and the runner may run swift as the wind,
but I cut him down,
crashing to his doom!

And as he falls,
he senses nothing,
blind,
blinded with pollution's evil;
darkness covers the man and his house,
the darkness of guilt,
the darkness of death;
and legend tells his tale through tears.

I leap from the heights with a crushing footfall,
and the runner may run swift as the wind,
but I cut him down,
crashing to his doom!

Our task is for ever,
our mission inalienable,
we,
the Law of Retribution,
unshakable,
unappeasable,
spirits of dread,
spirits of awe.
No evil escapes us,
we see all.
Disgraced, degraded,
we work in darkness,
banished from the gods of light,
we exact stern payment
from the living and the dead.

Where is he,
where is the man,
who fails to reverence the Law we uphold,
who fails to fear the power Fate gives us,
the power of Law allowed by the gods,
indelible to the far reaches of time?
Our power abides,
our ancient rights.
Honor us, give us your grace,
who live in the earth
in sunless night!

(The dance ends. ATHÊNA appears with her aegis.)
(Music out.)

ATHÊNA:
I heard your call from beside the Skamander.
I was taking possession of Troy,
    the hero's share of the war-loot
given me by the Greeks for all
    time, a rare gift to the sons of
                Thêseus.
I came from there sped on by the swift

             stallions of the winds and my
                 billowing aegis.
But what is this I see?
                 An odd gathering, to be sure, far less
             frightening than surprising.
                                 Who are you?
I address you all together.
This stranger here,
             clinging to my statue—and you who are
             surely the like of no other race, no mortals
                 bred by mortals, goddesses
unknown to the gods.
                                 But, no,
             I beg your pardon,
prejudice is unworthy of anyone,
             least of all a goddess.
             You've done nothing wrong.
I must be impartial.

FIRST FURY:

Daughter of Zeus,
             you will learn of us in few words.
We are the children of endless Night,
                 our mother, and in our
             home beneath the earth we are called
                                 Curses.

ATHÊNA:

I now know your name and lineage.

FIRST FURY:

And yet you know nothing of our powers.

ATHÊNA:

Then tell them to me, but tell me clearly.

FIRST FURY:

We drive from their homes men who take other men's lives.

ATHÊNA:

> And where does the murderer's flight end?

FIRST FURY:

> Where no joy is.

ATHÊNA:

> Is that where your screeching pursuit will drive this man?

FIRST FURY:

> He murdered his mother and called it just.

ATHÊNA:

> Was he forced? Did someone's anger goad him?

FIRST FURY:

> What could spur a man to kill his mother?

ATHÊNA:

> There are two parties here; we've heard only half.

FIRST FURY:

> He refuses to swear his innocence or admit to guilt.

ATHÊNA:

> You claim to be just, and yet you act unjustly.

FIRST FURY:

> Your words are subtle. Explain. You have wisdom.

ATHÊNA:

> Injustice must never win by technicalities.

FIRST FURY:

> Then question him for yourself, and judge.

ATHÊNA:

> You resign to me the right to judge this man?

FIRST FURY:
As you respect us, we respect you and your birth.

ATHÊNA:
It's your turn now, stranger.
Speak.
Tell us your name, your country, and your
circumstance. Defend yourself
against this accusation.
You came as a suppliant seeking protection,
took up a place at my
idol, like Ixion.
If it is justice you want,
then speak, speak the truth,
and clearly.

ORESTÊS:
Athêna, lady, guardian of Athens,
let me remove first
any misgiving you may have.
It isn't as a suppliant for
purification that I've come here to your temple.
Nor have I approached your image with
polluted hands. And I have powerful
proof of this.
A murderer is forbidden to speak
until he has been purged of
blood-guilt by a priest who washes it away
with the blood of a slaughtered
suckling.
My hands are clean.
I was purified long ago and many times,
at other shrines and swift-flowing rivers.

As for me,
my home is Argos, and my father
is one you know well,
Agamemnon, who marshaled the fleet
that together with you at their

side toppled Troy,
    destroying the city and its people.
He died a shameful death on his return.
Killed by my black-hearted
    mother who caught him up in a web of
        cunning design then hacked him to
    death as he stood naked in his bath.

And when at last I returned to my home from exile,
    I killed her, my mother,
    the one who gave me life,
            I can't deny it.
She killed him, I killed her.
I avenged a beloved father's
    death.

My accomplice in this was
    Apollo; he shares the guilt. He threatened me
        with unspeakable torments if I failed
    to pay back the murderers for their evil deed.
Whether I acted justly or not
    is for you to judge.
        Whatever your decision,
I abide by it.

ATHÊNA:
    This is a matter too difficult for any mortal;
        nor is it right even for me to decide
        in a case of murder that excites such
            intemperate passions.
    All the more so since,
        schooled by your sufferings, you come here
        unpolluted, infection-free, a suppliant who
            brings no danger to my house.
    I respect your rights.
    But these women cannot be dismissed.
    They have a duty to Destiny that cannot be put off lightly.
    And if they fail in gaining the victory,
        there will come a time when the

venom of their wounded pride will
seep into the land and poison it, and all my
country and its future will suffer a dreadful and
unbearable pestilence.

So there we are.
A crisis no matter what.
On both sides.
Do I accept the case, or do I reject it?
Do I let you stay or do I send you off?
Disaster either way.
Choice or no choice, I still must choose.
The matter must be faced and dealt with.

Very well.
I will establish here in Athens
a court to hold jurisdiction over homicide.
A tribunal to last for all time.

I herewith instruct you,
both of you,
to order your evidence and prepare
witnesses to assist justice.
After I have appointed the best men,
the most excellent among my citizens,
to serve as judges, I will return
and preside over a fair decision,
for they will have sworn on oath
to judge only in the interest of Justice.

(ATHÊNA disappears.)
(Music. Song. Dance.)

FURIES: (Sing.)
Now all is revolution!
New laws prevail and ancient laws destroyed!
Eternal laws of Justice are no more!
And it is just, they say, it is just.
A mother murdered, and it is just.

The matricide goes free, and crime is easy.
A new harmony reigns, and crime is the victor.
A bloody sanction.
An evil license.
Wound upon wound,
at children's hands,
await parents in time to come.

Once we were guardians who kept strict watch,
safeguard against man's evil.
Now no more will our rage send Wrath
to keep men sane.
Death will come in every form,
murder will strike in every quarter,
doom has slipped the leash and roams the land.
Man will ask man when evil will end,
but there will be no end in sight,
no end to pain,
but only distress,
no remedy,
all cure is useless.
Nothing is sure.
Consolation is dead.

Destruction is everywhere,
Ruin runs wild,
Murder never sleeps.
Let no man cry for Justice,
for Justice's house is falling,
the throne of the Furies is tumbled,
majesty is no more.
Fathers, mothers may cry for judgment,
but Justice—Justice is dead.

Where there is no Fear there is no Justice,
for fear teaches the heart and mind right action,
sometimes in pain,
but all for the better,
wisdom comes of pain,

we learn from constraint.
But what man, what city,
for they are one,
without Fear would reverence Justice?

Praise neither Anarchy nor Tyranny:
moderation is best,
the middle way,
strike the balance and god sends success,
though how he does who can tell.
The impious heart has an impious hand.
The honest heart knows prosperity and blessing.

And we tell you this,
we Furies of Darkness,
honor for all time the altar of Justice.
Do not in the lust for riches
dishonor it with an impious foot,
for revenge will come,
an end awaits you;
the cause will have its effect;
there is no escape.
And so I say:
Honor your parents,
respect the stranger guest to your house
and treat him with reverence.

*(The scene changes to the Areopagos. Enter ATHÊNA in procession with
the HERALD OF THE COUNCIL OF THE AREOPAGOS and a
TRUMPETER. She is followed by the twelve MEN OF THE JURY, who
take their places, the ESCORT OF ATHENIAN WOMEN, and the
CITIZENS OF ATHENS. Simultaneously ATHÊNA places ORESTÊS
on the Stone of Outrage at one side of the area and the FIRST FURY on
the Stone of Unmercifulness on the other, with the chorus of FURIES
near her. The two voting urns—one for conviction, one for acquital—are
prominently placed.)
(Music out.)*

ATHÊNA:

> The Herald will bring order!
> And let the piercing Etruscan battle-trumpet
> > sound to crack the heavens and
> shake to its foundations the City of Athens!

(The HERALD points his mace at the TRUMPETER who sounds a clarion call.)

> Now that this council is being convened,
> > it is fitting and proper that silence be maintained
> so that you, the judges, the litigants, and the entire
> > city may learn my ordinances that will
> > > adhere to you and to your progeny for all time,
> so that justice may duly be done.

(Enter APOLLO to stand with ORESTÊS.)

ATHÊNA:

> Lord Apollo, this is not your jurisdiction!
> Please state what part you play in this affair!

APOLLO:

> I come to bear witness.
> As custom has it, this man was a
> > suppliant at my hearth and I have
> > cleansed his murderous hands of blood-guilt.
> As the one responsible for his mother's killing,
> > I am here to plead for him.
> I called for it.
> I commanded it.
> > When you try him,
> > > you try me. And so, lady,
> bring on the trial. Let justice be done,
> > as best you know how.

ATHÊNA:

> > It is for you the prosecutors to speak first.
> State the charges so that all may hear.

FIRST FURY:

We are many heads, but speak with one voice:
we will be brief.
I call on you, Orestês.
You will answer our questions, one by one.
First: did you kill your mother?

ORESTÊS:

I killed her. There's no denying it.

FIRST FURY:

Ah! There's the first of three falls!

ORESTÊS:

You boast, but your man isn't yet on his back.

FIRST FURY:

Answer to how you killed her.

ORESTÊS:

With a sword. I slit her throat.

FIRST FURY:

And who persuaded you? Who planned the deed?

ORESTÊS:

Apollo's oracle. Apollo is my witness.

FIRST FURY:

The god of prophecy ordered the killing?

ORESTÊS:

He did, and to this moment I regret nothing.

FIRST FURY:

When the verdict comes in, you'll soon sing another tune.

ORESTÊS:

I'm confident. My father will help from the grave.

FIRST FURY:

    You killed your mother, and you have trust in corpses?

ORESTÊS:

    I do. She was tainted with a double pollution.

FIRST FURY:

    Double? You can explain?

ORESTÊS:

    When she killed her husband, she killed my father.

FIRST FURY:

    You killed her; she paid her dues. Now it's your turn.

ORESTÊS:

    Did you hound her when she was alive?

FIRST FURY:

    The blood of the man she killed was not her own.

ORESTÊS:

    And my blood and my mother's are one and the same?

FIRST FURY:

    How else could she have
        bred you in her womb?
    The blood you shed was yours!
    Do you disown it?

ORESTÊS:

    It's your turn now, Apollo!
        Be my witness!
    Testify if I had Justice on my side.
    I killed her, yes,
        I slit her throat. How can I
           deny that? But this matter of
    bloodshed. Was it just or unjust?
    Decide so I may prove my point to this court.

APOLLO:

    Gentlemen of the Court!

    High Tribunal of Athens!

    Protective goddess of this great city,

                      Athêna!

    As god's prophet, I, who see all

        things, Apollo, I speak only

        truth, I cannot speak falsely.

    Every word delivered from my mantic

        throne to man, woman, or city is

    beyond being questioned, for it is first ordained

        by Zeus, father of Olympos.

                    You ask, Orestês,

  was your action just or unjust.

  Just is my answer.

  It is Zeus who says this, and than Zeus'

        justice there can be no greater.

  The justice is his. All-powerful.

               Be warned, gentlemen of the jury.

  This is his will. Bend to the Father's

        design.

  No oath can surpass the power of Zeus.

FIRST FURY:

    This is Zeus' will, you say?

    That this man here, Orestês, should

        avenge his father and ignore totally any

    claims his mother might have,

        his mother's rights?

APOLLO:

               Rights?

  You speak of rights?

    What rights?

  This man is charged with killing a woman who

killed a king, a nobleman whose scepter, whose
authority, was god-given, whose birth was
blest by Zeus himself; and what's
more, she killed her husband,
a wife killing her husband, a man!

There's no comparison.
Killed, a king,
a husband, a man, but not in battle, not by a
far-reaching arrow, even of an Amazon,
but by a woman,
at the hands of a—woman!

And how he died, I'll tell you, Athêna, and you
gentlemen who sit here to deliberate and
decide this matter by vote.

Home after a long campaign, home in
triumph, to most men's eyes, after
a largely profitable expedition, he was
reunited with the welcoming, waiting
arms of his faithful wife,
his wife who led him
to a steaming marble bath in the palace, and—
and as he stepped naked from the bath,
just at the edge where he would have
raised his foot, she caused to toss around him,
to catch him up, to hood him, to put it more
precisely, in a vast and richly woven
tapestry that, as it were, shackled him in its folds,
netted her prey, and, thus entangled,
she struck,
three times she struck, into the steaming, battle-hardened
flesh of the king, the general, commander of the fleet,
a magnificent physical specimen of a man—
her husband.

I have spoken as I have just spoken,
I have described this woman meticulously in her evil,

in the interest of stinging to anger those of you
assembled here to bring this trial
      to a just conclusion.

FIRST FURY:

You claim that Zeus puts greater store
      in a father's death. Then how do you explain
      that Zeus threw into chains his own father,
            the aged Kronos?
Is it possible we have a contradiction here?
I call upon the jurors to take note.

APOLLO:

Evil, creatures!
Loathsome!
Hated by the gods!
            Chains can be undone! There are
keys for every lock! But when the
      earth has drunk deep of a man's blood,
there is no remedy, none, to raise him up.
For this Zeus has made no healing charms,
      no spells to bring him back,
            not even Zeus. All other things
he turns topsy-turvy at will
      without even straining for breath.

FIRST FURY:

Be careful how you plead for his
      acquittal! Is a son who has
            spilt his mother's blood then to
      live in his father's house in Argos?
What public altars of worship will he use?
What brotherhood will accept him into their
                              rites?

APOLLO:

Then hear the truth and
      note the correctness of my argument.
The woman you call the mother is

not the child's parent. She's a nurse, rather,
a stranger who shelters a stranger for the
true parent,
the male who mounts and sows the seed.
He is the begetter.
She protects and preserves the offspring,
unless some god blights the birth.
I offer as proof for the truth of this assertion,
that a father can father a child independent of a woman,
a witness close at hand:
the divine child of Olympian Zeus.
No dark womb nurtured her; rather, she
emerged full-blown from the head of Zeus.
No goddess could have born such an offspring.

Pallas, I will do all in my power to help
Athens and its people to achieve the highest
pinnacle of success.
For no other reason I sent this man to your
temple and hearth as a suppliant, a faithful
friend, he and his heirs to be your
ally forever, faithful to the covenant
sworn here.

ATHÊNA:
Is there anymore to be said?
Shall I ask the Court to cast its vote
as justly and fairly as conscience permits?

APOLLO:
Our arrows are all shot.
I wait here only to learn the
Court's decision.

ATHÊNA:
And you? What must I do
to avoid your censure?

APOLLO:

You have heard what you have heard.

Let the jury cast its votes,

and respect the oath they have sworn.

ATHÊNA:

Hear me, men of Athens,

and hear the law I establish for you and for

all the people of Attica.

It is your privilege, now, as jury,

to try the first case of

bloodshed.

And this assembly of judges will

endure for all time.

It was here that the Amazon women

descended in fury against Thêseus and

pitched their camp, erecting a new city to

rival his, building wall against wall,

tower against tower. And it was here they

sacrificed to Arês and called this hill the Areopagos,

the Hill of Arês.

It is here, too, that I establish this court,

a place where fear and reverence will

reign and rescue our people from injustice

day and night as long as no evil influx

perverts the laws of Athens.

Once a pure well is fouled,

a man must go begging for drink.

I urge you to banish

Anarchy and Tyranny from your midst,

choose, rather, Moderation,

the middle way, let it thrive with the

reverence you show it.

And when you banish Fear,

banish not all of Fear, for what man is so

just he need not tremble before Fear?

Respect this Court, fear it,

it is your strongest defense, no bulwark

stronger to protect your land, your city,
stronger than the discipline of Sparta,
stronger than the warrior might of Skythia,
none stronger known to man.

I direct that this Court rise above corruption by
bribery or any other means,
that it be ever worthy of respect,
quick to anger, forever wakeful in
defense of this land's sleepers.
This Court that will be the guardian of our land,
I now establish.
To my citizen people present and future,
however long my exhortation may have been,
I dedicate these words.

                                    Gentlemen,
rise now, take up your ballots, and
vote with respect for the oath,
for my words now are ended.

(The JURY rises, files to the urns and one by one casts its votes during the following.)

FIRST FURY:
Beware, we can be a danger to your land.
Don't dishonor us.

APOLLO:
And you beware in respect of
my oracles and those of Zeus.
Don't interfere.

FIRST FURY:
You dabble in deeds of blood that are
none of your right! Your oracles will be
pure no longer!

APOLLO:

> And was Zeus wrong to pardon Ixion,
> > the first one to murder?

FIRST FURY:

> The words are yours!
> But let us lose, deny us
> > justice, and this land will suffer.

APOLLO:

> You are nothing to us, nothing to the
> > gods of Olympos, nothing to the
> > > older gods!
> > I'll take the victory here!

FIRST FURY:

> This is nothing new to you! You did it
> > in the house of Admêtos! Persuading the Fates
> > to give men immortality!

APOLLO:

> It was a crime, then, to help that pious
> > man in mortal need?

FIRST FURY:

> You violated age-old dispensations!
> You fuddled the minds of ancient
> > goddesses with wine, mocking their primeval
> privileges!

APOLLO:

> You'll lose this case soon enough, so
> > spew your poisonous venom at your
> enemies,
> > you're harmless!

FIRST FURY:

> You, young god, you, you
> > trample me underfoot with your indignities,

me, your elder! But I'll wait, I'll
wait to hear the outcome, and then I'll
act, then I'll decide do I blast this land
or not.

ATHÊNA:
Since the last vote is mine,
I cast it for Orestês.
No mother gave me birth, and so I honor
the male principle above all.
Except for my virginity,
I am in all things my father's child.
And so I will give no preference to the
death of a woman who kills her husband,
the master of the house.
Orestês wins even if the vote is even.

You of the jurors assigned to count the vote,
do so quickly.

ORESTÊS:
Apollo, god, how will the verdict fall?

FIRST FURY:
Night, dark mother, do you see this scene?

ORESTÊS:
Death by hanging awaits me, or the light of life!

FIRST FURY:
Destruction awaits me now, or renewed honor.

APOLLO:
Count them fairly, friends,
honor Justice in your division!
One error can cause disaster, and a single
vote bring life to a fallen house.

(The counted ballots are brought to ATHÊNA.)

ATHÊNA:
> The votes are even.
> The man is acquitted,
> > cleared of the charge of
> > > bloodshed.

(Exit APOLLO.)

ORESTÊS:
> Athêna, you have saved my house!
> > I was an exile and you
> > brought me home! The Greeks will say:
> "This man is an Argive again, restored once
> > more to his father's halls, thanks to
> > Athêna, Apollo, and Zeus Savior, who brings
> all things to pass."
> > Zeus saw the horror of my father's death,
> > he saw these champions of my mother's cause, and
> > > preserved me from them.
> It is time for me now to return home to Argos.
> But before I go, I swear a solemn oath to the
> > city of Athens and its people, an oath
> > > that will be for all time.
> > > > No lord,
> > no ruler of my land will ever approach
> Athens with military might and lowered spear.
> > > I swear this.
> And if he does, and I am in my grave, as may well
> > be, I will rise from the tomb and wreak
> > vengeance on him of such magnitude that it will
> thrust him into blind confusion and stake out his
> > march with ill omens so dire that he will
> curse the very choice he made.
> > > But those who remain loyal to our oath,
> > who strive to uphold this city and its people forever,
> > > comrades in arms, them I will
> bless from the fullness of my heart.

Farewell, now, to you and the city's people!
I wish you good wrestling,
    holds that grapple your enemy to you with
no escape, that preserve you and bring you
                             victory!

(Exit ORESTÊS.)
(Music. Song. Dance.)

FURIES: *(Sing.)*
              Gods of Light!
           Gods of the New!
           Younger gods,
              younger,
              you, you,
           you trample,
         you ride roughshod
         our ancient laws,
          you snatch,
             tear,
     rip them from my grasp!
         Gods of Light,
         gods of the New,
      where is your shame?
       I am dishonored!
      I suffer bitter loss!
          AIIIII!
         In my rage,
        in my wrath,
    I will destroy this land!
My grieving heart will spill its venom,
        drop by drop,
     to lay waste the land!
    The land will not yield!
       Cancer spreads,
      blight descends,
        crops die,
      children dead,
     nothing grows!

Ah, Justice! Justice!
Infections spread to destroy the people!
AIIIII!
I weep! I groan!
What's left to do?
Mockery, unendurable mockery,
the city's fool!
We the ill-fated Daughters of Night
who bear what none can bear.

ATHÊNA: *(Speaks.)*
Great Daughters of Darkness,

listen,

why all this anguish, this
grief? What defeat did you
suffer?

None.

The vote was equal. Fairly decided
in the spirit of truth with no
dishonor to you.
Zeus himself gave shining testimony through
Apollo that even though Orestês
did the deed he should not suffer
harm.
And now you
threaten your anger against the land,
to spread your venom across it and
blight the soil with senseless fury,
cruel spears, destroying plant and seed.
I swear in Justice's name and by my rights
that you will have honor here,
a seat and dwelling in this just land.
You will
sit enthroned at lustrous hearths,
sacred caverns in the earth.
And all of Athens will
honor you.

FURIES: *(Sing.)*

Gods of Light!
Gods of the New!
Younger gods,
younger,
you, you,
you trample,
you ride roughshod
our ancient laws,
you snatch,
tear,
rip them from my grasp!
Gods of Light,
gods of the New,
where is your shame?
I am dishonored!
I suffer bitter loss!
AIIIII!
In my rage,
in my wrath,
I will destroy this land!
My grieving heart will spill its venom,
drop by drop,
to lay waste the land!
The land will not yield!
Cancer spreads,
blight descends,
crops die,
children dead,
nothing grows!
Ah, Justice! Justice!
Infections spread to destroy the people!
AIIIII!
I weep! I groan!
What's left to do?
Mockery, unendurable mockery,
the city's fool!
We the ill-fated Daughters of Night
who bear what none can bear.

ATHÊNA: *(Speaks.)*

                              Dishonor?
                    No.
No, not dishonor. You've suffered
        no dishonor.
You are goddesses, why visit your
        rage on this land, why
                destroy it with blight?
                              As for myself,
I place my trust in Zeus and—
        need I say it?—
I alone of the gods hold the key to the
                secret place where Zeus stores his lightning.
But why speak of that?
Better to let me persuade you.
Why parch this land with malicious
        curses that destroy every living thing?
        A foolish thought.
Hold back force. Lull to sleep
        the dark flood of your
fury, and know that together,
                co-residents,
        we will share honor and reverence.
You will approve my words when this
        city will offer and sacrifice to you forever
                its first fruits in thanks for
        birth and marriage.

FURIES: *(Sing.)*

                    Am I to suffer this outrage?
                    Wisdom, knowledge,
                    conscience of ages,
                    dug deep in earth,
                        outcast,
                    condemned,
                like dread pollution!
                    I loath you,
                    hate you,
                my rage runs wild,

I rise in anger!
OI OI DA, FÉU!
The pain,
the pain,
stabbing my sides!
AIIII!
Night, hear me!
Hear me, Mother Night!
Help me, I suffer!
Treacherous gods,
gods of light,
usurping gods,
gods of the new,
they rape my powers,
cunning gods,
they make me nothing,
make me count for nothing!

ATHÊNA: *(Speaks.)*
I understand and forgive your anger.
You are older and therefore
wiser than I. And yet, Zeus gave
me some sense and insight, too.

But I'll tell you this:
go anywhere else, set yourself up in a
foreign land, and in time you will
find you long for Athens like a lover.
Time will bring even greater honor to my people,
and with you enthroned near by the house of Erechtheus,
you will know these people to be more
generous to you than all the rest of the
world combined.
But never sow in our land the greed for blood,
for young men's lives are always the cost,
young men
whose rage is not the rage of wine
but of your venom.
Not here,

not in my city.
Never plant in their breasts the
    hearts of fighting-cocks, and with them
    the spirit of war, of civil
        strife, turning brother against
                brother.
Foreign wars, yes,
    and easy to find, too, wars to
    satisfy our passionate lust for
        fame.
But the violence of civil strife I will not
    tolerate.

Such is the choice I offer you.
    Take it.
Do good, receive good, and in goodly honor
    share in this land so loved of the gods.

FURIES: *(Sing.)*
        Am I to suffer this outrage?
        Wisdom, knowledge,
        conscience of ages,
        dug deep in earth,
        outcast,
        condemned,
        like dread pollution!
        I loath you,
        hate you,
        my rage runs wild,
        I rise in anger!
        OI OI DA, FÉU!
        The pain,
        the pain,
        stabbing my sides!
        AIIII!
        Night, hear me!
        Hear me, Mother Night!
        Help me, I suffer!
        Treacherous gods,

                          gods of light,
                         usurping gods,
                        gods of the new,
                       they rape my powers,
                         cunning gods,
                      they make me nothing,
                   make me count for nothing!

(Music out.)

ATHÊNA:
    No, I will never tire repeating to you
        the gifts and blessings I offer.
    You must never say that I, a younger goddess,
        and this city's people, drove you off,
    you, an ancient goddess,
                            dishonored,
            exiled from this land.
                                        No!
    But if you honor Persuasion,
        the majesty of Persuasion, and if my
        voice has the power to soothe and
    charm you, you will stay.
                But if not, and you leave,
        you could not in Justice's name bring down on this
        city and its people any degree of destruction,
            vengeance, or wrath.
                        No.
    For I offer you a royal share of this land,
        and honor and glory for all time.

FIRST FURY:
    Lady, what is this place that will be mine?

ATHÊNA:
    One free of pain and suffering. Won't you accept it?

FIRST FURY:
    And if I do, what honor will be mine?

ATHÊNA:

Such that no house will prosper without your approval.

FIRST FURY:

You would really do this; give me so much power?

ATHÊNA:

Whoever honors you will always flourish.

FIRST FURY:

I have your promise of this for all time?

ATHÊNA:

I never promise what I can't fulfil.

FIRST FURY:

Your persuasion is working its magic. My rage is fading.

ATHÊNA:

Live here, then, and help us, and we'll be friends.

FIRST FURY:

What song will you have me sing to bless this land?

ATHÊNA:

Sing of victory—
  a song of victory with honor.
Sing of the earth and the sea and the
  blessings they give; of the sky and gentle
   rain, and of soft winds blowing the
land on sun-drenched days,
  sing of these blessings.
Sing of the beasts of the fields, of endless
  herds and of grain-rich harvests,
  abundance of earth's fruits,
   blessings unending,
sing of them,
  of their blessings,
   for our city's people,

blessings that will know no end.
And sing of the preservation of human seed,
	the sowing of new life, and piety
		cultivated to make the good man thrive.
For like a loving gardener, I tend the good and
	pluck out the bad, and save the honest man
		from sorrow.

All these are yours,
	these gifts of peace. My task is to
	tend the arts of war, to see that this
city is forever honored
by bringing her glorious victory in battle.

(Music. Song. Dance.)

FURIES: *(Sing.)*

Goddess,
I accept,
I choose to live here,
side by side with you,
to share in your house.
No harm will come through us,
no pain, no suffering
no dishonor to Athens:
Athens will never suffer at our hands:
Athens ruled by Zeus Almighty
and war-proud Arês;
Athens defender of gods and the gods' altars.
For Athens I pray.
For Athens I make my kindly prophecies.
May life's blessings abound for her,
may the radiant sun smile on her fields
and make them flourish,
and may prosperity rule.

ATHÊNA: *(Chants.)*
	I welcome these powers,
	terrible goddesses,

implacable, unappeasable,
in my city's name
I welcome them,
I welcome them
for my city's good.
Their fate is to order
the ways of man.

Struck down by their blows
a man lives in misery, never
knowing the source of his
pain. But ancient crimes
haul him before them, crimes
unredeemed, sins of the fathers,
and in silence, regal in
wrath, they destroy him,
the judging goddesses,
grind him to nothing.

FURIES: *(Sing.)*

These are my gifts,
the gifts I bring you.
No bitter wind to blast your trees,
no scorching heat to sear the buds,
no pestilence to blight your crops.
May Pan bless your sheepfolds
and make them thrive,
and earth give up riches
hidden in her womb.

ATHÊNA: *(Chants.)*
Guardians of Athens,
do you hear? Do you
hear their promises, the blessings
they bring? The Furies' power is
great in the earth, with
gods above and gods below,
dread goddesses who
decide man's fate.

Laughter is theirs
to give, as well as tears.

FURIES: *(Sing.)*

I banish chance that takes men's lives,
young men dead before their time.
Give every lovely girl a husband,
and a marriage happy and rich in fulfillment.
Give it, gods who hold the power,
and sister Fates,
Daughters of Night,
hear us,
grant our prayers,
for you are great in every house,
you the keepers of Justice and Right,
you who are known to every season,
you who bear the burden of Justice,
you,
most honored by the gods.

ATHÊNA: *(Chants.)*
Rejoice!
I rejoice at your
gifts, the blessings you
rain on me and my land!
You turned away, you
scorned my offer,
but Persuasion,
kindly Persuasion,
came to guide my tongue:
Zeus Persuader
has won the day.
Our rivalry now will be for good,
and Athens will be
blest in our contest.

FURIES: *(Sing.)*

Let Civil Strife,
forever hungry for evil,

never divide fair Athens.
Let Attic dust not drink our people's blood,
let revenge not breed revenge
in an orgy of slaughter.
But let them rejoice in joy,
each to each,
united in love for the good,
united in hate for the evil.
Here is a cure for many human ills.

ATHÊNA: *(Chants.)*
Listen! Listen!
They're finding words,
words of blessing, words for
happiness! Fearful faces
alight with hopeful promise!
Be kind, kind to these
Kindly Ones, honor them
always, and you will be
beacons on the straight course
of Justice, and your city
will be great in all eyes!

(Groups of ATHENIAN CITIZENS begin to gather from offstage.)

FURIES: *(Sing.)*
Rejoice! Rejoice!
Rejoice, Athens and its glorious citizens!
Wealth will be yours,
and joy,
you sitting close to Zeus' throne,
you beloved of beloved Athêna,
you to whom wisdom comes in time,
you whom Father Zeus loves,
you, you,
beneath the watchful wing of Pallas.

(Enter an ESCORT OF ATHENIAN WOMEN carrying torches. Others bring intricately woven purple robes. Still others lead animals for sacrifice.)

ATHÊNA: *(Chants.)*

> Rejoice with me,
> great goddesses!
> Rejoice as by this procession's
> sacred light I lead you down to your
> chambers deep in this rock.
> Go now,
> sped on by our solemn sacrifice.
> Protect us from harm,
> give us good fortune,
> lead us to victory.

> Sons of Kranaos,
> keepers of Athens,
> lead them, lead down our sacred
> guests. Give them kindness
> who give kindness to you.

FURIES: *(Sing.)*

> Rejoice,
> rejoice once more for the city!
> For all in the city!
> Gods and mortals!
> Twin pillars of Athêna's proud land!
> Give us reverence,
> your immigrant guests,
> and happy fortune is yours forever.

ATHÊNA: *(Chants.)*

> I thank you for your prayers and blessings.
> Now in the dazzling light of flaming torches,
> I will lead you to your cave in this rock,
> deep down in the cool earth.
> Come with me to the core of my city,
> the heart of Athens.
> These women who guard my image
> will escort us. For this is your right,
> this is your privilege.

Children, young women, venerable ladies,
come, hang them with purple robes of honor.
Lead on with the light,
let the torches flare high.
Honor them, the Kindly Ones,
that in years to come they will
bless our land
with men of glorious courage.

(The FURIES are hung with the purple robes and the procession begins.)

ESCORT OF ATHENIAN WOMEN AND GIRLS: *(Sing.)*
Onward,
onward,
lovers of honor,
ancient, proud Daughters of Night,
on to your home,
we give you good escort!
Silence,
silence,
all here present!

Go under earth,
to earth's dark caverns,
where honor is yours,
and sacrifice yours,
and holy reverence!
Silence,
silence,
let no one speak!

Bless our land,
great Furies,
be kind, be kind,
great spirits,
come, o come,
exult, rejoice,
on your way bright with torches!

Exult, exult,
in triumph exult!
Cry a glad cry,
shout a great shout,
echoing our song!

Peace is forever now,
forever!
Peace for the people of Pallas,
of Athens!
Zeus and Destiny join to seal our truce.
Exult, exult,
in triumph exult!
Cry a glad cry,
shout a great shout,
echoing our song!

APPENDIX

The Casting Couch

by Hugh Denard

Little by little tragedy advanced, each new element being developed as it came into use, until after many changes it attained its natural form and came to a standstill. Aeschylus was the first to increase the number of actors from one to two, cut down the role of the chorus, and give the first place to the dialogue. Sophocles introduced three actors and painted scenery.

Aristotle *Poetics.* Tr. T. S. Dorsch

Aristotle was not born until seventy-five years after the *Oresteia's* first performance, and the *Poetics* is probably a late work, written in his mid fifties. Given that there was no "scientific" discipline of history (much less theatre history) as we would recognize it today, and that most of the surviving Greek tragedies do not accord with Aristotle's account of tragedy, we have to approach what he says cautiously.

If we look at the first sentence of the translated extract from Aristotle's *Poetics* above, we can see that Aristotle is working overtime to make the history of tragedy fit into his neat teleological scheme whereby the primitive gradually develops into the perfect. In other words, if time had revealed to Aristotle and his contemporaries that the "perfect" number of actors for tragedy is *three,* then tragedy must have evolved into this state from an earlier, "imperfect" state of one, and later two, actors. But the *Oresteia* required *three* actors, and some have argued that it even requires a fourth! Aristotelian acolytes, do not despair: By 458 B.C.E., Sophokles had already been competing against Aeschylus and his peers for a decade, so Aeschylus' use of a third actor could well have been following an earlier, Sophoklean innovation.

I am not going to get into the arguments for or against a fourth actor here, which largely center on the difficulty of one actor in *Libation Bearers* having to change from house slave to Orestês' companion-mentor-lover Pyladês in somewhere between three and thirteen lines. Let's work on the assumption that Aristotle is right and there are just three (very dexterous) actors at work. Does this information make any difference to the way in which we think about or perform the plays?

The first thing to be said is that there are several different theories about how the different parts were distributed among the three actors. They all start with the basic arithmetic (if Actor A and Actor B are already in the playing area when another character enters, then Actor C must play that other character, and so on). They then use different kinds of arguments to distribute the roles that math alone can't decide. The intriguing "problem" about Greek tragedy, they agree, is that the actors all wore masks that entirely covered their head, and that the costumes covered the rest of them, so that *any actor could play any role.* Not only that, but they could even *swap* roles in the course of a performance: Klytaimnêstra could be played by Actor A in Scene 1, but by Actor C in scene 6!

My difficulty with these arguments is that they often tend to base their reasoning primarily on "literary" and "thematic" considerations rather than thinking about what is involved in having three specific actors in performance. It's one of the unhappy facts of theatre-historical research that, in order to gain a sense of the four-dimensions of theatrical performance, we have to spend much of our time looking at a medium (paper), which exists only in two (or at a stretch three) dimensions, and does not visually, aurally, or temporally resemble what it documents (i.e., a chapter in a book does not *look* or *sound* like a performance, nor does the act of reading it produce the same effects of time). One of the dangers of such research is that we can become so absorbed by the particular properties and conventions that are attached to the acquisition of paper-knowledge, that we lose sight of the (quite different) properties and conventions that performance-knowledge demands. The casting of the three actors in Greek tragedy is where we could easily fall into this trap: what seem, in theory, like compelling thematic arguments for or against certain actors playing certain roles, unfortunately require us to treat the dynamic play of the particular, live actor's body and voice in time and space as if it were a merely mechanical function. This is problematic because, while masks and costumes may be interchangeable, *actors' bodies, voices, and performances are not.*

That is why I want to reverse the common approach by *starting* from an "actorly logic," and then working out from that to thematic concerns. I propose that we try out two simple additional "rules" that seem reasonably obvious corollaries of thinking about actors in performance (rather than characters on the page), and *then* see what kind of thematic patterns emerge from the probable casting patterns that these rules produce.

RULE 1. EACH ROLE IS PLAYED BY THE SAME ACTOR THROUGHOUT THE TRILOGY.

This eliminates the fun scholars have had for so many years with the interchangeable actor. Why? Each role in the trilogy requires a particular physical, gestic, and vocal style and vocabulary, not only to denote general factors such as gender and status, but also to particularize each role as a specific instance of these (and other) factors. Regardless of how "formalized" we imagine characterization in Greek theatre to have been (and Greek tragic acting was by no means "naturalistic" or "realistic" in our sense of the words), no amount of mask and costume can conceal the particular body-shape or nuances of voice and body of an individual actor, all of which are non-interchangeable, inalienable elements of what would have gone into making up a particular role in performance. Nor would it have made sense for several actors to have trained themselves to play the same role when *the plays do not require it of them*. Indeed, the fact that they do not require it is perhaps the most direct indication of the practice of "consistent casting."

We also know that as time went on, acting became highly prestigious in the Greek-speaking world: The "*protagonist*" (lead actor and impresario) was commissioned by other cities and rulers to bring his company (the *deuteragonist* and *tritagonist:* second and third actors) to perform at local festivals and other special occasions such as royal weddings. Before 449, only the playwright and *choregos* (producer) were awarded prizes at the City Dionysia. But in that year, just nine years after the *Oresteia's* first outing, the city also instituted a prize for "Best Actor." This suggests that these performances must have been attracting attention in their own right and that the work of the actor was acquiring prestige. How do actors and acting win such prestige? Through particular celebrated performances, and the actor's mastery would (very) arguably have been best displayed by his virtuosity in creating and delivering particular lead roles. If those lead roles were played by several actors, it is difficult to see how those memorable "star" performances could have taken place.

There are a number of objections that could be raised to this approach, above all, that, in an acting system not based on psychological realism, continuity of actor and role is not important. What *is* important is that the star actor gets a chance to show off his versatility in dealing with several different roles, rather than playing just one role or range of roles. Other traditions of performance do successfully interchange actors and roles, and this would make perfect sense for the evidence that we have for Greek performance. These arguments lead to a different sense of the performance aesthetics, and they provide a different, and at times highly attractive, way of reading the plays. While both theories can equally be argued from the efficacy and attractiveness of their different outcomes, and both can be equally well defended from the evidence, neither set of outcomes or arguments is sufficiently definitive conclusively to disprove the other. That is not, however, to say that the exercise is futile. Our investigations may not result in "the truth" (even if we were to get it right, we would have no way of knowing), but they do enable us to understand more clearly the kinds of variables with which we are faced, and to identify some of the broader implications of the different decisions we make.

That is not to say that I am entirely neutral: I inevitably have reasons for preferring my theories above those of others. Nor am I arguing for actor-role continuity in the Greek theatre out of some latent desire to impose contemporary notions of acting upon the ancient world, but rather out of considerations arising directly out of the kinds of theatrical and metatheatrical mappings of performative elements that are observable within the plays. (It is also worth noting that arguments for interchangeable actors and roles based on examples from other performance traditions are no less potentially anachronistic as evidence of theatre practice in Greece than the retro-imposition of contemporary norms of dramatic representation.) I do think that it is highly likely that, as tragedy increasingly became a highly prestigious international export in the course of the fourth century B.C.E., with companies of actors doing star-turns of the "highlights" of tragedy for various patrons (rather like the 1990s phenomenon of the "Three Tenors"), the case for a different kind of casting in response to these changes becomes stronger. That is quite different, however, from the decisions that might have applied to the casting of an entire play or trilogy for its original setting in the City Dionysia. In that context, it makes sense for the body and voice of the actor to recur in thematically connected roles in much the same way that other elements do in the *Oresteia*.

RULE 2. EACH ACTOR MAY SPECIALIZE IN PLAYING CERTAIN TYPES OF ROLES.

This is a pretty obvious corollary of the first rule. After 449, actors were officially placed within a hierarchy of prestige. It is not unreasonable to imagine that long before then the *choregos* and playwright, intent on securing the first prize for their efforts, would have placed the strongest actors available to them in the strongest roles. As such, the institution of the actor's prize in 449 must have been a natural recognition of a *de facto* hierarchy among actors, from which the terms *protagonist, deuteragonist,* and *tritagonist* emerged. (Since we don't know which set of major roles would have been taken by which actor, for the time being we should perhaps simply refer to the performers as Actor A, Actor B, and Actor C.) Without spelling out the mathematical logic of the argument at each point, these rules suggest the following preliminary alignments of actors and roles:

> **Actor A:** Klytaimnêstra; Êlektra; Pythia; Athêna.
> **Actor B:** Agamemnon; Orestês.

Immediately we note that each actor takes either the leading female or the lead male roles in the trilogy, so in addition to a logistical solution, each actor also has a primary range of roles that draws on a consistent set of skills. This is encouraging. If we look a little closer at each of these two sets of roles, we notice that there are much more striking similarities between the roles that each actor would have played. Most obviously, both female and male roles are in positions of authority. But, interestingly, of the female roles, all but the relatively small part of the Pythia are portrayed in some way as "mannish," while the men are portrayed as "womanish." Arguably, the Pythia, too, in authoritatively addressing men in public also falls into the range of behaviors that the Greeks would have deemed "mannish." Aeschylus, as a practical man of the theatre (Athênaeus, in about 200 C.E., reports earlier writers who recorded that Aeschylus acted in and choreographed his own plays), and conscious of the resources available to him, certainly wrote with particular role-alignments in mind. This casting arrangement would have allowed each actor primarily to concentrate on perfecting a particular kind of role: strong women and weak men, respectively.

If Aeschylus had not only particular role-alignments, but also specific *actors* in mind to play these roles (and the actors may have included Aeschylus himself, along with two actors called Kleandros and Mynniskos),[1] it is possible that this casting scheme may even be one of the few surviving traces of the particular acting skills and talents for which these individuals were known. This can be neither proved nor disproved. Nor does it even aspire, in this context, to fulfill the necessary conditions of "scholarly argument from evidence." But Aeschylus and his actors were real people working together in Athens in 458 B.C.E., and we *can* say with absolute scholarly certainty that the dearth of evidence imposes its own distortions: That where we have gaps, *there was something.* Speculative attempts to fill the gaps may not bring us any closer to the "verifiable truth," but it may help us more acutely to sense the presence and contours of those gaps.

To return to the actor-role alignments, it does no harm at all to the strength of this "actor-first" approach to casting that we find these role-groups also offering a strong, thematic symmetry between the two main sets of characters—one that accords well with the trilogy's major preoccupation with questions of gender. If Actor A plays both Klytaimnêstra and Êlektra, for instance, the shared body and voice will become a signal to the audience that helps them to recognize that these two characters are perilously alike. Both are driven by the ghosts of the past to commit murder against their closest kin. Both enlist the dead as their silent justifiers. The coincidence is so great that Êlektra even prays:

> And for myself
> I ask that I never be like my mother,
> in mind, in body, in act.

This reference does little to detract from the *theatai's* awareness of the correspondence between the two characters (or actors). The final play, the *Eumenides*, is one in which negative, deathly patterns on several levels are transformed into positive, regenerative patterns. In this scheme, some positive version of the deadly, city-destroying, mannish-women of the House of Atreus is required: warrior-goddess, civic-guardian Athêna, who breaks the cycle of revenge by placating Furies, rather than raising them, and by putting the needs of the city and its citizens above those of the royal house, provides the perfect answer. For their parts, Êlektra and the Pythia can be seen as moral staging posts between the negative pole of Klytaimnêstra and the positive pole of Athêna.

AIGISTHOS

Moving on, here is where our "actorly" logic begins to help out in casting other roles. Mathematically speaking, Aigisthos, for instance, could be played by either Actor B or Actor C. But if we take these alignments of roles as first and foremost alignments of *actors*, then there are good reasons for thinking that Aigisthos, who is also a lead male in position of authority and a "womanish man," should be played by the same actor that plays the similar role-types of Agamemnon and Orestês. So:

Actor B: Agamemnon; Aigisthos; Orestês.

Once we have done this, we can again observe that this will also provide a much stronger *thematic* doubling between these three roles, which accords with a veritable obsession for doubling that the trilogy displays in a variety of other ways (more about this later). So, again, the actorly logic also coincides with a persuasive thematic logic.

For instance, given that the subject of the trilogy is this tangled, sordid history of killings within the House of Atreus, it is fitting that Agamemnon, Aigisthos, and Orestês are brought together in one actor. There's an even more sinister, ironic symmetry to seeing the Agamemnon actor also play Agamemnon's (albeit indirect) killer, Aigisthos; and then in the next play seeing the Aigisthos actor also play *his* killer, Orestês. It also seems appropriate that Klytaimnêstra's two men—Agamemnon and Aigisthos—should be played by the same actor, to allow the obvious differences between them to be disrupted by the possibility of observing, through the actor's single body, disturbing similarities. This is then twisted into a further degree of ambivalence when the same actor returns as her son, Orestês, whom she has cause both to fear (as she feared Agamemnon) and to love (as she loved Aigisthos).

Indeed, all three men are worryingly alike. The *theatai* may have sensed a challenge to each of these three characters' masculinity when they saw how each has achieved victory by "feminine" means—namely, deception. We may have very different ideas about gender, but for the Greeks, deception was always primarily to be associated with the feminine. It might (as in the case of the Homeric "wily Odysseus") bring successes that could be measured in terms of male glory—but it was no less suspect (at the very best, ambiguous) for that. Half a century later, Sophokles would bring the problem into even sharper focus in his play, *Philoktêtês*. Here, in the *Oresteia*, the Old Men of Argos recount, graphically and at length, how Agamemnon used deception to lure his own daughter to her sacrifice in Aulis to maintain his own generalship over the Greek army. At the end of the same play, the Old Men openly jeer Aigisthos for having defeated Agamemnon by deception, and through the intermediary of a woman, rather than facing him "man to man." Even Orestês is not exempt: He, too, enters the house to do his bloody work by deception, on the advice, it might be pointed out, of Apollo—one of the decidedly less butch gods in Olympos (unlike Athêna). And what is his chief task? To kill a woman.

The masculinity of these three male characters is called into question in other ways. On his return to Argos as triumphant king, Agamemnon allows himself to be overruled by a woman. This demasculinization is then played out in gore inside the house: His body is violently penetrated like a sacrificial beast (apt recompense for his sacrifice of Iphigeneia), but by a "mannish woman" who describes killing him and his concubine as a sexual delicacy ("side-dish for his bed, / grand satisfaction for mine!"): their blood spurting onto her:

> He falls, his huge body,
>> and a sharp jet of blood spurting,
>>> falling on me, spattering, like a
>> dark shower of crimson
>> dew.

In the play that follows, we learn that before burying him, Klytaimnêstra has mutilated Agamemnon's body to deny his angry spirit power: The catalogue of savagery as recounted to Orestês by the Chorus includes the "detail" that even his "manhood" has been cut off:

> The she-wolf
> who
>> murdered also
> mutilated.
> Hands, feet,
> ears,
> manhood,
> lopped away,
> tied to his neck,
> slung through the
>> armpits!

While this does not render his body "female" (unless you follow the rather unsatisfactory Freudian line that the "female" is to be defined in terms of absence of male genitalia, rather than the presence of female genitalia), it does certainly physically strip it of most of what constitutes its masculinity.

Aigisthos, in his brutality and deception, is the mirror image of the Agamemnon described by the Chorus in the early part of the *Agamemnon*: the Agamemnon who by guile stole and slaughtered his daughter Iphigeneia so that he might lead the army to war. But moments after Agamemnon has been killed, Aigisthos allows Klytaimnêstra to overrule him just as she overruled Agamemnon—he is persuaded to permit the Old Men to impugn his honor with impunity. In *Libation Bearers*, Orestês has to "learn" how to become as deceitful and brutal as Aigisthos in order, like him, to kill a king and seize power. He, too, wins by deception, entering the house with a false story, and needs his friend Pyladês to help him steel his nerve for the task by warning: "It's better to have no friends / than the gods hate you." The difference between Orestês and the previous two is that, despite the strongest possible claim, that of maternity, he does not allow Klytaimnêstra to overrule him. In this, he acquires a degree of "masculine" power that had eluded his father and his uncle: Thus he survives, and she dies.

But what ultimately conjoins all three sinister figures, and is carried through the shared body-voice-presence of a single actor, is their willingness to sacrifice members—especially female members—of their own family in order to further their own ambition.

So beyond the "actorly" logic of having one actor play all the males in the House of Atreus, there are sufficient overlaps between the way in which the three roles are characterized in the trilogy, and how they would have had to have been performed, to make it worth arguing: The application of "actorly" logic is entirely congruent with a strong theatrical and thematic logic.

ACTOR C

If we work on the assumption of these actor-role alignments, then the math dictates that Actor C *must* play Kassandra, Pyladês, and Apollo. These are all significant "tragic" roles, but subsidiary or auxiliary to the lead roles—all quite appropriate to a tritagonist. All three roles are predominantly concerned with Apollo: Kassandra is his priestess. Because she denied him sex, he blighted her with a curse that her prophecies would never be believed. Pyladês' *only* words in the entire trilogy are to remind Orestês of Apollo's instructions—that he should kill his mother on pain of terrible punishment:

> Remember Apollo. You swore
>   oaths at Delphi.
>   It's better to have no friends
> than the gods hate you.

Finally, Actor C arrives in the person of Apollo himself, whose terrible justice we have seen, to justify himself by his own testimony at the trial convened (rather conveniently) by none other than his sister, Athêna.

Thematically, we find again that this actorly logic gives good theatrical and thematic results. For instance, although not explicit, the relationship between Pyladês and Orestês would have been recognized by the *theatai* as an instance of the kind of highly respectable, homoerotic companionship that existed in Athenian society, and other later classical sources explicitly list Orestês and Pyladês as exemplary among such relationships. The casting allows the sexual link between Agamemnon and Kassandra to be echoed in the link between Orestês and Pyladês: The same two actors (B and C) play out both of these relationships, enabling the *theatai* imaginatively to superimpose, compare and contrast them. In the case of Actors A and B, we saw how the proposed role-groupings allow a disturbing casting of victors and their victims in the same actor's body. Here, too, we see one single actor play both Kassandra and her victimizer, Apollo.

BIT PARTS

There has been a lot of discussion about the casting of the five remaining minor roles, and again, I am going to try to apply an "actorly" logic to see if this gives us any insight into how the trilogy may have been performed and what kinds of theatrical and thematic patterns this might have enabled. The five roles are: Watchman and Herald (*Agamemnon*); Gatekeeper, Kilissa, and Slave (*Libation Bearers*). Let's start with the observation that, among these roles, three are remarkably similar in range: Watchman, Gatekeeper, and Kilissa. All three are house slaves. All three, however briefly they appear, are given strong "earthy" characterization that mediates between pain and comic potential. Take, for instance, the Watchman's patter at the opening of the *Agamemnon*:

> And so I whistle, I hum,
> to guard against sleep,
> I moan, I sigh with the thought
> of how once this house
> was blessed by the gods,
> but now is cursed.

Or the Gatekeeper at a high-tension point in the *Libation Bearers* when we are about to see whether Orestês will be recognized and killed, or whether he will succeed in his deceit and become the killer:

> All right, all right, I hear you!
> Don't knock down the door!

Again, it is a momentary comic puncture in the high, tragic fabric. Or take the house slave Kilissa talking about nursing Orestês as a baby:

> They're like animals, babies,
>> do what they want, no
>> tongue to tell what's wrong.
>>>   Is he
> hungry, is he thirsty, does he
>> want his potty—how do I
>>> know, no way to know—and a
> baby's belly will have its own
>> way, a terror at both ends.

> Was I a prophet to know?
>> So I guessed, guessed and
>> guessed, sometimes right,
>>> sometimes—well—and so I was
> washerwoman, too, don't you know.

All three put into immediate physical terms the suffering of the House of Atreus, to which they are subject. These slave roles would then seem to suggest an actor who excels in "colorful" low-status characters—perhaps something of a comic talent. But also one capable of blending the comic potential into a tragic texture. Linking these three as a group of roles for a single actor might even suggest something about the way in which these roles were to be performed. And if the suggestion of comic elements seems too undignified for the Great Aeschylus, it is worth remembering that the selfsame Great Aeschylus is also a celebrated author of satyr plays!

If we check our math, we see that one of these is already decided for us: The role of the Gatekeeper must be played by Actor A. On paper, all four remaining minor roles *could* be distributed in various ways between all three actors, but if we stick with the idea that each actor is likely to have specialized in certain types of roles, then the roles of Watchman and Kilissa should also go to Actor A. This actor's profile would then encompass *two* role-types: (i) lead, "mannish" women, (ii) tragi-comic slaves. This would also distinguish this actor from the other two in both the power and range of his roles, which might point toward an identification of Actor A as the star-actor, or protagonist.

But thematically speaking, doesn't this confuse, or at best dilute, the kinds of associations between the lead-female roles that we have previously noticed?

And doesn't it weaken the theatrical impact of the plays? On the contrary, I think if we look at this distribution of roles we can see that it would actual-ly have served to *accentuate* the thematic and theatrical structure of the plays. The relationships between these three slave roles and Klytaimnêstra, all played by the status-actor, the protagonist, are strikingly similar. The Watchman starts off the trilogy, and the same actor will bring it to its conclusion in the role of Athêna. The Watchman is Klytaimnêstra's minion, set by her to give her advance warning of Agamemnon's triumph at Troy and imminent return: If she has been waiting and plotting for this moment for all these years, his is the actual, physical manifestation of that watch, so he acts as a kind of exten-sion of her fears and desires. In Greek social terms, that is all he—her slave—actually *is*. The connection is made even more direct when he describes himself as lying on the roof like a dog; it is a recurrent motif in the trilogy that Kly-taimnêstra is the hound keeping watch over the door to the palace. (Perhaps this is a kind of negative Argus, Odysseus' faithful dog, whom Homer has die with pleasure on his master's return: Hell Hound Klytaimnêstra ensures that it is her "master" who dies on his homecoming.) It is also the Watchman who introduces the motif of fire, the beacon-signals set up by Klytaimnêstra, which is also the sign that Klytaimnêstra gives as prelude to her own entrance, as the perplexed Chorus exclaim:

> The altars of the city's gods
> are ablaze with offerings,
> gods above and below the earth,
> gods of the marketplace.
> Torches everywhere leap
> heaven-high with flames
> fed by holy oils from the inner store.

Fire returns again at the end of the trilogy—on the instructions of none other than Athêna! There is also a nice irony that the Watchman is the first to com-ment on Klytaimnêstra's gender:

> Mykenê's queen, my mistress
>   Klytaimnêstra,
>   who rules here now
> with the confidence and the hard
>   will of a man—

As this same male actor will go on to play Klytaimnêstra, the "mannish woman" of which this Watchman is the anticipatory (male) extension, her gender is thus not only described, but in a sense *performed* by the casting coincidence.

The value of these kinds of connections is, as elsewhere in the trilogy, only fully realized when combined with significant disjunctions, contrasts, dissimilarities. This "compare and contrast" structure is used by Aeschylus over and over again to generate a multilayered texture of ambivalence, tension, and irony. In this case, although the Watchman acts as a precursive extension of Klytaimnêstra, he is also a foil. His spontaneous joy at the prospect of his King's return ("If only he were here now, / my master, Agamemnon, / and I could hold his dear hand in mine") stands in illuminating contrast to the calculating pleasure of Klytaimnêstra behind which, Goneril-like, lies only malice.

The theatrical logic is also compelling: Klytaimnêstra enters the playing area a long time before she first speaks to tell the Chorus about her beacon signal, a silence that gives her character mystique and power. But the *theatai* have already heard this actor in the role of Klytaimnêstra's "extension," the Watchman. Likewise, they have already heard all about the beacons, having themselves watched the moment the message arrived. These previews give the *theatai* an advantage over the other characters in the play, offering them the illusion of omniscience—an illusion that is always useful for an Athenian poet to cede to his sovereign, democratic audience. Rather than diminish in any way the dramatic suspense of Klytaimnêstra's silence, it creates a wonderful anticipatory effect: The *theatai* see the male slave transform into the female queen linked by shared but ambivalent tokens—the fire and actor.

These are then the main patterns that we will see repeated strongly in the *Libation Bearers* in the roles of Kilissa and the Gatekeeper: Like the Watchman, the parts will (i) in some way anticipate entrances by Klytaimnêstra, and (ii) act as both extensions and foils to certain important aspects of her character.

Like that of the Watchman, the appearance of the Gatekeeper in *Libation Bearers* becomes the occasion for attention to be drawn to Klytaimnêstra's ambivalent gender: Orestês instructs him:

> Bring someone in authority.
>   Your mistress, or better
>   yet, your master.
> A woman takes tact to speak to;
>   with a man you can say what you
>   mean and not mince words.

This in itself is a tenuous, "on paper" connection. But if the Gatekeeper and Klytaimnêstra are both played by the same actor, with only moments between the two appearing (the next lines after Orestês finishes speaking to the Gate-keeper are by Klytaimnêstra), then these otherwise arbitrary comments by Orestês assume a more complex layering of associations. The Gatekeeper and Klytaimnêstra must, in any case, be in almost exactly the same place at the same time backstage for this scene, and a mask-switch makes this simple to achieve—with two actors already onstage (as Orestês and Pyladês), and the third having exited into the house (as Êlektra) it would be perverse to imag-ine that the author would have considered casting anyone other than the Klytaimnêstra-Êlektra actor for the role of Gatekeeper. The scene might have been played as follows: Wearing the mask of the Gatekeeper, and perhaps an over-garment covering the costume of Klytaimnêstra beneath, the actor opens a hatch in the wall or door to address Orestês. Following Orestês' words, he withdraws. While stagehands slowly swing open the central doors, he switch-es masks and discards the over-garment, and then makes an unhurried, queen-ly entrance as Klytaimnêstra.

The visual difference between the opening of a minor hatch and the open-ing of both central doors, distinguishes dramatically between the status of slave and Queen. The immediacy of the juxtaposition of his and her arrivals at the door also heightens the thematic connection between the two characters, the Gatekeeper acting as an amplification of Klytaimnêstra's role as guardian of the door. The *theatai* would recall that she had conquered Agamemnon in the previous play by controlling access to this door; they would now sense that her failure to do so in this play—allowing the son of Agamemnon entrance on his own terms—would her her life.

As a slave nurse, Kilissa is the extension of Klytaimnêstra's maternal role toward Orestês, just as the Watchman and Gatekeeper have been extensions of other of her roles. In this case, too, she has delegated these roles to subor-dinates but continues to depend upon their successful execution for her own success and survival. Her failed maternal relationship to Orestês, however, will prove critical to her downfall, as her dream foretells:

> FIRST LIBATION BEARER:
> She dreamt she gave birth to a snake.

> ORESTÊS:
> And?

FIRST LIBATION BEARER:
> She wrapped it. In swaddling clothes. Like a child.

ORESTÊS:
> Did this monster cry for food?

FIRST LIBATION BEARER:
> She fed it at her breast.

ORESTÊS:
> Surely it didn't bite her?

FIRST LIBATION BEARER:
> No, but it sucked a clot of blood in the milk.

To this, the corporeal detail of Kilissa's description of nursing Orestês offers a touching, but pointed contrast. Kilissa's scene also precedes the crucial conflict in which Klytaimnêstra will attempt to use maternity as a defense against death at the hands of her son. As with the other two slave-roles played by the Klytaimnêstra actor, the tragic action to come is anticipated in tragi-comic mode. Not only that, but if Kilissa is to be believed, then there is a perverse distortion of tragic and festive feeling within the house on hearing of the supposed death of Orestês. Of Klytaimnêstra's response she says:

> Her face is all
> > tears—all for the
> > > slaves—but I saw it there, I
> > saw it, the smile she
> hides beneath her pain-mask, her
> > eyes, her mouth, smiling
> > inside for how well it has all worked
> > > out for her.

This duplicitous Klytaimnêstra with her crocodile tears contrasts starkly with Kilissa's own spontaneous response of pain:

> How can I bear it! All the ancient
> > evils this house has suffered
> joined as one, are not so terrible as

this that tears my heart.

He's dead!

Orestês is dead!

My baby, my boy!

The disjunction between the slave's spontaneous grief and the mistress' false grief closely resembles the spontaneous and false joy of slave and mistress at the opening of the *Agamemnon:* the different responses of the Watchman and Klytaimnêstra to news of Agamemnon's imminent return from Troy. And the correspondence between the dramatic technique and thematic functions of these two foil scenes does nothing to diminish the likelihood that they were identically cast, or that such a casting would have helped the correspondences to stand out. But the playwright does not merely reiterate the earlier scene. He "masterfully" turns the true grief of the slave into a false sign to Aigisthos, summoning him to his death at the hands of the "dead"; the dialectic of similarity and differentiation operates between, as well as within, scenes and plays.

HERALD

There remains the role of the Herald in the *Agamemnon* to cast. He could be played by either Actor B (the Deuteragonist) or Actor C (the Tritagonist), and it is clear from the other casting decisions that either of these actors could have played this reasonably extended, serious role. That he is a military man returning home would tend to identify him as a similar role-type to that of Agamemnon, Aigisthos, and, perhaps to a lesser extent, Orestês, to whom the homecoming motif is so central. This would all tend to identify the role as the type played by the Deuteragonist.

As we have seen, the overall casting pattern that I am proposing tends to give to a single actor the roles of both victors and their victims, both masters and their slaves. So in this scheme, the Protagonist plays Klytaimnêstra, who will be (indirectly) conquered by Êlektra. So, too, he plays the house slaves who are subject to Klytaimnêstra. Likewise, the Deuteragonist plays Agamemnon, who will be (indirectly) conquered by Aigisthos, in turn to be conquered by Orestês. And likewise, he plays the soldier who is subject to Agamemnon. Only the very minor bit-part of a Slave calling in panic in the *Libation Bearers,* which the Tritagonist must almost certainly play, escapes this symmetry, and the designation of this minor slave role to the most junior of the actors seems a good gradation of both high-status and lower-status characters, between the three actors in order of their range of roles and seniority.

This may be as far as actor-role typing alone can take us. However, if we conjoin it with other approaches, we can now see if this casting would be consistent with what we have learnt from the dramatic and thematic patterns created by the other casting decisions. Dramatically speaking, by bringing all the essential news from Troy, for instance, the Herald allows Agamemnon to make a grand, silent entrance unencumbered of all but mystique and power. Agamemnon's arrival can thus focus on the question of how he will deal with the city and how he will enter the house; the division of labor between the Herald and Agamemnon is a good means of providing dramatic focus upon these central issues. In this regard, the Herald plays a dramatic function in relation to Agamemnon that closely mirrors the dramatic function played by the Watchman in relation to Klytaimnêstra. Also, just as the Watchman's spontaneous joy at Agamemnon's return acts as a foil to Klytaimnêstra's false joy— the Herald's openly emotional homecoming acts as a useful foil to the imperious Agamemnon, who as general and king must conceal his emotions—and anticipates the emotional return of Orestês at the beginning of the *Libation Bearers*. Thematically speaking, the Herald's account of the storm at sea in which the greater part of the victorious fleet was lost figures as an ominous premonition of the disastrous homecoming of Agamemnon that the *theatai* are about to see. This ironic juxtaposition may also gain something from shared casting.

So, here is the proposed casting for each of the three plays:

Protagonist: Watchman, Klytaimnêstra, Êlektra, Gatekeeper, Kilissa, Pythia, Athêna.
Deuteragonist: Herald, Agamemnon, Aigisthos, Orestês.
Tritagonist: Kassandra, Pyladês, House Slave, Apollo.

In order to allow this proposed distribution of roles, and something of its logic, to be seen at a glance, I have included a scene-by-scene table (Table 1) showing the basic configurations of roles "onstage" at any one time, or those that follow each other so closely that it is highly unlikely that they could have been played by the same actor. For ease of reference, I have put in normal typeface the alignments that automatically follow if we accept the first of my two proposed additional "rules," i.e., that each role is played by the same actor throughout the trilogy. The italic sections show the casting consequences of the second "rule" about type casting, leaving only the Herald and House Slave, in bold type, to be argued from other (e.g., thematic) considerations.

Table 1: Casting hypothesis for the *Oresteia*

	Protagonist	Deuteragonist	Tritagonist
Agamemnon	*Watchman*		
	Klytaimnêstra	HERALD	
	Klytaimnêstra	Agamemnon	Kassandra
	Klytaimnêstra		Kassandra
	Klytaimnêstra	*Aigisthos*	
Libation Bearers		Orestês	Pyladês
	Êlektra	Orestês	Pyladês
	Gatekeeper	Orestês	Pyladês
	Klytaimnêstra	Orestês	Pyladês
	Kilissa		
		Aigisthos	
	Klytaimnêstra		HOUSE SLAVE
	Klytaimnêstra	Orestês	Pyladês
		Orestês	
Eumenides	*Pythia*		
		Orestês	Apollo
	Klytaimnêstra		
			Apollo
	Athêna	Orestês	Apollo

Key: Normal type = Rule 1. Italic type = Rule 2. Capped type = Argued from other considerations.

[1] Pickard-Cambridge, Sir Arthur. *The Dramatic Festivals of Athens*. Oxford: Oxford University Press, 1988, p. 93.

GLOSSARY

ACHAIANS: another name for the Greeks.

ACHERON: river in the underworld.

AEGEAN SEA: sea between Greece and Turkey; an arm of the Mediterranean.

AEGIS: a magical cloak worn by Athêna.

AGAMEMNON: son of Atreus and grandson of Pelops; co-ruler of Argos with his brother Menelaos.

AGON: contest or struggle.

AGORA: marketplace and city center of the city-states of ancient Greece; also the political and social center of Greek life.

AIGEUS: legendary king of Athens; father of Thêseus.

AIGISTHOS: a son of Thyestes, lover of Klytaimnêstra, usurped the throne of Agamemnon.

AKROPOLIS: fortified upper part of a city, as at Athens; means high city.

ALEXANDER: son of Priam and Hêkabê; his abduction of Helen began the Trojan War; also known as Paris.

ALTHAIA: daughter of Thestios and Eurythemis; she murdered her son Meleager by throwing a burning torch on the fire, thus ending his life.

AMAZONS: tribe of female warriors; they were known to cut off one breast to facilitate their aim as archers.

APHRODITÊ: goddess of love, beauty, and fertility; wife of Hêphaistos; said to have been born out of the seafoam; also known as Kypris after the island that was the seat of her cult.

APOLLO: born on Delos; one of the twelve Olympian gods; symbol of light, youth, beauty; synonymous with music, poetry, medicine, and prophecy; his temple of oracular prophecy at Delphi in central Greece was the most famous in the ancient world; twin brother of Artemis; archer known for his unfailing aim.

AREOPAGOS: "Hill of Arês" in Athens northwest of the Akropolis; the location of the supreme and most ancient court of Athens; the site of the final scene of the *Oresteia*.

ARÊS: god of war unpopular among the Greeks; son of Zeus and Hera; lover of Aphroditê and probably father of Eros.

ARGOS: ancient city in southeastern Greece in the northeastern Peloponnesos; in general terms mainland Greece.

ARTEMIS: daughter of Zeus and Hera; twin sister of Apollo born on the island of Delos; virgin huntress associated with wild places and animals; primitive birth goddess; known as an archer.

ATHÊNA: daughter of Zeus who sprang fully armed from his head; goddess of wisdom, skills, and warfare; chief defender of the Greeks at Troy; particular defender of Odysseus; in competition with Poseidon, who produced the horse, she won the favor of the Greeks by producing the olive tree, considered the more valuable, for which she was made patron of Athens, her namesake.

ATREUS: king of Mykenê; father of Agamemnon and Menelaos; to avenge the treachery of his brother Thyestes, he killed Thyestes' sons and served their flesh to him at a banquet.

ATTICA: a peninsula of southeastern Greece; in ancient times a region dominated by Athens, its chief city.

AULIS: ancient town in east central Greece, Boiotia; traditionally the harbor from which the Greeks set sail against Troy.

BAKKHANT: a female follower of Dionysos, whose ecstatic frenzy was brought on by the god; free of human fears and conventions, they roamed the mountains in celebration of the god, tore up trees by the roots and devoured raw flesh.

BOIOTIA: province of east central Greece northwest of Attica; dominated by Thebes.

CHALKIS: A city on the southwest coast of Euboia.

DAIMON: divine being; an attendant or ministering spirit; frequently associated with bad luck that shadows an individual or a house from birth; fate; what is unexpected and outside of one's control.

DAULIS: a small town in Phokis, near Apollo's shrine in Delphi, originally Pylos.

DELOS: Greek island in the southwest Aegean Sea; traditional birthplace of Apollo and Artemis.

DELPHI: Greek city on the southern slopes of Mount Parnassos; site of the most famous oracle of Apollo.

DELPHIC ORACLE: the primary source of oracles in Greece; sacred to the

Earth Mother and passed down through her to Apollo; located on the southern slopes of Mount Parnassos at Delphi.

DELPHOS: according to legend, the eponymous king of Delphi.

DIONYSOS: god of divine inspiration and the release of mass emotion; associated with wine, fruitfulness, and vegetation; son of Zeus and Semelê; leader of the Bakkhai; bestower of ecstasy; worshipped in a cult centered around orgiastic rites and veiled in great mystery; also known as Iakkhos and Bakkhos.

ÊLEKTRA: daughter of Agamemnon and Klytaimnêstra; sister of Orestês.

ERECTHEUS: in classical times considered the first or an early king of Athens; raised by Athêna; associated with earth; worshipped with Athêna on the Athenian Akropolis.

ERINYS: singular of Erinyës.

ERINYËS: snake-haired goddesses of vengeance who pursue unpunished criminals; furies.

EUBOIA: island in the west Aegean Sea; second largest island in the Greek archipelago.

EUMENIDES: name for the Erinyës in their benevolent aspect.

EURIPOS: strait that separates the island of Euboia from the mainland.

FATES: the three goddesses who ultimately control the destinies of humans; also known as the Moirai; their powers and those of Zeus overlapped.

FURIES: see Erinyës above.

GAIA: goddess of the earth.

GORGONS: three snake-haired sisters, monsters, who live in the Far East; daughters of Phorkys and Keto; of the three, Medusa is the best known; their glance turns people to stone.

HADES: underworld abode of the souls of the dead; also lord of the kingdom bearing his name; known also as Pluto; son of Kronos and Rhea; brother of Zeus, Dêmêter, and Poseidon; husband of Persephonê.

HARPIES: foul, winged female demons.

HELEN: daughter of Zeus and Lêda; half-sister of Klytaimnêstra; her abduction by Paris began the Trojan War.

HELLAS: classical Greek name for Greece.

HÊPHAISTOS: god of fire; son of Zeus and Hera; husband of Aphroditê.

HERA: goddess; daughter of Kronos and Rhea; sister and wife of Zeus; associated with women and marriage.

HERAKLÊS: son of Zeus and Alkmênê; of outstanding strength, size, and courage; known for the performance of twelve immense labors imposed upon him.

HERMÊS: god; son of Zeus and Maia; messenger and herald of the gods; associated with commerce, cunning, theft, travelers, and rascals.

IDA: a mountain and range southeast of ancient Troy; a favored seat of Zeus.

ILION: another name for Troy.

INACHOS: principal river of Argos.

IPHIGENEIA: daughter of Agamemnon and Klytaimnêstra; sister of Orestês and Êlektra; sacrificed by Agamemnon at Aulis so the Greek fleet could sail to Troy.

ITYS: son of Aëdon, accidentally killed by her while she tried to kill a son of Niobê.

IXION: a Thessalian king punished by Zeus for his love of Hera by being bound to a perpetually revolving wheel.

KALCHAS: seer and priest of Apollo who accompanied the Greek forces to Troy.

KASSANDRA: daughter of Priam and Hêkabê of Troy; priestess of Apollo; taken as a captive by Agamemnon to Argos and killed along with him by Klytaimnêstra.

KILISSA: old wet-nurse of Orestês.

KITHAIRON: a vast range of mountains stretching between Korinth and Thebes.

KLYTAIMNÊSTRA: wife of Agamemnon; half-sister of Helen; mother of Orestês and Êlektra.

KOKYTOS: river in the underworld whose name means "wailing."

KRANAOS: early ancestor of the Athenians.

KRONOS: Titan; son of Ouranos and Gaia; father of Zeus who dethroned him.

KYPRIS: Greek name for Aphroditê.

LÊDA: wife of Tyndareos; mother of Klytaimnêstra; with Zeus the mother of Helen.

LEMNOS: island in the northeastern Aegean Sea; famous for its medicinal earth.

LÊTO: Titaness; daughter of Phoibê; mother of Apollo and Artemis.

LIBYA: north African country on the Mediterranean.

LOXIAS: Apollo; a cult epithet that probably refers to him as one who speaks in riddles, indirectly, through his oracle at Delphi.

LYKEIAN: epithet for Apollo; wrongly believed to be derived from the Greek word for light, an attribute of Apollo; as Apollo Lykêios he was supposed to protect shepherds from wolves and pestilence.

MAIA: mother of Hermês by Zeus.

MENELAOS: son of Atreus; brother of Agamemnon; husband of Helen.

MIASMA: pestilence; pollution.

MYKENÊ: city in the northeast Peloponnesos on the plain of Argos, north of the city of Argos.

NAVELSTONE: the Omphalos in the temple of Apollo at Delphi; regarded as the earth navel.

NIGHT: born of Chaos; mother of Day and the Furies.

NIOBÊ: queen of Phrygia whose six sons and six daughters (in some versions seven) were killed by the gods Apollo and Artemis because she boasted they were more beautiful than the two gods.

NISOS: King of Megara; father of Scylla.

ODYSSEUS: son of Laërtes; father of Telemachos; leader of the Ithicans at Troy.

OLYMPOS: mountain in northeastern Thessaly; seat of the Olympian gods.

OMPHALOS: see "navelstone" above.

ORESTÊS: son of Agamemnon and Klytaimnêstra; brother of Êlektra and Iphigeneia.

ORPHEUS: legendary musician from Thrace whose music was so sweet it made trees and wild animals follow him.

OURANOS: a god who personified the heavens; son-husband of Gaia; father of the Titans, Furies, and Cyclopes; overthrown by his son Kronos.

PALLAS: name of unknown derivation associated with Athêna.

PAN: Arkadian god; son of Hermês; a man with goat's legs, horns, and ears; god of fields, woods, shepherds, and flocks.

PARIS: another name for Alexander; see above.

PARNASSOS: mountain in central Greece in northwest Boiotia; sacred to

Dionysos, Apollo, and the Muses; on its slopes are Delphi and the Kastalian Spring.

PELOPS: King of Argos; father of Atreus; grandfather of Agamemnon and Menelaos; gave his name to the Peloponnesos.

PENTHEUS: King of Thebes, son of Echion and Agavê, and grandson of Kadmos; because he denied the divinity of Dionysos, he was torn apart by maddened Bakkhants and his mother Agavê.

PERSEPHONÊ: daughter of Dêmêter and consort of Hades.

PERSEUS: the Argive hero who slew the Gorgon, Medusa, by looking at her in a mirror given to him by Athêna.

PHINEUS: a legendary king of Salmydessos in Thrace who blinded his sons when their stepmother falsely accused them; the gods punished him by sending the Harpies.

PHOIBÊ: grandmother of Apollo; a Titan.

PHOIBOS: cult title of Apollo; meaning "bright."

PHOKIS: region in central Greece surrounding Mount Parnassos.

PLEIADES: a major constellation visible in Greece between May and November.

PLEISTOS: the river that runs through the gorge below Delphi.

POSEIDON: brother of Zeus; god of earthquakes, water, and ocean.

PRIAM: King of Troy.

PYLADÊS: son of Strophios of Phokis; companion of Orestês since childhood.

PYTHIA: Apollo's priestess at Delphi.

SARONIC GULF: inlet in the Aegean in southeastern Greece.

SIMOIS: the second river of the Trojan plain.

SKYLLA: female monster who preyed on ships opposite the whirlpool Charybdis in the straits of Messina; daughter of Nisos and Megara.

SKAMANDER: the main river of the Trojan plain.

STROPHIOS: King of Phokis; father of Pyladês; raised Orestês from childhood.

STRYMON: large river that flows into the north Aegean.

TANTALOS: son of Zeus; father of Pelops; founder of the house of Atreus.

TARTAROS: the utter depths of Hades where the Titans were imprisoned; a part of Hades reserved for evildoers.

THEMIS: goddess of established law or custom; Right or Tradition; the Titan daughter of Earth whose function is to see that crime is punished; first dispenser of oracles at Delphi.

THESEUS: great national hero-king of Athens.

THRACE: mountainous region north of Greece in the Balkan peninsula.

THYESTES: son of Pelops, brother of Atreus, father of Aigisthos; his seduction of Atreus' wife is the beginning crime of the House of Atreus.

TITANS: pre-Olympian gods.

TRITON: river in Libya; traditional birthplace of Athêna.

TROY: city in northwest Asia Minor; destroyed by the Greeks during the Trojan War.

TYNDAREUS: King of Sparta; father of Klytaimnêstra.

ZEUS: King of the Olympian gods; son of Kronos and Rhea; brother and husband of Hera; brother of Poseidon; father of the gods and mortals as well; has many epithets arising from his many functions.

SELECT BIBLIOGRAPHY

Aristotle. *The Poetics* (tr. Gerald Else). Ann Arbor: University of Michigan Press, 1967.

Arnott, Peter. *Public and Performance in the Greek Theatre.* London: Routledge, 1989.

Arnott, Peter. *Greek Scenic Conventions in the Fifth Century BC.* Oxford: Oxford University Press, 1962.

Bieber, Margarete. *The History of the Greek and Roman Theater.* 2nd ed. Revised. Princeton: Princeton University Press, 1961.

Blundell, Sue. *Women in Ancient Greece.* London: British Museum Press, 1995.

Burkert, Walter. *Greek Religion.* Cambridge: Harvard University Press, 1985.

Bury, J. B. and Russell Meiggs. *A History of Greece to the Death of Alexander the Great.* Revised 4th edition. New York: St. Martin's Press, 1991.

Buxton, R. G. *Persuasion in Greek Tragedy.* Cambridge: Cambridge University Press, 1982.

Csapo, Eric and William J. Slater. *The Context of Ancient Drama.* Ann Arbor: The University of Michigan Press, 1995.

Denniston, J. D. and Page, D. *Agamemnon.* Oxford: Oxford University Press, 1957.

Easterling, P. E. (ed.) *The Cambridge Companion to Greek Tragedy.* Cambridge: Cambridge University Press, 1997.

Else, Gerald F. *The Origin and Early Form of Greek Tragedy.* Martin Classical Lectures, Vol. 20. Cambridge: Harvard University Press, 1965.

Ewans, Michael. *Aeschylean Inevitability: a Study of the* Oresteia. Ann Arbor: University of Michigan Press, 1971.

Ewans, Michael. *Wagner and Aeschylus: the Ring and the Oresteia.* New York: Cambridge University Press, 1982.

Fergusson, Francis. *The Idea of Theater: A Study of Ten Plays, The Art of Drama in Changing Perspective.* Princeton: Princeton University Press; London: Oxford University Press, 1949.

Fraenkel, E. *Agamemnon.* Oxford: Oxford University Press, 1950.

Garvie, A. F. *Libation-Bearers.* Oxford: Oxford University Press, 1986.

Goldhill, Simon. *Reading Greek Tragedy.* Cambridge: Cambridge University Press, 1986.

Goldhill, Simon. *Aeschylus: The Oresteia.* Cambridge: Cambridge University Press, 1992.

Goldhill, Simon. *Language, Sexuality, Narrative: The Oresteia.* Cambridge: Cambridge University Press, 1984.

Herington, J. *Aeschylus.* New Haven: Yale University Press, 1986.

Hesiod. *The Poems of Hesiod* (translated by R. M. Frazer). Norman: The University of Oklahoma Press, 1983.

Hornblower, Simon and Spawforth, Antony, eds. *The Oxford Classical Dictionary.* 3rd ed. Oxford: Oxford University Press, 1996.

Hornby, Richard. *Script into Performance.* Austin: University of Texas Press, 1977.

Jenkins, Ian D. "The Ambiguity of Greek Textiles." *Arethusa,* 18, no. 2: 109–32, 1985.

Jones, John. *On Aristotle and Greek Tragedy.* Stanford: Stanford University Press, 1980.

Just, Roger. *Women in Athenian Law and Life.* London and New York: Routledge, 1991.

Kitto, H. D. F. *Form and Meaning in Drama: A Study of Six Greek Plays and of Hamlet.* 2nd ed. London: Methuen, 1964; New York: Barnes and Noble, 1968.

Kitto, H. D. F. *Greek Tragedy: A Literary Study.* 2nd ed. New York: Doubleday, 1964; 3rd ed. London: Methuen, 1966.

Kitto, H. D. F. *Word and Action: Essays on the Ancient Theater.* Baltimore and London: The Johns Hopkins University Press, 1979.

Kott, Jan. *The Eating of the Gods: An Interpretation of Greek Tragedy.* New York: Random House, 1973.

Kuhns, Richard F. *The House, the City and the Judge: The Growth of Moral Awareness in the Oresteia.* Indianapolis: Bobbs-Merrill, 1962.

Lattimore, Richmond. *The Poetry of Greek Tragedy.* Baltimore: The Johns Hopkins University Press, 1958.

Lattimore, Richmond. *The Story-Patterns in Greek Tragedy.* Ann Arbor: The University of Michigan Press, 1964.

Lax, Batya Casper. *Elektra: A Gender Sensitive Study of the Plays Based on the Myth.* North Carolina and London: McFarland and Company, Inc, 1995.

Lloyd-Jones, Hugh. *The Justice of Zeus.* Sather Gate Lectures, Vol. 41. Berkeley and Los Angeles: The University of California Press, 1971.

Mastronarde, D. *Contact and Disunity: Some Conventions of Speech and Action on the Greek Tragic Stage*. Berkeley and Los Angeles: The University of California Press, 1979.

Neils, Jenifer. *Goddess and Polis: The Panathenaic Festival in Ancient Athens*. Princeton: Princeton University Press, 1992.

Neuberg, M. *An Aeschylean Universe*. Ann Arbor: The University of Michigan Press, 1981.

Pickard-Cambridge, A. W. *The Dramatic Festivals of Athens*, 2nd edition. Oxford: The Clarendon Press, 1968.

Pickard-Cambridge, A. W. *The Theatre of Dionysus in Athens*. Oxford: The Clarendon Press, 1946.

Plato. *Early Socratic Dialogues* (ed. Trevor J. Saunders). Harmondsworth: Penguin Classics, 1987.

Podlecki, Anthony. *Eumenides*. Warminster: Aris and Phillips, Ltd., 1992.

Podlecki, Anthony J. *The Political Background of Aeschylean Tragedy*. Ann Arbor: The University of Michigan Press, 1966.

Rehm, Rush. *The Greek Tragic Theatre*. London and New York: Routledge, 1992.

Scott, William C. *Musical Design in Aeschylean Theatre*. Hanover: The University Press of New England, 1984.

Smyth, Herbert Weir. *Aeschylus*. Vol. 2. Cambridge: Harvard University Press, 1963.

Sommerstein, A. H. *Eumenides*. Cambridge: Cambridge University Press, 1989.

Steiner, George. *The Death of Tragedy*. New York: Alfred A. Knopf; London: Faber and Faber, 1961.

Taplin, Oliver. *Greek Tragedy in Action*. Berkeley and Los Angeles: The University of California Press; London: Methuen, 1978.

Taplin, Oliver. *The Stagecraft of Aeschylus*. Oxford: The Clarendon Press, 1977.

Thucydides. *The Peloponnesian Wars* (translated by Rex Warner). Harmondsworth: Penguin Classics, 1972.

Vernant, Jean-Pierre and Vidal-Naquet, Pierre, eds. *Myth and Tragedy in Ancient Greece*. New York: Zone Books, 1990.

Vickers, Brian. *Towards Greek Tragedy*. London: Longman, 1973.

Vickers, Michael. "Images on Textiles: The Weave of Fifth-Century Athenian Art and Society." *Xenia* 42: 1-72, 1999.

Walcot, Peter. *Greek Drama in Its Theatrical and Social Context*. Cardiff: The University of Wales Press, 1976.

Walton, J. Michael. *The Greek Sense of Theatre: Tragedy Reviewed*. London and New York: Methuen, 1984.

Walton, J. Michael. *Greek Theatre Practice*. Westport and London: Greenwood Press, 1980.

Wiles, David. *Tragedy in Athens*. Cambridge and New York: Cambridge University Press, 1997.

Winkler, John, and Zeitlin, Froma I., eds. *Nothing to Do with Dionysus*. Princeton: Princeton University Press, 1990.

Winnington-Ingram. *Studies in Aeschylus*. Cambridge: Cambridge University Press, 1983.

CARL R. MUELLER has since 1967 been professor in the Department of Theater at the University of California, Los Angeles, where he has taught theater history, criticism, dramatic literature, and playwriting, as well as having directed. He was educated at Northwestern University, where he received a B.S. in English. After work in graduate English at the University of California, Berkeley, he received his M.A. in Playwriting at UCLA, where he also completed his Ph.D. in Theater History and Criticism. In addition, he was a Fulbright Scholar in Berlin in 1960–61. A translator for more than forty years, he has translated and published works by Büchner, Brecht, Wedekind, Hauptmann, Hofmannsthal, and Hebbel, to name a few. His recently published translation of von Horváth's *Tales from the Vienna Woods* was given its London West End premiere in July, 1999. For Smith and Kraus he has published volumes of plays by Wedekind, Schnitzler, Strindberg, Pirandello, Kleist, and he has also co-translated the complete plays of Sophokles. Forthcoming is a translation of Goethe's *Faust* and the complete plays of Euripides. His translations have been performed in every English-speaking country and have appeared on BBC-TV.

HUGH DENARD lectures in Theatre Studies at the University of Warwick (UK). He has published articles on ancient drama and its reception and the use of Virtual Reality in studying places of performance. He is Editor of Didaskalia: www.didaskalia.net. Currently he is working on a co-authored book on Roman wall paintings and Roman theater for Yale University Press with Richard Beacham (Warwick). He is also co-director of major research grants from the Leverhulme Foundation and the Joint Information Systems Committee (UK). His theater work includes a devised production called *Dionysos,* co-directed with Carl Mueller in August 2000 at the Warwick Arts Centre, and he is Resident Director for Two Hats Theatre Company.